School for
Prophecy

CW00550797

Discovering Prophecy

LEVEL 1
COURSE MANUAL

Mark Iles

School for Prophecy

Onwards and Upwards Publishers
4 The Old Smithy
Rockbeare
EX5 2EA
United Kingdom

www.onwardsandupwards.org

The first edition was published by Onwards and Upwards Publishers (2019) with the title 'Developing Your Prophetic Gift'.

Second edition, published in the United Kingdom by Onwards and Upwards Publishers (2023).

ISBN: 978-1-78815-956-2
Typeface: Sabon LT
Graphic design: based on an original design by Hunt Design, Canterbury, Kent.

 **School** for **Prophecy**

Endorsements

It is rare to find both a practitioner of prophecy (or any charismatic gift) who can also train and develop others in it. Having worked with Mark over many years, I can testify to both qualities in him. He has both a deep gift and is a humorous teacher who has combined those qualities into a holistic discipleship process. His training goes beyond simply learning how to prophesy, to understanding how to develop a prophetic ministry that will stand the test of time.

Rob Gardiner
Senior Pastor, Network Vineyard Church.

The Apostle Paul tells us to "eagerly desire gifts of the Spirit, especially prophecy". Mark takes this biblical statement seriously in his own life, and now his many years of prophetic ministry and equipping the saints (from which we have benefitted in Jersey) can serve a wider audience through the practical teaching and wisdom in these pages – I commend this excellent manual.

Paul Brookes (Rev.)
Minister of St. Paul's Church and Vice Dean of Jersey.

Mark has many years of experience teaching prophecy and knows the joys and struggles that this brings. This manual brings this experience together in a very biblical, practical and balanced way. Mark makes the area of prophecy accessible for the ordinary church member. I highly recommend it to all.

Michael Norman
Rector of St. Saviour's, Bath, UK.

What a useful manual; I wish I'd had this 40 years ago! I'm very happy to recommend my good friend, Mark, and his biblically based teaching. It's well illustrated with Mark's personal experience giving helpful insights to his own journey in giving and receiving prophecy. Each section has its own Q&A ending, which is so important because it shows our questions are not unique! I have found Mark's teaching enriching, stimulating, inspiring and faith-stretching.

Alan Baker
Senior Pastor of King's Church, Southampton [1980-2003]. Now retired.

About Mark Iles

Mark has been in prophetic ministry for over 30 years now. He has been leading and teaching on *Schools of Prophecy,* teaching at conferences and mentoring the prophetic, most of that time. He currently works with churches in the UK and overseas on a relational basis providing strategic teaching, prophetic ministry and mentoring support.

"My heartfelt prayer is that this manual will enable you
to comfortably, confidently and correctly move
in the biblical gift of prophecy;

for the glory of God,
the strengthening of his Church
and as a demonstration of power to the world."

To contact the author, please send an email to:
schoolforprophecy@gmail.com

More information can be found online:
www.schoolforprophecy.com.

Contents

School for **Prophecy**

Foreword by Graham Cooke

It is a great honour for me to endorse this valuable and substantive manuscript on developing the prophetic gift by my friend and former disciple, Mark Iles.

Mark was an excellent student who grew into being a key member of the prophetic team that worked around the UK and Europe for many years. We were together in the flagship church of C.Net based in Southampton, England.

As a businessman and an elder in this local church, Mark had a profound training path marked out for him even before we met. A loving husband and passionate family man are all part of his character credentials. His love of learning, and diligence to seek out the truth, meant that he never settled if there was more truth to receive and practise.

We had great dialogue about grace and the gift of righteousness being seen and heard in the prophetic.

Mark has been mentored by an excellent apostolic team, great leaders, church planters and trainers. How many consultants are also profoundly prophetic? He is a catalyst with a strong pragmatic and practical dimension to his spirituality.

All of this shows up in this impressive manual. It is so typically Mark! He is not content to just train in the prophetic gift by itself. He knows that training in a supernatural gift requires a holistic approach that prepares people to walk with God and therefore live above natural circumstances in a way that defines trust, faith and expectation.

The mindset of the believer is the key to transformation. The lens of the Christian is vital to understanding how God sees people and how to view life in Jesus. If we do not see as God sees, or think as He thinks, then we cannot hear consistently when He speaks.

There is a process to everything that God does, and it is vital that we do not just understand the principles of process but also that we practise the art of pursuing it in our relationship with God. It is the process that makes us rich in our life situations, not the outcome.

Impartation of anointing by itself is only half the lifestyle required to be a significant man or woman of God. Impartation will lift you to a new level in Christ but only process will keep you there. The practice of impartation and the absence of process are seen in the boom and bust theology of some Charismatic ministries.

This is what sets apart the building prophet from the blessing prophet. This is where Mark's apostolic and church experience plus his business and leadership acumen set him apart as being more than a prophetic gift and ministry.

He is a builder, laying foundations in the lives of individuals and the corporate man of the church.

This manual is full of wisdom, truth, principles and values for growing up into all things in Christ. It is packed with practical guidelines that will empower people to study the prophetic in the context of being children of God learning to become mature in the Spirit.

For anyone starting out in prophecy or for people who need to recalibrate their development process, this manual is a must read. The true value of a mentor is that they have gone before. They know the pitfalls, the dangers and the dead ends. They are cartographers who are defining the territory, not just following a sketch map. Good mentors can take years off your learning experience, saving valuable time and wasted effort in spiritual growth and relationship with God.

Mark has graduated with honours from being a diligent disciple to a master mentor. I could not be prouder of him and this excellent piece of work.

Graham Cooke
brilliantperspectives.com

INTRODUCTION

School for Prophecy

The Birth of a Manual

While you can trace the birth of this manual back to my original discovery of the gift of prophecy, its true source is undoubtedly in my journey with Graham Cooke and the many years I worked with him during his time at Community Church, Southampton. I was fortunate enough to grow up, develop and mature in a network-based, community-orientated and lively Charismatic church. My church provided me with considerable exposure to the operation of prophecy in public and personal settings, as well as plenty of opportunities to learn and practise the gift of prophecy myself. It laid a solid foundation for Graham to build on.

A significant part of my journey that was initially hidden from me was my many years of prior preparation. These were necessary to mature my character enough to safely manage my prophetic gift, as well as develop the important supporting teaching and pastoral ministries I would need. I recognize I am very fortunate to have found my primary calling, received experienced and anointed prophetic training and am now able to move in it as my occupation. However, I consider myself even more fortunate that my heavenly Father spent many hidden years preparing my character and related ministries before I had any idea I was prophetic!

An important element of my time with Graham was travelling to, helping to run and being a part of his many Schools of Prophecy. At a time when there was a dearth of prophetic training in the UK, I had access to something that was groundbreaking, extremely popular and internationally recognized. It was during this time that I learned the 'tools of my trade' and developed a vision for schools of prophecy. It was also the time that I discovered my calling, to help the wider Church to be able to confidently hear from God and comfortably move in the gift of prophecy.

When Graham moved to California, it was a very heart-searching time for me, and it could have easily all ended there. However, my colleagues stubbornly refused to give up what we had already achieved, even having lost our inspiration, so P.R.I.S.M. Training [Prophetic Resources Inspiring Spiritual Maturity] was born. Through learning about church consultancy, running schools of prophecy and leading prophetic conferences, I began to establish the principles of my way forward. I developed my 'relational only' approach to ministry, wrote three School4Prophecy courses [levels 1-3] and became heavily involved in prophetic mentoring.

In 2006, Julie and I felt God calling me to leave my career employment as a Group Financial Director, and I became an itinerant prophetic minister, i.e. self-employed church consultant. The story of the birth of this manual could have finished there, but there was still one more bridge to cross. I was poor at English throughout my education, and I frequently learned to survive by relying on my excellent maths skills. A university degree, Chartered Accountancy and a professional career had wallpapered over this 'crack' until Julie started to encourage me to write this manual. Then it all came back! Thanks to Julie I discovered my procrastination was due to my need for inner healing, and pushing through to the completion of this manual has profoundly changed me.

So here we are in 2023, and I am releasing the second edition. The level one course and this manual continue to prove their popularity due to their straight-talking, Bible-based teaching and practical application.

Structure of the Manual

The manual contains a detailed index of chapters and sections; an *Introduction;* four teaching topics containing three subject chapters each; and two final chapters covering our advanced courses. The three chapters in the last topic, *Prophetic Developments,* are only available in the extended course, and are designed to prepare you for level two. The *Introduction* includes how this manual was born; this page on the structure; *a Chapter Overview;* instruction on how to use the manual; *Essential Health and Safety;* and an explanation of *The 7 I's of Prophecy.*

The first teaching topic on *Prophetic Engagements* covers those areas of spiritual interaction with God which, while a normal part of our salvation and relationship with him, are an integral part of how we move in the gift of prophecy. It contains three chapters on *Battle for Your Mind* [1], *Seeing the Bigger Picture* [2] and *Hearing Your Father's Voice* [3].

The second teaching topic on *Prophetic Foundations* covers a set of core principles that, very much like the foundations of a building, are what all our other teaching, understanding and experience of the gift are based upon. It contains three chapters on *Understanding Biblical Prophecy* [4], *New and Old Covenant Prophecy* [5] and *Biblical Prophetic Culture* [6].

The third teaching topic on *Prophetic Protocols* covers the biblical guidelines that govern the operation of the gift of prophecy, and are fundamental to its safe, satisfactory and successful operation. It contains three chapters on *The Principles of Testing Prophecy* [7], *The Principles of Interpreting Prophecy* [8] and *The Principles of Responding to Prophecy* [9].

The fourth and final teaching topic on *Prophetic Developments* covers those areas of our anointing, training and calling that with proper investment can significantly shape and improve our consistency, maturity and longevity in the gift. It contains three chapters on *Preparing to Prophesy* [10], *Unlocking the Prophetic Process* [11] and *The Character Challenges of Prophecy* [12]. Being part of the extended course, these chapters are more advanced and necessarily build on the earlier chapters.

There is a full and detailed table of contents at the beginning of the manual, containing page references to all the chapters, and subjects within the chapters. Each chapter contains a chapter summary; seven subject sections; personal testimony; and frequently asked questions and answers. There is also a lined page for study notes at the start and end of each chapter.

The final two chapters [13 and 14] provide an overview of the *Growing in Prophetic Ministry* level two course [L2] and the *Engaging Your Prophetic Calling* level three course [L3]. They include a thorough profile and a detailed curriculum of all the teaching subjects covered for both courses.

There are three levels of reference used in the manual. Chapters are referenced by whole numbers, e.g. [3]. Sections [or pages] within a chapter are referenced starting with the chapter number and then the section number, e.g. [3.5]. Finally, paragraphs within a section are referenced starting with the chapter number, followed by the section number and then the paragraph number, e.g. [3.5.2].

I have employed footnotes as a means of providing full Bible references for those used in the text, and I also use them, on occasion, to provide the names of people I refer to and the authors of quotes and book titles mentioned.

Chapter Overview

TOPIC 1: PROPHETIC ENGAGEMENTS

Chapter 1: *Battle for Your Mind:* The first *Prophetic Engagements* subject explains the importance of our thought life as the primary battleground with our enemy. It describes his tactics, weapons and how to defeat him.

Chapter 2: *Seeing the Bigger Picture:* The second *Prophetic Engagements* subject lays the biblical principles of seeing the spiritual realm with our Father's eyes and the visible realm with our physical eyes.

Chapter 3: *Hearing Your Father's Voice:* The final *Prophetic Engagements* subject establishes the centrality of our relationship with God and explains the main biblical ways he communicates with us and how to engage with them successfully.

TOPIC 2: PROPHETIC FOUNDATIONS

Chapter 4: *Understanding Biblical Prophecy:* The first *Prophetic Foundations* subject introduces the biblical basis, definition and operation of the gift of prophecy while tackling many of the associated myths, misnomers and misunderstandings.

Chapter 5: *New and Old Covenant Prophecy:* The second *Prophetic Foundations* subject explains the crucial differences between New and Old Covenant prophecy, and reveals a biblical pathway for a confused church and a deceived world.

Chapter 6: *Biblical Prophetic Culture:* The final *Prophetic Foundations* subject identifies the core values, principles, and practices essential for the correct, complementary and complete operation of the gift of prophecy.

TOPIC 3: PROPHETIC PROTOCOLS

Chapter 7: *The Principles of Testing Prophecy:* The first *Prophetic Protocols* subject looks in detail at the biblical principles of testing prophecy, particularly their practical application.

Chapter 8: *The Principles of Interpreting Prophecy:* The second *Prophetic Protocols* subject provides biblical, practical and experienced guidance on the challenging but important area of interpreting prophecy.

Chapter 9: *The Principles of Responding to Prophecy:* The final *Prophetic Protocols* subject explains the importance, process and stages of how to respond to prophecy, from the often-ignored recipient's viewpoint.

TOPIC 4: PROPHETIC DEVELOPMENTS [EXTENDED COURSE ONLY]

Chapter 10: *Preparing to Prophesy:* The first *Prophetic Developments* subject looks at the many ways we can prepare to prophesy, the resulting benefits and how it helps us to develop a prophetic lifestyle.

Chapter 11: *Unlocking the Prophetic Process:* The second *Prophetic Developments* subject introduces the ingredients [I's] of prophecy, and helps us understand the process by identifying the importance of each of its seven key elements.

Chapter 12: *The Character Challenges of Prophecy:* The final *Prophetic Developments* subject looks at the ways the operation and environment of the gift of prophecy create specific challenges and pressures for our character.

How to Use the Manual

This Training Course Manual contains all the teaching from my *School for Prophecy* level one course, *Discovering Prophecy*. It includes the nine subjects [Chapters 1 to 9] from my standard course program and the three additional subjects [Chapters 10 to 12] from my extended course program. Therefore, it is an ideal companion for those attending this school course or those who are not able to but would still like to have access to all the teaching material.

The *Introduction* section includes important information which will significantly improve your use of the manual and is not just 'the starter before the real meat'. I strongly recommend you read all the other parts of the *Introduction* before starting on the teaching material, because each one serves a specific purpose in helping you get the maximum benefit from this manual.

The first eight sections [or pages] within each chapter match the PowerPoint slides I use when teaching that subject, and the paragraph references match the bullet points on the relevant PowerPoint slide. It will enable you, if you can attend a course, to comfortably use the manual for clarification, reinforcing and revision of the teaching from the matching student notes issued for each subject. Furthermore, each chapter begins and ends with a lined page for your study notes, which you can use whether or not you attend a course.

If you are not able to attend a course, this manual does include all the teaching material from the extended course curriculum. Unfortunately, it cannot include the one-hour workshops, i.e. activations, that are part of each meeting, but please refer to the advice in *Essential Health and Safety* opposite. In these circumstances, it could form the basis for your training and instruction, or act as a support and supplement to what is currently available to you.

This manual is an excellent reference resource and can be used to provide specific answers to specific questions. The manual contains an exhaustive chapter and subject table of contents, extensive use of chapter and section referencing within the text, Bible references and even quote sources. Therefore, before or after you have read the whole manual, it can easily be used as a reference resource, by referring to the chapters, sections or even paragraphs that your circumstances require, for answers, clarification, guidance and revision.

At the end of each chapter there are *Frequently Asked Questions* and answers arising from that chapter. Over the many years of ministry, I have become accustomed to the more frequent questions inevitably raised by each chapter's subject, usually to do with their practical application. While I have not been able to cover them all, the manual does include the main ones, my suggested answers and associated references.

If you are interested in taking your training further, the penultimate chapter [13] provides an overview of the *Growing in Prophetic Ministry* level two course [L2], including an introductory profile and a detailed curriculum of all the teaching subjects included.

School for Prophecy

Essential Health and Safety

While this manual contains all the biblical principles, parameters and practice that you need to grow in prophecy, it is simply not adequate on its own. To enable you to develop your prophetic gift fully, this *Essential Health and Safety* section advises you of the other training resources I believe you will need to do this.

The Bible teaches that practice is an essential ingredient for us to reach maturity,[1] or as is colloquially translated, "Practice makes perfect."[2] An essential addition to this manual's teaching is copious amounts of relevant, applied and reviewed practice. It is for this reason that in my *School for Prophecy* I spend as much time on workshops, i.e. activations, as I do teaching the manual. Without the opportunity to practise, the development of your gift can be slow, stunted and unsatisfying. If your circumstances are challenging, you may need to be creative in finding ways to practise your gift in meetings, ministry and moments of opportunity.

While practising is easily the most important health and safety addition, the opportunity for other training in the prophetic can help the process. Although I am very experienced, I cannot teach you everything, and attendance at other prophetic training will provide you with the opportunity for questions, clarification and personal issues which the manual may not cover. For similar reasons, the attendance at prophetic conferences can also be helpful, by providing an encouraging atmosphere, further training and the opportunity for observing prophetic ministry in action.

Something I strongly recommend, and have found extremely helpful for my health and safety, is to walk your journey with an encouraging, honest and mature friend. They are not easy to find, but 'worth their weight in gold' in helping you to grow and develop properly. I am famous for referring to them as your 'Bad Breath' counsellor. Let me explain. The problem with bad breath is that everyone knows you have it, but no-one is going to tell you. If you have bad breath, i.e. a problem with your character or ministry, you need a friend who is loyal enough to tell you the truth and in a loving way. Feedback is the 'life blood' of successful growth, and this one is pretty important!

Another important element of health and safety is to recognize how prophecy works in your church environment, combined with having a healthy relationship with your leadership. Every movement, denomination and church has 'their' way of doing things, and although it is unlikely to be documented, it can be discerned by observation and enquiry. There will be different levels of the three key ingredients, expectation, encouragement and example, which you will need to harmonize with initially, even if you are seeking to change them. It is also important to develop good lines of communication with your leadership, through trust, commitment and service.

Finally, there is no easier way to grow than by finding somewhere to serve practically, inside or outside of the church, and watch for the prophetic opportunities to 'pile up'. It is a great way to learn how to use your gift in many different circumstances, as well as teaching you to recognize when the Holy Spirit is moving around you. It also protects us from over-spiritualizing our gift, develops a servant-hearted approach and keeps us actively involved in our community outside of ministry.

---

1. Hebrews 5:14 | 2. John Adams; *Diary and Autobiography of John Adams* [USA: 1761]

The 7 I's of Prophecy

This manual seeks to establish a clear biblical framework for the complete operation of the gift of prophecy. To assist this objective, I have broken the prophetic process down into its seven essential ingredients using a system I call *The 7 I's of Prophecy*. It paves the way for us to look in more detail at the individual stages in the prophetic process, helps you to identify where you are at any time in the different stages and encourages a more thoughtful and active involvement in the particular stages of the process. The essential ingredients of prophecy are:

- *Inspiration* – how revelation is received from the Holy Spirit, which will form the basis of the prophetic message. [11.3]
- *Interpretation* – the process by which the revelation received is translated into its full meaning in a prophecy. [11.4]
- *Initiation* – when, where and how the prophecy is delivered to the identified audience. It is lovingly fashioned, creatively presented and has a servant's heart. [11.5]
- *Investigation* – the selective process through which the recipient tests the prophecy to clarify what they believe the Holy Spirit is saying to them. This is such an important subject, it has its own chapter, *The Principles of Testing Prophecy* [7].
- *Implication* – the process that identifies the significance, purpose and timing of the prophecy for the recipient. [11.6]
- *Implementation* – involves the identification of any actions required by the prophecy and then actually following through with them. [11.7]
- *Investment* – the process whereby we learn to occupy, implement and defend whatever new territory God has moved us into as a result of the prophecy. [11.8]

The 7 I's may seem daunting at first, but the system is quite straightforward actually. Only the first three [*Inspiration, Interpretation* and *Initiation*] apply to the person delivering the prophecy, and are comfortably distinct stages. The *Investigation* stage, while inevitably in our minds when bringing a prophecy, is the responsibility of the recipient and happens independently. This then leaves the last three [*Implication, Implementation* and *Investment*] which only apply to the recipient and are relatively discrete stages. So, depending on where you are in the process, you are only ever considering one or two of them at any one time.

It is important not to get lost in the detail of the 7 I's teaching. The real purpose is to help you break down the prophetic process into easily manageable parts. This will assist your understanding of the process, facilitate your training and practice, and help you deliver a greater level of anointing in accuracy, detail and timing.

1

BATTLE FOR YOUR MIND

Study Notes

School for
Prophecy

1.0   Chapter Summary

1.0.1   *Introduction* – The *Prophetic Engagements* topic covers those areas of spiritual interaction with God which, while a normal part of our salvation and relationship with him, are an integral part of how we move in the gift of prophecy. The first *Prophetic Engagements* subject explains the importance of our thought life as the primary battleground with our enemy, and explains his tactics, weapons and how to defeat him.

1.0.2   *The Battlefield* – The most important principle we need to grasp is that the main battle of life takes place in our minds. Our enemy, through the propagation of lies, seeks to build strongholds in our lives to undermine, impede and disable the important biblical values we should live by.

1.0.3   *Know Your Enemy* – Satan's reliance on lies as his primary weapon against us has earned him the title 'Father of Lies'. Learning to differentiate between your thoughts, Satan's lies and our heavenly Father's gentle voice is the critical component in winning the battle for your mind.

1.0.4   *The Power of Lies* – The power of lies is that they can degrade, displace and replace the truth in our lives if we let them, consciously or unconsciously. Lies, as from the very beginning, seek to undermine our trust, security and relationship with our heavenly Father.

1.0.5   *The Three Great Lies* – We can learn some critical lessons about the devil's methods from his first major encounter with Jesus and the specific lies he utilised. The tests he put Jesus through reveal what I believe are the 'Three Great Lies' in his armoury.

1.0.6   *The Power of Truth* – Fortunately, the truth is far more powerful and effective in our lives than lies can ever be. Jesus taught us that if we hold [condition] to his teaching then we will [promise] know the truth, and the truth will [promise] set us free.

1.0.7   *Know Your Defences* – The first three parts of the armour of God are your defences. The biblical truth, our righteousness in Christ and our relationship with God [through the peace of the gospel] are automatic defence mechanisms against the lies of the enemy.

1.0.8   *Know Your Weapons* – The next three parts of the armour of God are your weapons. A shield that extinguishes fiery darts or lies, a guard for our mind [the truth of salvation] and our Bible knowledge are available offensive weapons we can use against our enemy's lies.

1.1   Introduction

1.1.1   To help you use this manual it is subdivided into four teaching topics: *Prophetic Engagements; Prophetic Foundations; Prophetic Protocols* and *Prophetic Developments.* This first topic on *Prophetic Engagements* covers what classically would form the core teaching of a training course on hearing God's voice. Inevitably, its key role in our relationship with God means there is a symbiotic relationship with moving in the gift of prophecy. In my experience, addressing these subjects before the next topic on *Prophetic Foundations* significantly improves our understanding, and consequently can accelerate our growth in the gift.

1.1.2   In the first topic of the manual we will cover the three core subjects of *Prophetic Engagements: Battle for Your Mind* [this chapter], *Seeing the Bigger Picture* [2] and *Hearing Your Father's Voice* [3]. *Prophetic Engagements* covers those areas of spiritual interaction with God which, while a normal part of our salvation and relationship with him, are an integral part of how we move in the gift of prophecy. The first *Prophetic Engagements* subject explains the importance of our thought life as the primary battleground with our enemy, explains his tactics, weapons and how to defeat him.

1.1.3   This chapter examines how our enemy engages in battle with us through our thought lives, using his weapon of choice, "lies, damned lies and statistics"[3]. Our enemy has made our minds the front line in his opposition to our relationship with our heavenly Father, and consequently the operation of the prophetic gift, through his undermining use of doubt, confusion and fear. The battle for your mind is a key area to appreciate, cultivate and dominate if we want to develop our prophetic gift to its full potential. Inevitably this will involve identifying and defeating the very weapons trying to hold us back.

1.1.4   As you will discover, I have often been fascinated by the sequence of events that play out during the construction of a new building, and have found there to be a remarkable number of biblical principles illustrated. At the very start of construction, a nicely painted fence is erected around the site with many signs about security and safety, and the area inside becomes a 'hard hat' area. This chapter is very much about setting clear boundaries to our thinking; adopting clear and well signposted biblical 'health and safety' procedures, and the importance of wearing a safety head-guard at all times.

1.1.5   In many of the chapters in this manual, what is essential for the development of the gift of prophecy actually helps to reinforce our Christian identity and growth. However, the battle for our mind is essential as part of our proper development and growth in Christ, so there is an obvious 'benefit in kind' of growth in this area as the foundation for the development of our prophetic gift. Accepting, understanding and engaging in this battle during the development of our prophetic gift consequently achieves the same goal for our character and relationship with our heavenly Father.

3. Mark Twain; *Chapters from My Autobiography* [USA: 1906]

1.2   The Battlefield

1.2.1   The most important principle we need to grasp is that the main battle of life takes place in our minds. Even great philosophers and thinkers of the world have long known that "as [a man] thinks in his heart, so is he"[4]. How we think defines and controls who we are and what we do. The first great battlefield is in the mind. We are encouraged to experience transformation by renewing our minds,[5] or literally 'changing the way we think'. Given our minds are our primary means of communication with our heavenly Father, this battle is key in developing your prophetic gift.

1.2.2   The attacks on our mind target fundamental areas of our lives, our identity in Christ, our intimacy with the Holy Spirit and our inheritance through the Father. They seek to undermine our understanding, confidence and application of core biblical truths in these areas through copious applications of caution, condemnation and confusion. Our minds are an important area of attack, because of the considerable impact of any 'toxic thinking', 'cycles of doubt' and 'paralysis by analysis'. Recognizing, engaging and defending this battlefield is consequently an essential area in the development of our gift.

1.2.3   The primary weapon that our enemy uses, and for good reason, is that of 'lies'. Lies are effectively anti-truth, and include untruths, misinformation and false-hoods. If we believe a lie, it creates a doorway through which our enemy can deliver more deception and create giants, i.e. areas of fear in our lives.[6] Whereas the truth leads to faith, lies lead to fear, the opposite of faith. Lies seek to challenge the truth we have been taught, learned or read in the Bible, using leading questions and subtle misdirection[7]. They feed on our fears.

1.2.4   Undermining the truth in our lives allows our enemy to import and reproduce giants in our lives. His long-term plan is to use the giants to build strongholds in our personality or specific areas of our lives. These can over time become places where the kingdom of God is inhibited or prohibited from functioning properly, such as addictions, unhealed hurts and systematic disobedience. A lie, if allowed to take root, can become the very foundation of a stronghold of fear in our life, which can then be fortified and defended by our enemy.

1.2.5   While we are saved by Grace, and live by Grace, our enemy through the propagation of lies seeks to build strongholds in our lives to undermine, impede and disable the important biblical values we should live by. Weakness in these areas inevitably creates wrong thinking, wrong expectations and wrong decisions that could affect how we move in the prophetic gift. The starting place is to recognize the battlefield, understand our role in the battle and humbly recognize our own weaknesses are covered by Grace. Next is to learn to distinguish between lies and the truth by changing the way we think.

1.2.6   Be careful how you are talking to yourself because you are listening.

4. Proverbs 23:7 [AMP] | 5. Romans 12:2 | 6. Numbers 13:27-28 | 7. Genesis 3:1-6

1.3   Know Your Enemy

1.3.1   Like everyone, you will often have had thoughts about how weak you are, what a failure you are and how bad you are compared to others, completely unaware that most of them are not your own. They come from our enemy, Satan, sometimes called the devil. The Bible calls him "the accuser of God's people"[8], and so he is, both day and night. His name also means 'adversary', hence Jesus referred to him as our "enemy". Our precious 'free will' allows him access to us and our thought lives, but not any authority over us.

1.3.2   The Bible teaches us that his goal is to kill, steal and destroy all the important things in our lives,[9] the opposite of Jesus who came to bring us life and in abundance. Satan was once a very significant spiritual being, with glory and authority. But now, because of his pride, he has fallen and is seeking revenge on God by thwarting his purposes in us. This is not a scary matter, as some would like to portray him. He does not have horns or a tail, but is particularly devious in his use of lies and accusations.

1.3.3   We are taught that he is a murderer, who has abandoned the truth, and that there is no truth in him. Satan's reliance on lies as his primary weapon against us has earned him the title "Father of Lies"[10]. Lies are such a significant part of his existence that they are described as his native language. His first encounter with Jesus teaches us that he is skilled at lies, half-truths and even misquoting the Bible. It is important to grasp, no matter how genuine and sincere he appears, you simply cannot trust anything he says. He is a liar. Period.

1.3.4   Our enemy seeks to deceive our minds, using lies, to lead us astray[11] from what we honestly believe God's will is in our lives. If we succumb to and believe his lies, we become deceived. As a result, we start making decisions based on misinformation, head in the wrong direction and misinterpret the true facts of our circumstances. Being led astray need only have a very minor impact to start with, but as time goes by, the distance from the true path becomes larger and larger. Once nudged off course, he can 'let nature take its course'.

1.3.5   We therefore need to get to grips with the fact that our enemy can put thoughts, i.e. lies, directly into our minds. Fortunately, he cannot make us believe them, accept them or act on them. This means that there are effectively three voices in your mind which, interestingly, all sound like yourself. Your own thoughts, the persistently toxic voice of our enemy, and the 'still, small voice' of our heavenly Father. Therefore, learning to differentiate between your thoughts, Satan's lies and our heavenly Father's gentle voice is the critical component in winning the battle for your mind.

1.3.6   No one can make you feel inferior without your permission.

8. Revelation 12:10 | 9. John 10:10 | 10. John 8:44 | 11. 2 Corinthians 11:3

1.4 The Power of Lies

1.4.1   The power of lies is that they can degrade, displace and replace the truth in our lives if we let them, consciously or unconsciously. Lies seek to degrade and undermine the truth by casting doubt on what we believe and feeding on any uncertainty. They then try to displace and dislodge the core truths in our lives from being our guide, using poor experience and disappointment. Finally, they seek to completely replace and erase the 'real' truth with 'new' truths that are easier and more appealing. The result is that we end up believing a lie, something that is not true.

1.4.2   This then is their goal: to replace the genuine truth in our lives with false truths we believe, and act on, as if they were true. Believing something that is not true is the simple definition of being 'deceived'. Believing a lie means you are deceived. It may only have a minor impact at first, but lies are like weeds; they spread rapidly unless forcibly removed. Once a lie has taken root, it will seek to spread to the neighbouring or related thoughts around it and multiply that way. As with any lawn, without regular attention you can end up with patches of weeds where there is no grass left.

1.4.3   This leads directly to the next feature of lies: they actively seek to turn our faith into fear. Lies are our enemy's tools of harm and, being 'ungodly beliefs', will gradually undermine our lifestyle of faith and breed fear instead. Lies, as from the very beginning, seek to undermine our trust, security and relationship with our heavenly Father. They generate fear as we unconsciously move away from positions of faith. Lies will take us on a journey from doubt to anxiety, anxiety to worry, and from worry to fear. Our enemy's lies seek to destroy our foundations of trust and release fear in our lives.

1.4.4   The next logical consequence is that being deceived gives birth to us making bad decisions. Believing a lie means 'not believing the truth but believing an incorrect fact'. We make decisions based on what we believe, and because we now believe something that is not true, we will inevitably make poor decisions. For example, if through difficult times the lie that God will not provide[12] for us starts to take root, fear will begin to grow in our heart and lead to us focussing on our perceived problem.

1.4.5   The final stage is for lies to occupy core values in our lives so that we become self-harming. If our enemy can replace some of our core values with lies, unbiblical beliefs, this potentially has the impact of making our decisions so bad that we will harm ourselves as a result. We can easily demonstrate this by using the example of learning to drive a car. If our enemy, impersonating as your driving instructor, teaches you that a green traffic light means 'stop' and a red traffic light means 'go', then you can see that he does not need to do any more than let nature take its course.

1.4.6   Don't let your thoughts rob you of what his blood has bought you.

12. Philippians 4:19

1.5   The Three Great Lies

1.5.1   We can learn some critical lessons about the devil's methods from his first major encounter with Jesus[13] and the specific lies he utilized. The tests he put Jesus through reveal what I believe are the 'Three Great Lies' in his armoury. This encounter teaches us about the lies the devil uses which, while there are many variations, actually all have the same DNA as the 'Three Great Lies'. By acknowledging, analysing and understanding them, we can prepare ourselves to recognize his attacks and defend ourselves more effectively.

1.5.2   The first great lie, and the source of many variations, says to you, "Go on, it will not do you any harm; it's only a small thing." It is the 'Steal Lie' and is designed to steal your clean conscience, freedom and values. Like a thin end of the wedge, it encourages you to abandon your principles. The devil challenged Jesus' identity and then suggested he turn a stone into bread to prove his identity and deal with his hunger issue.[14] Jesus' reply reveals to us the importance of knowing our own identity and trusting God for his provision.

1.5.3   The second great lie and the DNA of its many variations whispers to you and says, "You will never be any good because you are a failure." This is the 'Kill Lie'. It is designed to kill your hope, trust and identity; to get you to leave the straight path, by encouraging you to take an apparent shortcut to your goals. The devil offered Jesus immediate worldly authority and glory, without any effort, in exchange for worshipping him.[15] Jesus' reply, succinct as it is, reveals the high price being paid in this exchange and the importance of the first commandment.

1.5.4   The third and final great lie, and the father of many variations, announces to you at critical moments, "Nobody loves you; nobody truly cares about you." This is the 'Destroy Lie'. It is designed to destroy your sense of self-worth, belonging and family, to cleverly isolate you by encouraging you to abandon your greatest gift. The devil returned to questioning Jesus' identity by using his current circumstances, and called Jesus to prove it by testing his relationship with his Father.[16] Jesus' reply cleverly reveals how needing to prove we are loved undervalues and undermines its truth.

1.5.5   The common feature of the 'Three Great Lies' is that they test our knowledge and belief in what Jesus achieved for us on the cross. They test the depth of our belief and the level of our knowledge in the application of salvation in our daily lives. True, as with Jesus, the devil chooses opportune moments to lie to us, trying to use our circumstances against us. However, there is an undeniable benefit of growth in this area: we are better able to denounce the lies like Jesus did and better empowered to enjoy the fruit of the incredible 'good news'.

1.5.6   Believe the truth and it protects your past. Believe a lie and it poisons your future.

13. Luke 4:1-13 **| 14.** Luke 4:2-4 **| 15.** Luke 4:5-8 **| 16.** Luke 4:9-12

1.6   The Power of Truth

1.6.1   Fortunately, the truth is far more powerful and effective in our lives than lies can ever be. Jesus taught us how to harness its power in a key teaching, which includes a condition but also two very important and powerful promises. He said that if you hold to [condition] his teaching, then you will [promise] know the truth, and the truth will [promise] set you free.[17] Learning to believe, embrace and apply Jesus' teaching releases revelation about ourselves and our situation, as well as bringing freedom into our character and experience.

1.6.2   When the Bible describes the "armour of God", it reveals an important aspect of 'holding to' that is essential to appreciate.[18] It explains that the whole purpose of the armour is 'to be able to stand your ground'; not to advance, but to hold your ground. Too many Christians, not understanding the finished work of the cross, are tricked by our enemy into leaving their ground, not holding to it, under the misapprehension that they are still trying to get somewhere better. Holding to Jesus' teaching involves standing your ground and digging into the inheritance Christ has already won for you.

1.6.3   I believe another key principle that enables us to hold to his teaching was explained by Jesus when he said, "Seek first [God's] kingdom and his righteousness."[19] This inevitably questions any self-seeking, self-kingdom or self-agenda thinking which is contrary to the first commandment and consequently conflicts with holding to his teaching. It challenges our vision and values to make sure that they are in alignment with the kingdom of heaven and its purposes. Seeking first his kingdom, and not ours or anyone else's, helps us align with heaven, and consequently guides us to stay within Jesus' teaching and values.

1.6.4   To be able to fully 'know the truth' we must recognize the principle that we need to know it in our hearts, not just in our heads. You can only truly 'know' something when you have seen it with your spiritual eyes, i.e. the eyes of your heart, not with the eyes in your head [2.3.5]. Holding to Jesus' teaching brings us to a place where we believe. Belief is the birthing place of faith, and that enables us to see with our spiritual eyes the truth that may or may not be visible with our physical eyes.

1.6.5   Finally, we need to understand our spiritual authority, so that knowing the truth has its full impact in setting us free. Jesus reinforces his key teaching about the truth setting us free shortly afterwards, when he declares that if he sets you free, you will be free indeed.[20] It is therefore important that we recognize in our hearts that Jesus has set us free from the guilt and power of sin, our old selves and desires. To experience our true freedom, we must comprehend and exercise the spiritual authority Jesus won for us on the cross.

1.6.6   Believing the truth opens a door of potential, perspective and power.

17. John 8:31-32 | **18.** Ephesians 6:13 | **19.** Matthew 6:33 | **20.** John 8:36

1.7   Know Your Defences

1.7.1   After re-emphasising the principle of standing your ground [1.6.2], the Bible then identifies the first three parts of the armour of God, which are our defence against our enemy's lies.[21] These are the belt of truth, the breastplate of righteousness and the gospel of peace. The biblical truth, our righteousness in Christ and our relationship with God [through the peace of the gospel] are automatic defence mechanisms against the lies of the enemy. While they are a natural part of our salvation, we should be consciously wearing and relying on them daily.

1.7.2   Another defence we have is our ability to control what we think [1.3.5]. Simple as it may seem, this has far-reaching consequences. We are encouraged not to conform to the way the world thinks, but to be transformed by the renewing of our minds.[22] Simply put, changing the way you think changes who you are. This is a powerful truth the world has come to recognize but lacks the power of the Spirit of Truth within it to achieve. By recognizing the enemy's lies in our thoughts, we can renew our mind by thinking differently and consequently become transformed.

1.7.3   A defence mechanism that is often missed by many, and deliberately ignored by the world, is our conscience. This is the gentle whisper in our hearts that guides our actions and comments on our values. When you deliberately tell a lie, your conscience alarm starts going off. Our conscience is a form of 'virus checker' for lies living in our minds. Our enemy is obviously instructing us to ignore our conscience, but it's still there, repeatedly, disturbingly and persistently! Our conscience is there for a purpose, so it is no surprise that during a mentoring subject I will often encourage people to listen to their heart.

1.7.4   It is essential to appreciate that the battle for your mind is a journey, and not a single event. At the first sign of a mistake, our enemy will pronounce that it is not even worth trying, when we have only just begun to fight. The Bible delightfully teaches that, providing you are seeking the truth, practice does make perfect.[23] It says that the mature have trained themselves to distinguish between the truth and a lie *by practice*. The battle for your mind is a journey of practice, learning from your mistakes and embracing the real truth.

1.7.5   Finally, I believe during my 40+ years as a Christian I have discovered four distinctive hallmarks of our enemy's lies which have considerably helped me in identifying them in my thoughts and deliberations. Whenever I am experiencing anxiety, confusion, impotence or condemnation, I immediately start examining my thoughts for the enemy's lies, because I do not believe these ever come from God. For me they are a reliable tell-tale sign that he has deposited lies into my thinking. I believe God only ever gives us the opposites, which are faith, conviction, hope and endorsement.

1.7.6   F.E.A.R. is "False Evidence Appearing Real".

21. Ephesians 6:14-15 | **22.** Romans 12:2 | **23.** Hebrews 5:14

School for
Prophecy

1.8   Know Your Weapons

1.8.1   After covering the three defensive parts of our armour, the Bible then identifies the next three parts,[24] which are our offensive weapons against our enemy's lies. These are the shield of faith, the helmet of salvation and the sword of the Spirit. A shield that extinguishes fiery darts, i.e. lies, a guard for our mind [the truth of salvation] and our Bible knowledge are available offensive weapons we can use against our enemy's lies. While you 'wear' the defensive armour, the Bible instructs us to 'take up' the offensive armour, because we are meant to 'wield' it.

1.8.2   While Roman armour is used to illustrate our spiritual weapons, we do not wage war like the world does, and consequently our weapons are not like the world's.[25] Our weapons are designed to demolish lies that argue against the truth, lies making claims contrary to biblical values and lies trying to take control of our thoughts. There is a formidable array of supernatural weapons available to us through the offensive power of the armour of God, the indwelling power of the Spirit of Truth and the freedom from our old nature Jesus won on the cross.

1.8.3   It is worth looking closely at what our offensive weapons destroy, because this helpfully identifies what we should be looking out for. Firstly, they demolish arguments that try to tell us what we believe is wrong. A well-timed doubt is a powerful grenade we need to be alert for. Secondly, they demolish the assertions of the many voices around us that claim there is an easier way and ours is fatally flawed. Assertions can create prison walls. Finally, they enable us to take captive our enemy's lies, take control of our thoughts and become the free people we were born to be.

1.8.4   Bottom line: we need to 'think about what we are thinking about'. To put it another way, we need to 'listen to ourselves'. This is not so strange when you acknowledge that our enemy is putting thoughts and lies into our minds that sound exactly like us! While our defensive armour helps us to take hits and bounce back, with our offensive weapons we can literally go 'looking for trouble' and deal with it when we find it. The Bible refers to lies as fiery darts, and the raging forest fire caused by a thrown-away cigarette butt is a sobering illustration of the emotional reality.

1.8.5   One specific ability our weapons have is the "divine power to demolish strongholds"[26]. Unfortunately, through pain, disappointment or failure some lies evade our weapons and make it through our defences. They then take root and replace the truth with a lie, thereby becoming a stronghold in our lives. These can frequently be identified as areas of our life where we are struggling, bear poor fruit or have ongoing hurts from the past. We need to identify and break them with our offensive weapons, if necessary assisted by courses like *Freedom in Christ*[27] and *Restoring the Foundations*[28].

1.8.6   T.R.U.S.T. is "Total Reliance Upon Spiritual Truth".

24. Ephesians 6:16-17 | 25. 2 Corinthians 10:3-5 | 26. 2 Corinthians 10:4b | 27. *www.ficm.org.uk*
28. *www.restoringthefoundations.org*

1.9   Personal Testimony

1.9.1   My journey with the battle for my mind began by accident and progressed in stages. I had an intense childhood of anxiety, fear and stress, and my life was built around it with the usual coping mechanisms. Saving for a rainy day, anticipating the worst and being stressed by exams was my normal diet. I was in a kind, loving and caring family, but I lived like the Gauls in *Asterix,* with a fear that "the sky may fall on my head tomorrow"[29]. Panic attacks were one of the more unpleasant symptoms I experienced.

1.9.2   Having been saved for just under a year, I moved to university for a very difficult and emotional first year. I then had an epiphany and made a momentous decision which was to set me on a different path from then on. Not only did my doctrinal position say that my experience was just not biblical, but I also realized the tradition of fear I was beginning to develop. So, I made a decision to change, to live by faith, not in fear, and to trust God every day. In hindsight, this was clearly birthed by inspiration from the Holy Spirit as part of my maturing.

1.9.3   This quite literally transformed me over my student years from an introvert to an extrovert, and from a pessimist to an optimist. I consumed the Bible; I worshiped intensely; I read every Watchmen Nee book I could find; I learned off by heart many key Bible promises [including the whole of Philippians 4]; and I spent hours with strong Christian friends. The more I broke free, the easier it became to change. I was soon trusting my heavenly Father for my failing student finances, poor study results and confusion about my future.

1.9.4   My student years came to an end, and after qualifying as an accountant I settled down. I developed the normal family, mortgage, car and job lifestyle and noticed that the anxiety, fear and stress started to take control again, especially through my work. This triggered the next eureka moment, when I realized that not all the thoughts in my head were mine and I was becoming self-destructive. It was an intense period as I fought to get control of my thought life back and break out of the ungodly thought patterns I had acquired.

1.9.5   Fortunately, I had developed a love for computers, or what they were back then, and my familiarity with antivirus software helped me to understand the concept of the battle for my mind and the importance of the truth. I researched this area more thoughtfully, and with more experience discovered our enemy, his weapons of lies and the importance of the armour of God in my life. This changed things. I now better understood the environment I was living in, the nature of the spiritual battle and my freedom to choose what I think.

1.9.6   While it is still an ongoing journey, the battle for my mind has been significant in my growth as a son of God and confidence in my prophetic ministry. Engaging in it has helped me sharpen the core biblical values I live by, deepen my understanding of our enemy's tactics and broaden my appreciation for the love of God. Interestingly, in recent years it has become significant again as an essential part of my role as a mentor to the people I journey with.

29. Chief Vitalstatistix

School for
Prophecy

1.10 Frequently Asked Questions

1.10.1   How do I know if a thought is mine or it is someone else's?

1.10.2   Just recognizing that there are three potential sources for your thoughts is a great step forward [1.3.5]. The majority will be yours, but you will learn by practice to identify our enemy's and the Holy Spirit's. Their name gives you a big clue to start with. Our enemy is an accuser and a liar, and these are features you should be alert for. He is trying to throw 'grenades' into your mind at critical moments.

1.10.3   Are you really saying there are other voices in my head?!

1.10.4   These are not voices in your head; that is something completely different. These are thoughts in your mind that, although they sound and feel like all the others, they are not from you. God is whispering to you through his Holy Spirit, to encourage and guide you [3.5.3]. Our enemy is trying to mislead, misinform and misdirect you through ideas that you think are your own [1.3.1].

1.10.5   How can I recognize when one of my thoughts is a lie?

1.10.6   The page describing the 'Three Great Lies' [1.5] is a good place to start. This explains the major types of lies that our enemy uses, because they are most effective. Listening for what I call the 'darkness' in your thoughts will help you identify them. Remember, our enemy likes to lie to us at times when we are emotional, particularly distracted or upset, and when things go wrong.

1.10.7   How can I learn not to let myself overthink these situations?

1.10.8   The foundational change we all need to make is not to conform to how the world thinks, and change the way we think to be more like Jesus [1.6.1]. I have recommended you imagine you are running spiritual antivirus software in your mind, that uses the truth to detect and destroy the lies that try to make your thoughts their home. Bottom line: give yourself time, it takes practice.

1.10.9   I feel very weak in this area; is there anything I can do to be stronger?

1.10.10 Fortunately, we have been given a shield, helmet and sword as weapons[30] [1.8.1] that we can use in this conflict. These weapons have divine power to help you demolish arguments in your mind, lies that seek to take root, and help you have self-control over your thought life. Bottom line: there is no better solution than a healthy, regular diet of Bible reading, study and meditation.

1.10.11 How can I find lies in my past that I let in before I realized the danger?

1.10.12 This is more challenging because these are lies that have already become part of your life. I suggest you look for barrenness [the effect of lies] in those areas that have a bigger impact on your life, such as your identity, intimacy and inheritance. Also, you should consider the courses I have mentioned [1.8.5] which are designed for this purpose, and others like it, e.g. SOZO.

---

30. Ephesians 6:16-17

Study Notes

2

SEEING THE BIGGER PICTURE

Study Notes

School for
Prophecy

2.0   Chapter Summary

2.0.1   *Introduction – Prophetic Engagements* covers those areas of spiritual interaction with God which, while a normal part of our salvation and relationship with him, are an integral part of how we move in the gift of prophecy. The second *Prophetic Engagements* subject lays the biblical principles of how to see the invisible realm with our spiritual eyes, as well as the visible realm with our physical eyes.

2.0.2   *The Bigger Picture* – One of the consistent features of Jesus' early ministry was that despite the profound things he taught, people regularly did not understand him. Those around Jesus could not see the bigger picture and as a result their understanding was based on incomplete information – hence the problem. *Prophetic Engagements* are about seeing the bigger picture.

2.0.3   *The Eyes of Our Heart* – To be able to see in the Spirit and to see into the spiritual realm, we need to see with the eyes of our heart. To see the bigger picture, you need to see the physical world with your physical eyes and the spiritual realm with your spiritual eyes, i.e. the eyes of your heart.

2.0.4   *The Problem with Our Eyes* – We face an immediate problem because our physical eyes are such an important and powerful tool in our lives that they usually dominate, dictate and define how we see our world. We do need to recognize that they are not the only pair of eyes we have and they do not always tell us the whole story.

2.0.5   *Living by Faith and Not by Sight* – The definition of 'faith' in the Bible makes this point very clearly. Faith is confidence in what we hope for and assurance about what we do not see. Faith is fundamentally all about what you cannot see with your physical eyes but you can see with your spiritual eyes.

2.0.6   *Understanding How God Works* – To help us see with the eyes of our heart, we also need to learn to recognize when and where God is at work. Seeing with the eyes of your heart involves sensing, feeling and recognizing spiritually when God is doing something different and letting the Holy Spirit guide you.

2.0.7   *Opening Our Spiritual Eyes* – Learning to see with the eyes of your heart may involve opening your spiritual eyes for the first time, and stepping out in faith and trust where you have never been before. It involves learning to see beyond the facts as presented by the eyes in your head, and to recognize that "there is more than meets the eye".

2.0.8   *The Spiritual Dimension* – There are two different realities available to us. We can limit ourselves to just seeing the visible world with our physical eyes, or we can see with our spiritual eyes into the invisible realm. Seeing the bigger picture, i.e. seeing in the Spirit, is recognizing that there are times when our physical eyes do not tell us the whole story, and on occasions completely mislead us.

School for Prophecy

2.1   Introduction

2.1.1   Following the previous chapter on *Battle for Your Mind* [1], the next subject in the *Prophetic Engagements* topic is the equally critical means of encounter, *Seeing the Bigger Picture*. *Prophetic Engagements* covers those areas of spiritual interaction with God which, while a normal part of our salvation and relationship with him, are an integral part of how we move in the gift of prophecy. The second *Prophetic Engagements* subject lays the biblical principles of how to see the invisible realm with our spiritual eyes, as well as the visible realm with our physical eyes.

2.1.2   A key part of our spiritual sonship [3.2], which enables us to engage in the gift of prophecy, is to learn how to be able to 'see the bigger picture'. Some would call this learning to 'see through Father's eyes' or, more commonly, 'see in the Spirit'. In doing this, we recognize the reality that we are not only physical beings, but spiritual beings as well, and need to be able to see in both dimensions. This is not a spooky or flaky subject but a simple recognition that God is spirit[31] and has given us a living spirit to be in relationship with him.

2.1.3   One of the interesting features of a building site [1.1.4] is that not a lot seems to happen for a long time, other than a big hole. However, this is a key stage, where the necessary utilities are being installed before the foundations are laid or any building work commences. While some utilities can be added at a later date, with some limited success, once the foundations are laid it is very difficult and expensive to back install them for universal availability. Seeing the bigger picture is well illustrated by the early installation of utilities, as it provides adequate resources for whatever we might need in the future.

2.1.4   The two common errors associated with this subject are both extreme versions of the principle, but in different directions, which result in them both failing miserably. The first approach is so uncertain about what is from God and what is unspiritual imagination that it limits its experience to only what our physical eyes can see. This makes the bigger picture so insignificant it becomes ignored. The second approach sees significant meaning in everything, whether there is one or not, a form of super-spirituality, making the bigger picture so intense and extensive it becomes overwhelming.

2.1.5   Of all the subjects covered in this manual, *Seeing the Bigger Picture* has the most capacity to have a profound, positive and permanent impact on people's lives. The lack of teaching in this area, non-supernatural traditions and the focus on meetings often does not allow disciples to connect with their spiritual and supernatural roots. I therefore often use the teaching in this chapter outside of my *School for Prophecy* courses, admittedly in a shorter form, when helping churches teach about identity and intimacy. The acceptance of a spiritual realm outside of the physical world, let alone being able to see into it, can change people's lives profoundly.

---

31. John 4:24

School for Prophecy

2.2   The Bigger Picture

2.2.1   One of the consistent features of Jesus' early ministry was that despite the profound things he taught, people regularly did not understand him. This was particularly true of his disciples, who you would have thought would have had a better grasp of his life's message. Even his day-to-day conversation would often be completely incomprehensible to them. This demonstrates the key principle of this chapter. Those around Jesus could not see the bigger picture and as a result their understanding was based on incomplete information, hence the problem. *Prophetic Engagements* are about seeing the bigger picture.

2.2.2   A good and helpful illustration of this is the time Jesus was approached and questioned by a rich ruler in front of his disciples.[32] He asked Jesus what he had to do to inherit eternal life, and it seems to me that he was pretty confident he had already satisfied the anticipated answer. Jesus gave him an overview of the Mosaic commandments he needed to obey and, sure enough, he immediately answered that he had followed them since childhood. Up to this point everything was going well, and everyone was probably on the same page.

2.2.3   However, it is at this point that the conversation took a weird turn and everyone lost the plot. Jesus unexpectedly told him to sell everything he owned, give it to the poor, and then come and follow him. The rich ruler became very sad because of his great wealth, and as a result Jesus announced that it is hard for the rich to enter the kingdom of God. From the disciples' point of view, he looked a 'dead cert' to become the next disciple. He would be a good source of income for them; he would have had a significant standing in the local community and probably substantial political influence.

2.2.4   Jesus, however, was able to see what the disciples, and those with them, were unable to see. In fact, what the disciples did not realize, because of their limited perspective, was that all Jesus was doing was *actually* answering the rich ruler's question! Jesus could see with his spiritual eyes that the rich ruler had an idol of wealth in his life that stopped him from inheriting eternal life. So, to be able to inherit eternal life he needed to be delivered from his idol and recognize Jesus as Lord, i.e. sell everything, give it to the poor and then follow Jesus.

2.2.5   This story explains the conundrum of why people regularly did not understand what Jesus said. Jesus was able to see more than others; he was able to see the bigger picture. Consequently, he was making conversation based on information those around him did not have. They were only able to see, at that stage, with their physical eyes, i.e. the eyes in their head. Jesus, on the other hand, was able to see in the Spirit, which meant he had more accurate information than those around him which, if known, would have turned his inexplicable actions into obvious ones.

2.2.6   Only engaging with the physical world sacrifices the eternal for the convenient.

32. Luke 18:18-23

School for Prophecy

2.3 The Eyes of Our Heart

2.3.1   When we are moving in the gift of prophecy, we are seeking to bring God's message, which will naturally be from his perspective. Seeing the world as the people around us are seeing it will not necessarily achieve this. Effectively, we need to see the world as God sees it to properly reflect his perspective and purpose. To do this we need to see things through, or with, our Father's eyes, called 'seeing in the Spirit'. This involves seeing the physical world with our physical eyes but also seeing the spiritual world through our Father's eyes.

2.3.2   Jesus established an important foundational principle on this subject when he said to his disciples, "The Son can do nothing by himself; he can only do what he sees his Father doing."[33] This reveals how Jesus knew what to do, i.e. what God's will in his life was. He looked to see what his Father was doing and followed suit. Given how exclusive this statement is, if we want to be Jesus' disciples and follow him, then we too need to be able to see what the Father is doing. We need to learn to see the bigger picture.

2.3.3   If we can only see with our physical eyes, the eyes in our head, we will miss much of what he is doing in, through and around us. God is spirit[34] and to see the bigger picture we need to be able to see in the Spirit. Unfortunately, having discovered this clearly important principle in my life, without knowing how to see in the Spirit, it became a source of much frustration to me. A number of years later, while studying what I consider to be the greatest three-point sermon in the Bible, I came upon the key to seeing in the Spirit.

2.3.4   Fortunately for us, the Bible explains how we can practically do this in our lives. While praying for the Ephesians to receive the spirit of wisdom and revelation, Paul identifies the key principle of how to see in the Spirit: "I pray that the eyes of your heart may be enlightened."[35] To be able to see in the Spirit, to see into the spiritual realm, we need to see with the 'eyes of our heart'. To see the bigger picture, you need to see the physical world with your physical eyes, and the spiritual realm with your spiritual eyes, i.e. the eyes of your heart.

2.3.5   This does require a radical change in our approach, especially if we have previously predominantly relied on our physical eyes. Seeing with the eyes of your heart does not have the filmlike quality that we are used to our physical eyes providing. The eyes in our heart recognize the invisible realm, and provide a sense, a conviction and feelings about the spiritual world around us as inspired by the Holy Spirit living within us. This can feel like learning to drive a car all over again but, combined with the principles established in the previous chapter [1.1.3], releases a God-given solution.

2.3.6   To see what our Father is doing, you have to see through his eyes.

33. John 5:17-19 | 34. John 4:24 | 35. Ephesians 1:18-19

School for **Prophecy**

2.4 The Problem with Our Eyes

2.4.1 We face an immediate problem because our physical eyes are such an important and powerful tool in our lives that they usually dominate, dictate and define how we see our world. Our physical eyes are undoubtedly a wonderful gift from God and an essential part of our five physical senses. I am in no way suggesting that the next time you go driving you close your eyes to see how seeing in the Spirit works! However, we do need to recognize that they are not the only pair of eyes we have, and they do not always tell us the whole story.

2.4.2 Jesus made this point very clearly when he said, "The eye is the lamp of the body." He pointed out that, "If your eyes are healthy, your whole body will be full of light."[36] While he is drawing a comparison between the two extremes, light and darkness, the truth still applies between these two points. The light or darkness in our worldview depends on how good our eyesight is. The quality of the sight of our physical eyes and spiritual eyes, being the 'lamp of the body', determines the amount and quality of the light in our life.

2.4.3 The challenge with our physical eyes is that, no matter how important and essential they are, their power enables them to define the world around us based only on what they see. However, no matter how accurate our physical eyes are, they do not always tell us the whole truth. They sometimes miss so much it is misleading, and on occasions they simply lie to us by denying the impossible is possible. Relying on our physical eyes will inevitably limit our perspective to our level of knowledge, the laws of the science of our age and our experience to date.

2.4.4 Jesus once berated his disciples for this mistake, when he said, "Do you have eyes but fail to see, and ears but fail to hear?"[37] They had not yet learned to see into the spiritual realm, with the eyes of their heart, and were consequently completely missing the point. By relying on their physical eyes' interpretation of their world, they misunderstood Jesus. Interestingly, instead of emphasising the impossibility of feeding the five and four thousand with very little food, he drew their attention to the physical impossibility of having more than they started with left over afterwards!

2.4.5 I am not saying we should not use our physical eyes to perceive our world, but I am saying we cannot see everything, i.e. the bigger picture, without the inclusion of our spiritual eyes, 'the eyes of our heart'. Our physical eyes can only see into the visible realm, so we need our spiritual eyes to see into the invisible realm, sometimes referred to as 'seeing in the Spirit'. We need to learn to see with the eyes of our heart, as the Bible teaches, so we are able to see the bigger picture, and specifically follow Jesus [2.3.2] by looking to see what the Father is doing!

2.4.6 Relying on our physical eyes limits God to our level of understanding.

36. Matthew 6:22-23 | 37. Mark 8:14-21

2.5   Living by Faith and Not by Sight

2.5.1   In contrast to the powerful impact on us that our physical eyes can have, as disciples we are called to live by faith. It is a core principle of our Christian lives that we live our life by what we believe, not just by what our eyes tell us. As the Bible famously puts it, "We live by faith, not by sight."[38] As a corollary, living by faith requires us to see the bigger picture. We are called to rely on what our faith sees in the invisible, and not just depend on what our eyes see in the visible.

2.5.2   Our calling is a lifestyle of faith, of trusting in God. The definition of faith in the Bible makes this point very clearly: "Now faith is confidence in what we hope for and assurance about what we do not see."[39] Faith is fundamentally all about what you cannot see with your physical eyes, but you can see with your spiritual eyes. All born-again Christians do this quite naturally and comfortably every day, as we believe in an invisible God we cannot prove with any of our five senses, let alone our eyes.

2.5.3   One disciple made himself famous for refusing to see the bigger picture and acquired the nickname 'Doubting Thomas' as a result. When the other disciples told Thomas that they had seen the risen Jesus, he firmly replied he would not believe them until he had seen this with his own eyes.[40] Thomas dogmatically took the position of only believing what he could see with his physical eyes and denied the bigger picture. The kindness of Jesus was that he later appeared to Thomas and gave him the required physical evidence so that Thomas would believe the miracle of his resurrection.

2.5.4   After Thomas had publicly acknowledged the miracle, Jesus then reinforced the principle by stating that, "Blessed are those who have not seen and yet have believed." Jesus was directly addressing the mistake Thomas had made and was calling us to believe what we have seen with the eyes of our heart, i.e. eyes of faith, even if we have not seen it with our physical eyes. You need to see the bigger picture. You need to see the invisible world with the eyes of your heart, as well as the visible world with the eyes in your head.

2.5.5   Another good example of the importance of seeing the bigger picture is when Jesus declared, "I have not found anyone in Israel with such great faith."[41] What made him say this? He had met a centurion who had come to him to request he heal his seriously ill servant. However, unlike many others, he was able to recognize the divine authority in Jesus, by seeing with his heart what he could not see with his eyes. On explaining the basis of his revelation, and consequent faith, this triggered the above profound statement from Jesus.

2.5.6   Faith is making decisions based on what we see in heaven, not what we see on earth.

---

38. 2 Corinthians 5:7 | 39. Hebrews 11:1 | 40. John 20:24-29 | 41. Matthew 8:5-13

School for **Prophecy**

2.6 Understanding How God Works

2.6.1 To help us see with the eyes of our heart, we also need to learn to recognize when and where God is at work. Seeing with the eyes of your heart involves sensing, feeling and recognizing spiritually when God is doing something different, and letting the Holy Spirit guide you. This acknowledges that some of the unusual thoughts we have are actually the Holy Spirit speaking, directing and leading us [3.3.3]. Understanding how God works, and the principles he moves by, will obviously help us recognize more easily when and what he is doing. The challenge we face is that God works in very different ways to us.

2.6.2 There is a well-known verse that points out how challenging understanding God's ways can be, but I am not convinced its significance is really fully grasped. It says, and then repeats for effect, "My thoughts are not your thoughts, neither are your ways my ways."[42] Put simply, God does not think like we do, and he does not do things like we do. His omniscience, omnipresence and omnipotence put him in a completely different dimension to us. However, we can learn to recognize where he is at work. Learning to see when God is moving is one thing, but we still may not fully understand what he is doing.

2.6.3 Resting in a place where you comfortably accept that God is beyond your understanding, experience and imagination opens up a whole new season of unexpected coincidences, God appointments, supernatural surprises and miraculous outcomes. We are clearly taught that God is beyond our thinking and our full understanding, but I wonder if we take this seriously. This specifically means that why, what and how we do things are usually very different from why, what and how God does things. My experience of trying to predict how and when God will do something has a very low success rate!

2.6.4 Another well-known verse that reinforces this point, and yet again I am not sure how often it is applied, states that we are to "trust in the Lord with all [our] heart and lean not on [our] own understanding"[43]. Alternatively, this could read, trust in what you see with the eyes of your heart and don't just rely on the eyes in your head. Given that God is seriously beyond our understanding, this is wise counsel. It is interesting that it goes on to say, "Don't be wise in your own eyes," i.e. don't think you know better than God!

2.6.5 This means that letting the eyes in our head guide us is often going to be a very unfruitful journey and has specific implications for how we perceive things. While our minds are a remarkable and wonderful resource for us, relying on our own understanding will severely limit how much we can see what the Father is doing. Looking for the invisible is an act of faith and trust, recognizing the Father can do a lot of things we can't. Seeing in the Spirit involves seeing things in the light of God's nature, God's purposes and God's abilities, so we can recognize what he is doing.

2.6.6 God works with consistent motives, but with unpredictable methods.

42. Isaiah 55:8-11 | **43.** Proverbs 3:5-8

School for **Prophecy**

2.7 Opening Our Spiritual Eyes

2.7.1   Learning to see with the 'eyes of your heart' may involve opening your spiritual eyes for the first time and stepping out in faith and trust where you have never been before. It involves learning to see beyond the facts as presented by the 'eyes in your head', and to recognize that "there is more than meets the eye"[44]. This is not always an immediate process and can happen over a period of time. I have found the story of David and Goliath very helpful in watching someone gradually see more in the Spirit over time and be more directly led by the Holy Spirit. This is called progressive revelation.

2.7.2   David's journey began while he was delivering lunch to his ungrateful brothers and he got talking to the other soldiers around them. He was probably being nosey, but there came a moment when he saw something the 'eyes in his head' could not see and which the Spirit had revealed to him. "Who is this uncircumcised Philistine that he should defy the armies of the living God?"[45] He saw a deep spiritual reality that contrasted profoundly with how everyone else around him saw the situation, and opened up a whole new avenue of understanding, possibilities and action.

2.7.3   This awakening goes nowhere until Saul calls for him to come and meet him in his tent. David bravely volunteers to face Goliath, but during the conversation continues to see more and more of the spiritual truth he has not understood before. He begins to see that when God rescued him from the lion and the bear during his day job, he was actually being prepared to face and fight Goliath.[46] He is still only talking about being rescued, but he is seeing more and more with the 'eyes of his heart', as revelation builds on revelation.

2.7.4   Finally, David is in "the valley of decision"[47] facing Goliath, and the adrenaline speeds up the pace of his growing spiritual sight. He comes to the realisation that Goliath is actually fighting God, not him, because he has defied God publicly. Declaring that he will kill Goliath would be enough, but his inner sight continues to grow and he starts prophesying the immediate doom of the whole Philistine army, not just Goliath.[48] He at last grasps the full extent of God's ultimate purpose, that "the whole world will know that there is a God in Israel".

2.7.5   We may well face reasonable criticism from others when we genuinely follow the leading of the Spirit contrary to other people's physical and logical interpretations. Our journeys will be a lot easier if we learn to recognize that the Spirit works according to God's kingdom principles, and is not limited by our human understanding, experience or knowledge. We will then be better equipped to see his footprints on the path, feel his fingerprints in our life and hear his whispers in our soul.

2.7.6   We need to see the invisible, to be able to do the impossible.

44. W. H. Auden; *At Last the Secret is Out* [Poem, UK] | **45.** 1 Samuel 17:25-26 | **46.** 1 Samuel 17:31-35
47. Joel 3:14 | **48.** 1 Samuel 17:45-47

School for
Prophecy

2.8   The Spiritual Dimension

2.8.1   There are two different realities available to us. We can limit ourselves to just seeing the visible world with our physical eyes, or we can see with our spiritual eyes into the invisible realm. Seeing the bigger picture is recognizing that there are times when our physical eyes do not tell us the whole story, and on occasions completely mislead us. Being able to see with our spiritual eyes will help us be alert to those situations and circumstances when God is doing something different, unexpected or impossible.

2.8.2   The feeding of the 5,000[49] is a wonderful example of the disciples, who only used the 'eyes in their head', trying to talk to Jesus, someone who only used the 'eyes of his heart'. For once the disciples are showing some solid wisdom and suggest that Jesus sends the crowds away from their remote location to get some food and rest ready for another day tomorrow. But Jesus replies, "They do not need to go away. You give them something to eat." Now, you don't say to the Son of God, "Don't be silly!" even when you want to. They probably guessed they were missing the point but had no idea what it was.

2.8.3   So, they politely try to point out how ridiculous this request is by replying, "We only have five loaves of bread and two fish" [and 5,000+ people – hint, hint!]. You know the story. Jesus prays over the five loaves and two fish, and then makes the point by letting the disciples themselves feed 5,000+ people *and* have more left over than they started with. I am convinced they would have been staring incredulously at the baskets they were carrying as they began to realize they were not only not using up the food, but it was actually multiplying somehow in the baskets at the same time!

2.8.4   While the advent of technology like mobile phones has transformed my children's world, back in the late 70s when computers filled rooms and we talked to them by punched cards, a greater technological innovation occurred called 'WYSIWYG' [pronounced wiz-e-wig]. Back then we produced documents on word processors without any formatting, and consequently they then had to be transferred to a separate formatting program with fonts, margins, spacing, tabs etc. before they could be printed. Someone realized it would make life so much easier if what you printed was the same as what you could see on the screen.

2.8.5   WYSIWYG was birthed and soon became a normal part of everyone's lives. WYSIWYG stands for 'what you see is what you get' and sums up the principle of this chapter, seeing the bigger picture. If all you see is through your physical eyes [the eyes in your head], then that is all you are going to be able to experience. But if you can see into the invisible world with your spiritual eyes [the eyes of your heart] as well, then you will be able to engage, experience and enjoy the whole spiritual truth, and not just some of it.

2.8.6   We need to learn to see the truth with the eyes of our heart, and not just the facts with the eyes in our head.

49. Matthew 14:13-21

2.9   Personal Testimony

2.9.1   Some years ago, I went to an *Encounter More* conference at Causeway Coast Vineyard in Northern Ireland with a good friend of mine. It was at a time when I was seeking God for some big decisions in my life, so I was making space for myself. I found myself near the back of the main hall on my own and lost in my thoughts, when a group of men came in and sat down two rows right in front of me. With a hall that was nearly empty this felt unusual and, believing that God appointments are more frequent than we realize, I began to wonder if the man sitting in front of me was there for a purpose.

2.9.2   So, I began to quietly ask the Holy Spirit if he wanted me to do or say anything. Not much happened and then the group started chatting in friendly banter until the man in front of me became quite engrossed in a serious conversation. *Phew, well that ends that,* I thought, *I don't have to do anything.* Then quite suddenly into my mind jumped the thought, "Tell him that the plant may be dead, but the roots are still good." My heart rate rose immediately and I started to think of a hundred reasons why I couldn't share that. An image of a plant with a lady maybe, but a man, no.

2.9.3   Just to make things worse, he turned around and said hello to me. Heavens! I decided to go what I call 'fishing' first. Yes, lack of faith, I know. I introduced myself politely – *Please, don't think I am weird!* – and said I felt God had given me a word for him and wondered if something in his life had died recently, as I felt God was speaking life into it. He looked at me intently – *Yep, he thinks I am weird!* – and said they had just come straight from court, where his business had been wound up. They had lost everything and had spontaneously come to the conference to seek God's wisdom.

2.9.4   You could have heard a pin drop; everyone in the group was now looking at me. I shared with him, and them, what God had said to me about the plant, and how it easily fitted into his current situation with his business. My word grew at that moment, as did my confidence, into a more significant prophecy for him and his wife as I drew out the implications of 'good roots'. He immediately shared that relocation had been one of the options they had been considering but had been too overwhelmed by their recent financial loss. The group dynamics completely changed. Furious conversations soon left me well behind as they began to sense the possibilities of God in their situation.

2.9.5   I have learned time and time again that the Holy Spirit knows so much more than we do, and that trying to make decisions based on the limited information we have, rather than simply trusting and obeying him, is a recipe for missed opportunities, disappointment and confusion. I could recount numerous stories in which God has whispered to me thoughts that just could not be right, did not make any sense, or would make me look stupid. By simply being faithful in my gift, God has brought heaven to earth time and time again.

School for
Prophecy

2.10 Frequently Asked Questions

2.10.1 How do I know what I sense is from God?

2.10.2 Assuming that we can agree that there is a gift of prophecy today, and therefore we recognize that our heavenly Father speaks through us to others, then it is a matter of trusting our heavenly Father [3.3]. Jesus taught that he will give you what you ask for, not something worse, and that he is much more generous than us in giving to those who ask him.[50]

2.10.3 What if I get it wrong?

2.10.4 Chapter 7 teaches that prophecy should not be acted on until it has been tested and confirmed, so New Covenant 'health and safety' helps here [4.7.5]. However, if you stay within the definition of biblical prophecy[51] to strengthen, encourage and comfort, and you stay within your anointing,[52] then the worst that can happen is that you encourage someone in the wrong area of their life!

2.10.5 I am afraid of hurting someone…

2.10.6 Usually this means you have had a bad experience or heard of one. God only gives good gifts, and this is one of the best! If the giver and receiver stay within the very clear biblical principles and guidelines [6.2.2], everyone will be better off. It is only when independent characters, super-spiritual individuals or over-the-top ministries are involved that there is a real danger.

2.10.7 Am I just making up fantasies in my head?

2.10.8 Any prophecy inevitably starts in God and comes from his Spirit into our minds at some stage. It therefore inevitably feels and sounds like one of our own thoughts until we learn to recognize it. You are simply recognising that there is 'a bigger picture' and your spiritual eyes [2.7.1] are enabling you to see more than the physical reality around you.

2.10.9 I have heard that this sort of thing opens you up to the enemy…

2.10.10 This is actually scaremongering by the enemy to keep you away from the gift of prophecy [1.3.2]. There is no danger in focussing on, seeking and listening to Jesus; the danger comes when we set our minds on other things. Similarly, don't give the enemy too much credit. He is the father of lies and our accuser primarily.

2.10.11 Doesn't this make you vulnerable to manipulation by others?

2.10.12 Manipulation happens when you give your authority to someone else. This tends to happen when we are insecure in our guidance and rely on someone else's gift instead of our own sonship. It can also happen when we believe 'celebrities' have Old Covenant powers, which is unbiblical. Sticking to the biblical requirement of testing will keep you safe [7.8.4].

50. Matthew 7:7-11 | **51.** 1 Corinthians 14:3 | **52.** Romans 12:6

Study Notes

School for Prophecy

3

HEARING YOUR FATHER'S VOICE

Study Notes

3.0 Chapter Summary

3.0.1   *Introduction – Prophetic Engagements* covers those areas of spiritual interaction with God which, while a normal part of our salvation and relationship with him, are an integral part of how we move in the gift of prophecy. The final *Prophetic Engagements* subject establishes the centrality of our relationship with God, explains the main biblical ways he communicates with us and how to successfully engage with them.

3.0.2   *Being Sons of God* – Talking to our heavenly Father is one of the greatest rights, privileges and experiences a Christian can have, and yet it is one area where many are insecure and seem to struggle. How easy we find hearing from God depends to a great degree on our understanding and experience of our sonship in Christ. Being clear about our being a son or a daughter is therefore crucial in communicating with God.

3.0.3   *So How Does It Work?* – Developing his previous teaching on the coming of the Spirit of Truth, Jesus specifies that the Spirit *will* guide us into *all* truth, which is not a small claim by any means. He will promote Jesus by taking his teaching and making it known to us. This is a significant promise for us, and not one to be taken lightly.

3.0.4   *God Speaks to Us Through Sight* – Visions are one of the powerful ways that God uses our sight to speak to us. Dreams are another very significant way that God speaks to us using our sight. Finally, impressions are probably the most common way, in my experience, of how God speaks to us through our sight.

3.0.5   *God Speaks to Us Through Words* – The audible voice of God is the one everyone wants but very few have ever had – hearing God speak with your ears. The still small voice is another common way our heavenly Father speaks to us. We meet this in the story of Elijah. The Bible is the final way that God speaks to us through words – last but by no means least.

3.0.6   *God Speaks to Us Through Others* – Angels, or God's Messengers, are a significant and consistent way that God uses to guide his people. The gifts of the Spirit are an obvious and common way God communicates with us in our lives. Wise Counsellors, e.g. trustworthy friends, spiritual fathers and related leaders, are a valuable resource of God's wisdom.

3.0.7   *Listening Skills* – We can improve the process of hearing by developing our listening skills and being better listeners. There are some very helpful biblical principles we can learn that will make a big difference in this area. We need to cultivate active listening and always being alert for the still small voice, and not just passive listening when we only pay attention if God breaks in.

3.0.8   *Tuning into God* – Another way we can increase our listening capacity is by learning how to tune into God better, i.e. have stronger Wi-Fi! Often the problem is not being able to hear the Holy Spirit above the internal noise generated by our circumstances. Learning to be still, or to take time to do so, will really help our hearing capacity.

3.1 Introduction

3.1.1   The third and final *Prophetic Engagements* subject I want to cover after *Battle for Your Mind* [1] and *Seeing the Bigger Picture* [2] is *Hearing Your Father's Voice*. *Prophetic Engagements* covers those areas of spiritual interaction with God which, while a normal part of our salvation and relationship with him, are an integral part of how we move in the gift of prophecy. The final *Prophetic Engagements* subject establishes the centrality of our relationship with God, explains the main biblical ways he communicates with us and how to successfully engage with them.

3.1.2   This chapter looks at the more common and frequent, but extremely varied, ways that God can and does communicate with us. It is naturally a 'tour de force' through the Bible of how God communicates with us, guides us and reveals himself to us. Conversation is an essential and important part of any loving relationship, and we will look at how it biblically operates. Some of the ways, while biblical, may be outside the traditions of your church or the realms of your own experience. However, I pray this chapter encourages you to be more creative in your intimacy with your heavenly Father.

3.1.3   In my illustration of a new building construction, where *Prophetic Engagements* represents the establishing of the site [1.1.4] and the prior installation of utilities [2.1.3], *Hearing Your Father's Voice* is best represented by the telephone cabling required for communication. Our communication with God is on an 'anytime and anywhere' basis, so the extensive installation of telephone cabling throughout our foundations is essential. While our sonship is a very important part of our salvation through Christ, our right to be with God and converse with him is even more incredible and one of our great inheritances.

3.1.4   I have found on many occasions that people who obviously have the potential to be prophetic will not come to an introduction to prophecy course due to their misunderstanding of what the gift is. However, if I advertise the same course, but entitled *Hearing Your Father's Voice*, including all three *Prophetic Engagements* subjects, they will come and soon realize that biblical prophecy is easily within their reach. Hearing your Father's voice is a fundamental part of your daily relationship with God and yet at the same time a key element in how you develop your prophetic gift.

3.1.5   While improving how you hear from God is not as obviously transformational as the previous two chapters are, it does, in my experience, address an acknowledged inadequacy or fear that is far too common. It is therefore easy to see how learning to grow in the prophetic gift, by increasing and improving your ability to hear from God, is a significant benefit in kind. By developing in just one of the ways we can serve God [what you do], you are automatically growing in a fundamental part of your relationship with God [who you are].

 **School** for **Prophecy**

3.2   Being Sons of God

3.2.1   Talking to our heavenly Father is one of the greatest rights, privileges and experiences a Christian can have, and yet it is one area where many are insecure and seem to struggle. Our enemy seeks to flood our thoughts and minds with doubt as interference, when everything is already in place to make this a normal, natural and easy experience. How easy we find hearing from God does depend to a great degree on our understanding and experience of our sonship in Christ. Being clear about our being a son or a daughter is therefore crucial in communicating with God.

3.2.2   The Bible makes it very clear that the Spirit we received does not make us live in anxiety, but confirms our adoption as sons or daughters so we can talk to our heavenly Father.[53] The fact we call him 'Abba', i.e. 'Daddy', is indicative of the level of intimacy that we are meant to experience in this relationship. His Spirit, living within us, reassures us that we are his children and heirs to his inheritance. As children of God, we should expect and experience two-way conversation with our heavenly Father on a regular basis, out of our relationship and intimacy with him.

3.2.3   There are some important biblical principles about our salvation we need to fully grasp to make the process of hearing God easier. Jesus explained to his disciples, just before his arrest, that it was better for them that he left them; otherwise the Holy Spirit would not come.[54] I don't believe the disciples were at all convinced that losing the Son of God, his miraculous powers and his role as the Christ was better for them. However, this very point emphasizes how incredibly important the Holy Spirit coming is for us who believe.

3.2.4   Jesus explained the significance to his disciples a little earlier when he said that we would know the Spirit of Truth, and he would live *with* us and *in* us.[55] The omnipresent God occupies the same time and space as we do making communication easier than with a mobile phone! This is simply amazing on its own if you realize God cannot be closer than with us and inside us! We may not feel close to him at times, as our feelings are not always a reliable source of information, but the reality is we are.

3.2.5   However, that is not the whole story; there is more. To make communication even easier, Jesus explained to his disciples that the Holy Spirit would teach us all things and remind us of everything he has said to us![56] He stated that this should bring us peace, and not a worldly but a deep peacefulness. We all probably use Google much more than we should, and we would have to change our lifestyle considerably without it. However, the Spirit of Truth is way beyond Google. We actually have a mentor, teacher and counsellor with us 24/7 who is seeking to communicate with us about all things.

3.2.6   Talking to God should be as natural as walking with God.

53. Romans 8:14-17 | 54. John 16:7 | 55. John 14:15-17 | 56. John 14:25-26

3.3　So How Does It Work?

3.3.1　Fundamentally, you find out what type of God you believe in. Is he a cold, distant and harsh God, or is he a warm, intimate and generous father? The Bible makes the obvious point that it only works if you believe that he wants to talk and rewards those who speak to him.[57] Many of us have had the opposite journey with our own families and may unconsciously transplant this into our relationship with our heavenly Father. Our recognition of a loving and caring God, combined with being able to recognize his voice, should make communication for us an easy daily activity.

3.3.2　Jesus taught clearly on this subject[58] and specified he would call us by name, we would recognize his voice and, furthermore, we would not be led astray by voices we do not recognize. This has become something my wife Julie and I have grown confident and relaxed about, rather than striving over. It is now normal for us to hear thoughts like, "You have left the front door unlocked," or, "Your driving licence is in the top left drawer," and act accordingly. We do not always get it right, we are not perfect, but we do have a good hit rate.

3.3.3　There is much encouragement for us in the Bible's teaching that should help us to communicate with God with confidence and expectancy. Developing his previous teaching on the coming of the Spirit of Truth, Jesus specifies that the Spirit *will* guide us into *all* truth, which is not a small claim by any means.[59] He will promote Jesus by taking his teaching and making it known to us. This is a significant promise for us, and not one to be taken lightly. The combination of the words 'will' and 'all' are remarkable, but often missed by so many.

3.3.4　Furthermore, Jesus challenged any negative views of God when he pointed out that our heavenly Father is so much more generous than any earthly father, and will give us the things we ask for when we seek him.[60] My confidence has grown strong in the love of my heavenly Father and my security as his adopted son. When I am 'genuinely' seeking first the kingdom of God, and getting it completely wrong, he has consistently broken in and redirected me on the right path. He never sits and watches me crash and burn just to teach me a lesson, unless I won't learn any other way!

3.3.5　Finally, and specifically in times of persecution and challenge, Jesus reassures us that we will hear his voice so accurately that we will actually be given the words to say at the time.[61] There are many different ways that God can speak to us and in fact the sheer variety is challenging at times. We will now look at the more common ones, which are not exclusive, under the headings of how *God Speaks to Us Through Sight, Words* and *Others*.

3.3.6　God shouts at his enemies, but whispers to his friends. He wants us to come close.

---

57. Hebrews 11:6 | **58.** John 10:3-5 | **59.** John 16:13-15 | **60.** Luke 11:11-13 | **61.** Mark 13:11

3.4 God Speaks to Us Through Sight

3.4.1   *Visions* are one of the common ways that God speaks to us using our sight. It feels a bit like dreaming when you are not asleep. Sometimes you are still aware of your current surroundings, while on other occasions it is so consuming that you are not. They are strong, powerful images and can be still or moving. Ezekiel's experience of hearing from God included seeing visions.[62] He saw other locations in the world, including inside buildings, futuristic experiences he struggled to describe, and normal objects and places with prophetic meanings.

3.4.2   Probably his two most well-known visions are 'the valley of dry bones'[63] and 'the river from the Temple'[64]. These are not just Old Testament experiences, but are applicable today. The Apostle Peter was given a vision, effectively supernatural daytime television, to help him break through the cultural limitations of his understanding of the gospel so it included the rest of the world.[65] Visions are probably the closest we are realistically going to get to guidance through 'writing in the sky'.

3.4.3   *Dreams* are another common way that God speaks to us using our sight. Most of us will have had experiences of dreams, so this is a much easier subject to understand. While dreams appear to be a way our minds process information while we are resting – and we all know the weird type of dream you have after 'too much pizza' – God often uses them to communicate with us. Job refers to them as "visions in the night"[66]. In fact, dreams happened regularly in the Bible at key moments of decision or direction in people's lives. Having a notebook near you when you sleep is a key part of our journey with dreams.

3.4.4   *Impressions* are the final way that God speaks to us using our eyesight that I am going to cover. They are very similar to visions, but they do not have the same scale, detail or HD quality of visions. They are simple, powerful images that the Holy Spirit shows us in our minds. My experience is that around three-quarters of personal prophecies start in this form, as the majority of us are visual learners. An example of this is Jeremiah's first two prophetic training sessions, in which God said to him, "What do you see, Jeremiah?"[67]

3.4.5   This is quite similar to the TV quiz program called *Catchphrase,* where the host gradually reveals pictures and encourages contestants with, "Say what you see." The first time Jeremiah9 saw an almond branch and the second time a boiling pot tilting to the north, and out of this, two prophecies are born. The impressions-type experience of 'say what you see' could also include Bible verses, stories and characters; song titles or lines; movie titles; advertising slogans; single words; people's names; famous landmarks etc.

3.4.6   God opens our eyes so he can put his purposes into our hearts.

62. Ezekiel 1:1 | 63. Ezekiel 37 | 64. Ezekiel 47 | 65. Acts 10:9-23 | 66. Job 33:14-18 | 67. Jeremiah 1:11-19

3.5 God Speaks to Us Through Words

3.5.1 *The audible voice of God* is one of the ways that God speaks to us through words. When I listen to people, this is the one everyone wants, but very few have ever had – hearing God speak with your ears. It is clear from Moses' journey with God that they spoke to each other as anyone else would,[68] and Moses could hear God's voice as they talked face to face. Another precedent for this in the Bible can be found in the story of Samuel.[69]

3.5.2 This makes the point that God's voice is not spooky, unusual or frightening, but actually like everyone else's. There are sufficient precedents in the Bible of this. An example would be God speaking to the Apostle Paul at his conversion.[70] My own experience is that the audible voice of God is as special today as it was in the Old Testament, despite people's enthusiasm to hear it. However, it is in the Bible; so as long as we don't make an idol of it, it is still of benefit to us today.

3.5.3 *The still small voice* is a common way our heavenly Father speaks to us through words. We meet this in the story of Elijah[71] after he has fled from Jezebel into the wilderness and is feeling seriously sorry for himself. As part of his restitution, God appears to him, yet not in the Charismatic whirlwind, earthquake or fire, but in a 'still small voice'. For those of you who don't recognize this phrase, it is from the RSV, as I have not yet adapted to the more modern 'gentle whisper' translation.

3.5.4 I have found that, along with impressions, this is probably the most common way that we hear God. We learn that sometimes a simple, gentle thought in our mind is not ours but the Holy Spirit speaking to us, using the 'still small voice'. My experience is that God rarely raises his voice, so if your attention is elsewhere, it can be easy to miss. Just as Samuel learned to recognize God's voice from others' [Eli's] when he was a boy, we need to learn to hear him in our minds and recognize it's him.

3.5.5 *The Bible* is an obvious way that God speaks to us through words – last but by no means least. Our Bibles are a readily accessible and comprehensive resource; consequently, we call the Bible 'God's Word'. It is a resource for hearing from God that cannot be stressed enough. It is both Logos, the eternal and permanent truth of God, and Rhema, the today and living truth of God. Paul encourages Timothy, his spiritual son, to continue living what he has learned from the Bible as a child because it contains everything you need to know.[72]

3.5.6 While I would prefer the Bible to be structured like a textbook, it is a wonderful gift to have God's wisdom available to us 24/7 in such an accessible form. The Logos element means that it can answer many of our questions, and teach us biblical principles and practices whenever we want. However, the Rhema element releases the 'now' word of God. I regularly describe prophecy as finding the one verse in the Bible you need today, and that is often the experience of many.

3.5.7 "The pen is mightier than the sword." – Edward Bulwer-Lytton, 1839

68. Numbers 12:7-8 | **69.** 1 Samuel 3:1-11 | **70.** Acts 9:4 | **71.** 1 Kings 19:1-12 | **72.** 2 Timothy 3:13-17

School for
Prophecy

3.6   God Speaks to Us Through Others

3.6.1   *Angels,* i.e. God's messengers, are a significant way that God speaks to us through others. Angels were a consistent and significant way God talked to and guided his people in the Bible, even if it must have felt a very unusual and special occasion. Angels appeared with messages at some profoundly critical times in people's lives and the purposes of God. A good example is the commissioning of Gideon.[73] It starts a journey with a very unconvinced Gideon that leads to the complete annihilation of a vast invading Midianite army.

3.6.2   This is not only an Old Testament experience. The angel Gabriel appeared to Mary and told her that she was going to give birth to our Saviour, even though she was a virgin, which changed the course of history. There are many precedents in the Bible of God using angels as a means of speaking to us through others. Unfortunately, a lot of negativity has arisen out of fear that people might worship angels or that our enemy can appear disguised as an angel of light;[74] or from knowing too many intense friends who become consumed by their interest in angelic encounters.

3.6.3   *The gifts of the Spirit* are a common way that God speaks to us through others. Through being baptized in the Holy Spirit[75] we are empowered with the ability to move in supernatural gifts. The three obvious communication gifts, often described as the wisdom gifts, are prophecy, wisdom and words of knowledge. In my experience, their definitions overlap each other to some extent, and they often operate in tandem making them hard to differentiate at times. I define words of knowledge as simply knowing facts that you have never been told, seen or realized. Jesus talking to the Samaritan woman at the well[76] would be a good example.

3.6.4   *Wise counsellors* are the final way that God speaks to us through others that I want to cover. It may well feel more exciting to receive wisdom through supernatural gifts, but we are foolish to ignore the considerable godly wisdom in those mature and experienced members of the church family around us. Proverbs teaches us, on more than one occasion, that an abundance of counsellors is good news.[77] Not everyone knows everything, but there may well be people around us with considerable knowledge and experience in an area we need advice.

3.6.5   I have had three spiritual fathers who had a significant impact on the development of my life, calling and gifting over a twenty-five-year period, and I would not be where I am today without them. As a result, mentoring has become a substantial part of my work over the years, and I now have mentoring clients I walk with on a professional basis. The character limitations of our gift, which are much more critical in level two training, have brought my mentoring role more and more to the fore as I have trained people in their prophetic gift.

3.6.6   God's toolbox contains many unusual people with some remarkable gifts.

73. Judges 6:11-12 | 74. 2 Corinthians 11:13-14 | 75. Matthew 3:11 | 76. John 4:4-26
77. Proverbs 11:14; 15:22; 24:6

3.7 Listening Skills

3.7.1   We can improve the process of hearing by developing our listening skills and being better listeners. There are some very helpful biblical principles we can learn that will make a big difference in this area. One of the most important principles is to be clear we are seeking to build God's kingdom and not our own. Otherwise, we are effectively listening to the wrong telephone line and will miss what God wants to say. Is it our agenda or God's agenda? Aligning ourselves with heaven's purposes[78] is important. Otherwise, we may just get static on the line.

3.7.2   The Bible teaches that when we are listening to God's wisdom, it is not like the wisdom of this world or the leaders of this age.[79] As previously highlighted [2.6.2], God does not think as we do, and he does not do things as we do. Furthermore, God reveals things to us by his Spirit, and our minds may struggle to understand it at times even though our spirits experience peace through it. Fortunately, the Spirit within us will interpret and explain the spiritual truths to us so that we can understand them.

3.7.3   The Bible also instructs us not to live the way the world does, but to be transformed by changing the way we think.[80] We can recognize the hand of our enemy in our thought lives, particularly when his lies create anxiety [fear], impotence, confusion or condemnation. In contrast, our heavenly Father will give us faith, hope, conviction or endorsement, where we should always focus our thinking. Changing how we think to match biblical principles and practices will make it much easier to hear our heavenly Father because we are 'talking his language'.

3.7.4   We need to cultivate active listening, i.e. always being alert for the still small voice, and not passive listening, i.e. only paying attention when God breaks in; particularly for those strange quiet, lone thoughts that pop into our mind and get dismissed. Let me explain the 'pink car' principle [the UK only, sorry]. God's voice in our minds is like a pink car. It looks like every other car, it is doing what every other car is doing, but it just looks that little bit different. Why, in a crowd, does one person seem to stand out more than any other? Pink car.

3.7.5   My experience is that God speaks to me in three main ways, and I have learned over time to be sensitive and alert to them. The first, as above, is in my thought life. I often hear the Holy Spirit in my mind, and if it seems reasonable, peaceful and biblical, I will seriously consider it and look for confirmation or repetition. Secondly, I have found that I experience a considerable number of God-appointments, and find that many people I meet unexpectedly are for a purpose. Finally, I experience coincidences, or God-incidences, on a regular basis where God speaks to me, without using words, using my surroundings.

3.7.6   The advantage of listening skills is that you hear more than is being said.

78. Matthew 6:31-34 | 79. 1 Corinthians 2:6-10 | 80. Romans 12:2

3.8   Tuning into God

3.8.1   Another way we can increase our listening capacity is by learning how to tune into God better, i.e. stronger Wi-Fi! The lessons learned in the previous chapter on seeing in the Spirit [2.3.1] will obviously significantly increase our ability to hear God more clearly, specifically as we practise and learn to see with the 'eyes of our heart'. Learning to see the bigger picture will enable us to tune in to how and when God is speaking, and what he is saying, more accurately. As we grow in tuning into God, we will become more confident in hearing him.

3.8.2   Often the problem is not being able to hear the Holy Spirit above the internal noise generated by our circumstances. Lack of peace, urgency, anxiety, pressure or difficult decisions can all create internal noise that drown out the Holy Spirit. Learning to be still, or to take time to be still, will really help your hearing capacity. The psalmist encourages us to, "Be still, and know that I am God."[81] Being still leads to knowing God. It helps us change our perspective to seeing the situation from God's viewpoint, which then will help us hear and understand what he is saying more clearly.

3.8.3   We often forget that listening to God is not a one-way event but a two-way conversation. We need to learn to talk to him as much as he is talking to us. Our friends would consider us very odd if we never talked to them! One of the interesting side-effects of verbalising our thoughts is that it frequently brings greater clarity to them, helps focus them and highlights any fuzzy or fearful thinking. Engaging in conversation helps us to ask the right question, so that we can then hear the real answer.

3.8.4   Another way that helps us tune into God and get our thoughts, emotions and perspective into alignment with heaven is reading and meditating on the Bible. The very first Psalm states that valuing the Bible and meditating on it day and night creates an environment where we are fruitful, protected and prosperous.[82] Not an offer to be taken lightly. The impact of regular, but not legalistic, Bible reading, study or meditation is profound due to the effect of the regular intake of spiritual truth. Biblical principles, historical stories and apostolic teaching will keep our thinking, emotions and values on course.

3.8.5   The regularity of our conversations builds familiarity, experience and confidence. While there will no doubt be times when we will have serious conversations, I prefer to chat throughout the day and encourage myself to engage with the Holy Spirit as much as possible. Another way of tuning into our heavenly Father is to study the significant prophecies we have had. It is a good discipline on its own and reminds us of how much he has done and is still going to do. Lastly, the Bible teaches that when we speak in tongues, we build ourselves up,[83] so please don't miss the opportunity to benefit from its personal use.

3.8.6   God does not need words to communicate.

81. Psalm 46:10-11 | 82. Psalm 1:1-3 | 83. 1 Corinthians 14:4-5,18

School for Prophecy

3.9 Personal Testimony

3.9.1 Julie and I were on a camping holiday in the Gower, Wales, during August 2008, and enjoying some good weather together. We had a detailed Ordnance Survey map of the Gower, a guidebook of local walks and comfortable walking boots just in case. We were about three miles into a walk, having circumvented a few fields with herds of cows in, and all seemed to be going well. We came through a large gate to a field and headed over to the other side in accordance with the instructions. We then stopped to get our bearings and, on looking around us, realized we could not figure out where we were. We were in the middle of a large number of similar fields, no buildings on the horizon as potential markers and, as hard as we tried, could not match either our map or the guidebook to our location. A sense of doom was settling in on me, and I started to consider if we should hit reverse and try to find our way back the way we had come.

3.9.2 We had wandered away from the centre of the field in our desperation to figure out where we were. It was at this point a cyclist, carrying his bicycle, came into the field we were in over a stile. He looked professional, head to toe in logo-covered spandex, and clearly had a lightweight bike from the way he easily carried it. As he approached us, I realized he had something like a GPS device on his handlebars, so we started walking towards him. I asked him if he could help us discover where we were, but he replied in French that he did not speak English – the one bit of French I know! I resorted to the English tourist technique of speaking slowly with lots of hand signals, pointing at the map with my hands in the air to show we were lost.

3.9.3 He seemed to understand and, without a word, started looking at his GPS device and then the map we were holding between us, as we formed a scrum. Suddenly, he put his finger on the map and said something like, "Il est là!" twice. I need to pause the story at this moment, as it is very important. We are now standing in a circle of three people near the centre of the field, Julie and I holding a map between us, and our cyclist pointing at the map where he presumably thinks we are. Okay! We must have both looked at the map intently for only three seconds tops when I realized he was right and I knew where we were and looked up to find Julie smiling back.

3.9.4 We both then immediately turned to the cyclist to say thank you, only to find he had vanished. *What!* We instinctively circled to look 360 degrees all around us for him, back quizzically at each other, and then around us again. No cyclist. Impossible. *What!* We just stood there in silence. He could not have covered the distance to any of the field's fences, assuming he could have got over them. We just stood there stunned. Then slowly it simultaneously began to dawn on us what had just happened. *No...* Surely not. Neither of us wanted to say what had just happened. We went back to the map and confirmed we were where he had shown us, and began to continue on our journey in accordance with the guidebook. We finished the rest of the walk uneventfully and went back to our tent. There was no way to avoid the truth that we both recognized, but do you want to admit you met a cyclist angel in racing spandex carrying a bike with a GPS? You just couldn't make it up, could you?

School for Prophecy

3.10 Frequently Asked Questions

3.10.1   How do I know what I hear is from God?

3.10.2   If you are openly and honestly simply seeking God's will, then it is a matter of trusting him that what you ask you will receive and that your heavenly Father is kind and generous[84] and will give you what you need. If it is significant, you should seek confirmation as well, but we learn by practice and that means giving it a try [3.3].

3.10.3   I have tried but I just can't hear anything...

3.10.4   I actually consider this good news. My God is a really kind and loving father, and if I needed to know something, he would find a way to tell me. All I have to do is keep doing the last thing he told me to do until he tells me otherwise. However, it is always worth considering a couple of 'just in case' items [3.8.2]. (1) Make sure there is nothing obvious he has asked you to do that you haven't done. (2) Also consider whether there are any options that God has suggested that you are just not willing to contemplate. Otherwise relax.

3.10.5   I am never really sure I have got it right...

3.10.6   This is really another variant of the first question above [3.10.1]. Accuracy comes from practice and experience,[85] so don't be afraid to press on and learn from your mistakes. You can always find someone with godly wisdom [3.6.5] and get their perspective on your circumstances and guidance before making a decision. Finally, remember, if you are genuinely and simply seeking to do God's will, and you make a mistake, he promises to work things out for our best in the end.[86]

3.10.7   My friends or family don't agree with me...

3.10.8   This may not be a problem, although their opinion should be considered if they are loyal and reliable friends. If they don't 'like' your guidance, it does not necessarily mean it is wrong, just unpopular. In this case, what to do with what you have heard is the issue. If on the other hand they don't 'feel' it's right, given they hopefully know you well, then caution should be engaged. Either way, the biblical requirement of testing [4.7.5] will guide you to a solution.

3.10.9   It's a bit strange but it has been confirmed a number of times...

3.10.10 If you mean you have never done anything like this before, this is not necessarily a bad thing but means your journey will be more involved. If on the other hand it is weird, while not on a daily basis, it may be no different from many of the stories and experiences in the Bible. Both circumstances are cause for seeking confirmation, and probably more importantly, seeking wisdom and counsel from someone with experience in this area. Engaging in the process of testing the prophecy with others [4.7.5] is essential.

84. Luke 11:11-13 | 85. Hebrews 5:14 | 86. Romans 8:28

Study Notes

4

UNDERSTANDING BIBLICAL PROPHECY

Study Notes

School for
Prophecy

4.0   Chapter Summary

4.0.1   *Introduction – Prophetic Foundations* are a set of core principles that, very much like the foundations of a building, are what all our other teaching, understanding and experience of the gift are based upon. The first *Prophetic Foundations* subject introduces the biblical basis, definition and operation of the gift of prophecy, while tackling many of the associated myths, misnomers and misunderstandings.

4.0.2   *A Supernatural Gift* – The Bible's traditional and most frequently used list includes the nine more well-known gifts of the Spirit. Prophecy is included in this list, and is therefore the working of, empowered with and distributed by the Holy Spirit for the good of everyone.

4.0.3   *Biblical Definition* – While the Bible is not a textbook, it fortunately does provide us with a clear definition of prophecy. It says that all prophecy is for strengthening, encouraging and comfort. This is what I call the 'essential flavour' of prophecy, and inevitably is a key factor in the testing of prophecy.

4.0.4   *The Covenant Change* – The introduction of salvation by faith through the New Covenant has inexorably changed the purpose, operation and environment of the gift of prophecy. Specifically, the promise of Jesus that the Holy Spirit would live with us and be in us obviously changes the way we relate to God and, as a result, how the gift of prophecy works in this environment.

4.0.5   *Receiving Revelation* – The Bible explains that prophecy comes spontaneously by spiritual revelation to the person, meaning it starts off in the spirit realm with the Holy Spirit and moves into the physical realm through our minds. Prophecy is God speaking through us to others, as we are led by the Holy Spirit.

4.0.6   *Levels of Gifting* – I recognize three different levels of prophetic gifting specified in the Bible that help us to measure our progress. First, the Bible teaches that everyone who wants to can move at some level in the prophetic gift. Second, the Bible describes having a prophetic ministry, not just a gift. The final level is described in a well-known teaching, often referred to as the 'five-fold ministry'.

4.0.7   *Testing Prophecy* – The requirement and process of testing prophecy is the second of the three major areas of confusion about the gift of prophecy in the church today. As a result, I will cover this in some detail in *The Principles of Testing Prophecy* [7], but it is important at this stage to learn the concepts and implications involved in this requirement.

4.0.8   *Responding to Prophecy* – While responding to prophecy is covered in detail in *The Principles of Responding to Prophecy* [9], it is helpful to highlight the New Covenant principles here. They all begin with 'P' and are participation, perspective, patience, perseverance and prayer. The most significant and misunderstood of these is the need for participation.

4.1 Introduction

4.1.1 We have now completed the first teaching topic of this manual on *Prophetic Engagements* and can start the next topic on *Prophetic Foundations*. Having established the important concepts and practices of *Prophetic Engagements*, I now want to cover the essential biblical teaching of our *Prophetic Foundations*. These teachings will establish the core values and principles that undergird everything we do in the prophetic, guide us in new situations and protect us from deception. I hear too many people, who think they understand them, say, "I have already done that," and move on without a real grasp of the biblical principles involved. This leads to an immature, emotional and inconsistent gift.

4.1.2 In the second topic of the manual we will cover the three core subjects of *Prophetic Foundations: Understanding Biblical Prophecy* [this chapter], *New and Old Covenant Prophecy* [5] and *Biblical Prophetic Culture* [6]. *Prophetic Foundations* are a set of core principles that, very much like the foundations of a building, are what all our other teaching, understanding and experience of the gift are based upon. The first *Prophetic Foundations* subject introduces the biblical basis, definition and operation of the gift of prophecy, while tackling many of the associated myths, misnomers and misunderstandings.

4.1.3 This chapter will look at what the Bible teaches about the gift of prophecy in its many forms. This will include subjects like *New and Old Covenant Prophecy* [5] and *The Principles of Testing Prophecy* [7] that are so significant they have their own chapters. It is an area that often requires the realignment of our understanding of the principles in the Bible. One important principle I need to clarify is that I will feel free to use the whole Bible, and not just those verses which specifically refer to prophecy, as the whole Bible applies to the nature, function and operation of the gift of prophecy.

4.1.4 I have found the foundations of a building [3.1.3] to be a very helpful example of the principle of *Prophetic Foundations*, and in some depth. I have often noted, when passing a building site, the inordinate amount of time that is taken to get the foundations right when all you can see is a fence. This includes the excavation down to bedrock, laying down all the utilities necessary and then preparing the concrete foundations. However, when this is done, the building seems to magically appear out of nowhere and at a remarkable pace. This illustrates the importance of our foundations and their impact on the accuracy, maturity and anointing of our gift.

4.1.5 My experience of teaching the gift of prophecy for over 20 years has taught me that the priority is often to 'un-teach' people's poor experiences, unbiblical presumption and bad practice and then, after laying secure biblical foundations, 'let nature take its course'. Often, if I go ahead and teach the prophetic gift on poor foundations, it makes its understanding more difficult, produces thinking out of alignment with the Bible, and needs regular support and adjustment.

4.2 A Supernatural Gift

4.2.1 There is considerable teaching in the Bible on, and examples of, spiritual gifts, i.e. supernatural gifts. They were a serious hallmark of the continuing ministry of Jesus in his disciples. The Bible explains that we are not to be uneducated or confused about gifts of the Spirit.[87] It explains that they are all very different in nature, used differently and work differently, but they all come from the same Holy Spirit and it is the same God who empowers them in everyone. Almost as reassurance, it points out that they are present in our lives for the good of everyone, not just for us.

4.2.2 The Bible's traditional and most frequently used list[88] includes the nine more well-known gifts of the Spirit. These are wisdom, knowledge, faith, healing, miracles, prophecy, distinguishing between spirits, speaking in tongues and the interpretation of tongues. It then reiterates that they all come from and are all empowered by the same Spirit, who distributes them, which is clearly meant to reassure us due to their supernatural nature. Prophecy is included in this list, and is therefore the working of, empowered with and distributed by the Holy Spirit for the good of everyone.

4.2.3 Prophecy is also mentioned in another list[89] as one of the common gifts of service. This list of gifts is used to encourage us not to think too highly of ourselves, i.e. compare ourselves to others, but in accordance with our faith. To illustrate this point, it specifies that we all have different gifts according to God's grace and that although we have different functions, we are all still part of the same body. Interestingly, and I will refer to this again later [6.5.5] when mentioning prophecy, it repeats that we should use the gift in accordance with our level of faith.

4.2.4 The Bible specifies a list of five significant church-building ministries,[90] now commonly referred to as the 'five-fold' ministries, in which the prophet is listed as the second one after the apostle. This is another example of the significance of prophecy, not only as a spiritual gift but also as a church-building ministry. As long as the church continues to struggle to understand and accept the full biblical meaning of these two ministries, the lack of apostles and prophets will keep the church in a weakened state. Quote me!

4.2.5 However, the 'coup de grace' undoubtedly comes during a key chapter in the Bible on the operation of gifts in meetings. It clearly states that we should eagerly desire spiritual gifts, especially the gift of prophecy.[91] We are therefore specifically encouraged by the Bible to seek after the gift of prophecy. Given the gift of prophecy is essentially a gift of encouragement, I can understand its emphasis in this statement.

4.2.6 Prophecy is partnering with the Holy Spirit, to provide us with power for Christ's purpose.

87. 1 Corinthians 12:1-6 | 88. 1 Corinthians 12:7-10 | 89. Romans 12:3-8 | 90. Ephesians 4:11-12
91. 1 Corinthians 14:1

4.3   Biblical Definition

4.3.1   One of the main differences I have found between my teaching and the teaching I have received about prophecy is that many seem to focus only on those Bible verses that mention prophecy. I believe the whole Bible is the truth and therefore all of it, where relevant, applies to our understanding of the gift of prophecy. For example, for me, a core principle in the operation of prophecy is the second most important commandment,[92] or the more practical variant, "Do to others as you would have them do to you,"[93] or, "Do as you would be done by."[94]

4.3.2   However, while the Bible is not a textbook, it fortunately does provide us with a clear definition of prophecy. It says that all prophecy is for strengthening, encouraging and comfort.[95] This is what I call the 'essential flavour' of prophecy, and inevitably is a key factor in the testing of prophecy. Older translations referred to edification, encouragement and comfort, so it became known down the years as 'EEC' prophecy. This had to be abandoned when the UK joined the European Economic Community [E.E.C.], but you may still hear it.

4.3.3   This birthed another definition, which has lasted down the years due to its simplicity and usefulness. This says that prophecy is to 'build up, stir up and cheer up'. Prophecy is fundamentally a gift of encouragement, and after the love of God, encouragement is one of the most potent forces in our lives. Having played in football teams that encouraged and supported one another, compared to teams that criticized and complained about each other, I have learned that the difference in their team potential and performance is dramatic.

4.3.4   I have noticed that a different definition is often used in the United States, drawn from the end of the book of Revelation: "For it is the Spirit of prophecy who bears testimony to Jesus."[96] The spirit, i.e. the heart, of prophecy is to lift up, push us towards and help us understand Jesus. This is different to my previous definition [4.3.2], but complimentary and helpful in increasing our understanding. It is also a warning not to subtly worship the person prophesying, which can happen when we allow ourselves to rely on them for guidance or lose sight of the fact they are just a messenger, admittedly with supernatural impact.

4.3.5   The first biblical definition I referred to [4.3.2] helpfully goes on to point out that the gift of prophecy is designed to strengthen the church.[97] It is one of the primary reasons prophecy is so important to the church family: its main purpose is to make us stronger, full of encouragement and comforted by each other. It is a potent instrument in the health, vitality and vision of the church family, and will keep us focussed on God's kingdom.

4.3.6   Prophecy should point to Jesus, portray him and promote him.

92. Mark 12:31 | 93. Luke 6:31 | 94. *The Water Babies* by Mary Wakefield | 95. 1 Corinthians 14:3
96. Revelation 19:10 | 97. 1 Corinthians 14:4-5

School for
Prophecy

4.4 The Covenant Change

4.4.1   After explaining the biblical definition of prophecy, the next important foundation to establish is our understanding of the fundamental change in the gift of prophecy between the Old Covenant and the New Covenant [5.1.2]. It is important at this stage to understand the concepts and implications involved in this change. One of the significant results of my journey with mentoring clients is that I have concluded that the majority of our weaknesses and problems as Christians come from a poor, or lack of, understanding of this very subject: what Jesus achieved on the cross!

4.4.2   The introduction of salvation by faith[98] through the New Covenant has inexorably changed the purpose, operation and environment of the gift of prophecy. Salvation by grace has brought us into a family;[99] a personal and intimate relationship with our heavenly Father; unhindered, unlimited and unrestricted access to his love, presence and purposes. Amen. Specifically, the promise of Jesus that the Holy Spirit would live with us and be in us[100] obviously changes the way we relate to God and, inevitably as a result, how the gift of prophecy works in this environment.

4.4.3   In the Old Covenant a priest was your means of accessing the presence of God, his prophets how you heard from God, and the King ruled over you, led you and settled disputes. As a result of the fundamental shift in our relationship with God between the covenants, all the gifts of the Spirit have changed to some degree or another. However, prophecy has changed more than any other because under the Old Covenant it was our means of hearing from God, whereas now under the New Covenant we can talk to God ourselves. Prophecy's supernatural anointing and objective have not changed but its expression, equipping and the environment has.

4.4.4   This is one of the three main areas of confusion about the gift of prophecy in the church today. Many still act as if they are Old Covenant prophets speaking the exact words of God, move in judgement and direction, are powerful individualistic ministries, and are not a living part of any church. The Internet is full of them, many faith-inspiring conferences tend to reinforce this image unhelpfully, and unwise leaders allow it to continue due to the apparent supernatural impact. When someone announces, "Thus says the Lord," what do you think?

4.4.5   Some Evangelicals are concerned that those moving in the prophetic are claiming their prophecies have equal authority with the Bible because they speak messages from God. However, because the final authority has moved from the spoken word (prophets) in the Old Covenant to the written word (the Bible) in the New Covenant, there can never be any conflict between the Bible and biblical prophecy. The Bible is a written record of what was spoken.

4.4.6   Prophecy should call out our potential, and not our performance.

98. Ephesians 2:8-9 | 99. Galatians 5:6-7 | 100. John 14:16-17

4.5   Receiving Revelation

4.5.1   The next area I am going to look at in understanding biblical prophecy is its operation or, put simply, 'how it works'. Too much of our learning is based on assumption, how we feel at the time and what experience we have had. The Bible helpfully explains that biblical prophecy does not come from the human will, but we spek as the Holy Spirit leads us.[101] While it refers to Old Covenant prophecy, the operational principle still stands today. Prophecy is God speaking through us to others as we are led by the Holy Spirit.

4.5.2   The Bible reinforces this principle by explaining that prophecy comes spontaneously by spiritual revelation to the person,[102] meaning it starts off in the spirit realm with the Holy Spirit and moves into the physical realm through our minds. The meeting context the Bible is speaking about helpfully makes two other important points. First, the prophets are speaking in an orderly way, and are therefore under their own control to be able to pick where and when the prophecy is given. Second, this control even extends to stopping in favour of another, if the circumstances require it.

4.5.3   When we hear for ourselves, it is hearing from God; when we hear for others, it is mainly prophecy. They both work identically to how Jesus taught we would hear from him: through the Spirit of Truth, who will guide us into all truth.[103] One of the reasons I started this manual with *Battle for Your Mind* [1] is because hearing from God and prophesying are both spiritual revelation from the Holy Spirit, that inevitably goes through our minds – and hence the battle. Jesus, in this particular teaching, also specifies that the Holy Spirit will tell us about what is yet to come.

4.5.4   My experience is that when many people start prophesying, they are often limited by their background and theology, i.e. only able use Bible verses, characters or stories to start with. However, seven out of ten of us are visually inspired and will soon find it easy to see in our minds impressions, pictures, objects and words. I have covered this previously under *Hearing Your Father's Voice* [3]. This is not a simple form of prophecy, as some teach. It is actually a sound basis to grow and develop our gift in the detail, accuracy, timing and meaning of the impressions we see in the Spirit.

4.5.5   A good example of this is described in what I call 'Jeremiah's lesson 101'[104], his first lesson in the gift of prophecy. God asks Jeremiah for the first time, "What do you see?" and after he describes the simple picture he sees, God explains to him the interpretation. The second time God asks Jeremiah, he describes another more complicated image that he sees. When God interprets the image, he does start based on what Jeremiah has described seeing, but then the revelation flows into an insight above and beyond the initial image.

4.5.6   Receiving revelation results in the reorientation of our reality.

101. 2 Peter 1:20-21 | 102. 1 Corinthians 14:29-32 | 103. John 16:13 | 104. Jeremiah 1:9-19

4.6 Levels of Gifting

4.6.1 We can only fully develop our prophetic gift in an environment of expectation, encouragement and example. Unlike teaching and pastoring, where to some degree our progress and development can be measured by the size of numbers involved, there is no such rough and ready measure of our prophetic gift. I recognize three different levels of prophetic gift specified in the Bible that can help us measure our progress. They divide our prophetic development into three defined ranges of gifting. They are ranges of gift, rather than specific points, for example 10-30 mph instead of any specific speed.

4.6.2 Firstly, the Bible teaches that everyone who wants to can move at some level in the prophetic gift.[105] At a beginner's level, this includes prayers that turn into prophecy, inspiration received during times of worship and Bible verses that leap off the page. Up to an intermediate level, that includes sharing spoken or written personal prophetic words, seeing pictures with interpretations and being more regular in contribution than others. This is the level of anointing that this manual is designed to develop, from beginners to those at an intermediate stage, which I call level one.

4.6.3 I do believe that there is sufficient teaching in the Bible to come to the conclusion that 'everyone can prophesy'. The Bible's encouragement above is rather decisive, and in conjunction with the policy statement[106] and the later repetition[107], I feel confident enough to be able to make this claim. However, I prefer to add the caveat 'if they want to', to avoid being drawn into any unnecessary controversy similar to my Charismatic renewal experiences. As my prophetic mentor would say, "If you can pray, you can prophesy."

4.6.4 Secondly, the Bible describes people who have a prophetic ministry,[108] not just a gift, and I refer to this next range of gifting as level two. This is different to level one and is where others recognize that one of your main gifts, and potentially your calling, is the gift of prophecy. This level could include being part of the appointed ministry or prayer team, having experience and a good track record in personal prophecy, sharing words for the whole church in meetings and possibly being asked to pray into specific situations for the leadership.

4.6.5 The final level of gift is described in a well-known teaching[109] often referred to as the 'five-fold ministry'. Here prophets are described as the second group of people given to the Church to bring us to unity, maturity and fullness of Christ. This does not mean people who can move in the gift (level one), or who have the gift (level two), but who *are* the gift. Unsurprisingly, I refer to this as level three. These are people, both men and women, whose lives are given to the church as master builders and trainers for service.

4.6.6 We can all cook, but only some of us are chefs!

105. 1 Corinthians 14:31 | 106. 1 Corinthians 14:1 | 107. 1 Corinthians 14:39 | 108. Romans 12:6
109. Ephesians 4:11-13

School for
Prophecy

4.7 Testing Prophecy

4.7.1 The requirement and process of testing prophecy is the second of the three major areas of confusion about the gift of prophecy in the church today. As a result, I will cover this in some detail in *The Principles of Testing Prophecy* [7], but it is important at this stage to learn the concepts and implications involved in this requirement. We need to clearly establish that all New Covenant prophecy, all prophecy as far as we are concerned, is required by the Bible to be tested before it is acted upon – no matter how simple or complicated this process might actually be.

4.7.2 Jesus warned us to watch out for false prophets[110] but, more alarmingly, he warned us that they will come disguised in 'sheep's clothing' when they are really 'ferocious wolves'. Humorously, I once heard a friend gasp at this point, "What maniac is making sheep's clothing in wolf's sizes!" Interestingly, I have found many people disturbingly easily and thoughtlessly impressed by the supernatural and celebrity nature of prophetic ministry. Jesus taught, in his warning above, that we will be able to identify them by the fruit of their lives. We should be asking whether they are they living what they preach, rather than 'tasting' the anointing on them.

4.7.3 The church has always wrestled with the conundrum that without *Quality Control* you don't have control of the quality; however, applying quality control, as in testing prophecy, has proved difficult and unsuccessful down the years. Many variants of two historical extreme approaches have been spawned to solve this dilemma. The first approach restricts the operation of the gift wherever possible, thereby removing any risk of damage through error. The second approach is to simply allow and enjoy the majority of prophecy, but never take it seriously, or act on it, so that there is never any harm done.

4.7.4 The key biblical principle for testing prophecy comes from a teaching[111] that actually specifically and helpfully refers to prophecy. The point I want to draw out here is, *be selective*. I have found many people believe a prophecy is either completely right or completely wrong, which does not fit in with what the Bible teaches. Most prophecy is not all right or all wrong. It often does not fit with our circumstances due to reasons of timing, progressive revelation and 'around the corner events'. Wonderfully, the Bible teaches that when we are served a Sunday roast, we can take any food we don't like off our plate and only eat the rest!!

4.7.5 Testing prophecy involves applying a health check of biblical principles, which I will explain later in great detail [7]. The Bible's guidance gives us a very simple and clear set of instructions as a result. Putting it bluntly, a prophecy is not a prophecy until it has been tested and confirmed to the extent that we are confident we know what God has said. The considerable benefit of testing prophecy is that it makes sure we hear what was actually said, enables us to 'hear between the lines', and brings us naturally to a place of faith in what we believe.

4.7.6 I gave my new car an RAC vehicle inspection before I risked my life in it.

110. Matthew 7:15-20 | 111. 1 Thessalonians 5:19-22

School for
Prophecy

4.8 Responding to Prophecy

4.8.1   While responding to prophecy is covered in detail in *The Principles of Responding to Prophecy* [9], it is helpful to highlight the New Covenant principles here. The most significant and misunderstood of these is the need for *participation*. Just because someone claiming to be prophetic has said it, this doesn't mean that it is going to happen. We live in a Covenant based on faith. The Bible[112] teaches that faith, if not accompanied by action, e.g. participation, is dead. While this does not involve 'making' your prophecy happen, it does involve being available, alert and applied to all aspects of its journey to fulfilment.

4.8.2   The next 'P' in the principles of responding to prophecy is *perspective*. Most importantly, perspective is learning to see the journey in our prophecy from our heavenly Father's point of view. This involves understanding what our Father is seeking to achieve in us, where He sees us actually starting from, and what He intends us to learn during the journey. It sometimes involves understanding the requirement for 'prior preparation' and 'proper placement' to create the right conditions for our prophecy to activate in our lives. Too often, our focus is completely on the destination instead of the process initiated by the journey.

4.8.3   Prophecy, even one fulfilled in the short term, releases a process of transition in our lives, which frequently requires some elements of the next 'P', *patience*. Patience ensures that we allow the process of transition to complete its full work in us as intended. It also helps us to discover and embrace the 'progressive revelation' encountered during the journey, which can change our understanding and perspective considerably. Patience, perhaps most importantly, enables us to overcome the biggest prophetic assassin of frustration. Patience talks to us about trusting our heavenly Father and experiencing His peace in our hearts.

4.8.4   *Perseverance*, while not a common subject in Church, is the response our heavenly Father is looking for in us with some prophecies. He understands there can be a world of difference between receiving and possessing new territory in our lives, and perseverance enables us to push through to acquisition. Perseverance is about keeping going when things turn against us. Perseverance helps us recognise the authority of our tested prophecy over our circumstances, not our circumstance's authority over our prophecy. The biblical reality is that God uses[113] trials to test our faith because it produces perseverance in us.

4.8.5   The last 'P' in the principles of responding to prophecy is *prayer*. Prayer involves us in a deliberate, conscious and active conversation with the Holy Spirit, the Spirit of truth, about our prophecy. As a result, this keeps us open to an environment of progressive revelation, greater insight, deepening interpretation and further confirmation. Prayer helps keep our prophecy alive and fresh in our hearts and minds. Prayer is very capable of being a strong supporter of the other 'P's, particularly perspective and patience. Prayer creates a healthy atmosphere to engage with the change, transition and challenges we will encounter.

4.8.6   Responding to prophecy is about being part of the solution and not part of the problem.

112. James 2:14-17 | 113. James 1:2-5

4.9 Personal Testimony

4.9.1 Probably one of the most personal and longstanding principles in my ministry, especially as it differentiates me from most of the other ministries I meet, is that I record everything I share in prophecy whenever possible. This is a principle I inherited from my prophetic mentor who introduced me to it back in 1996 and proved very conscientious and thorough in its application. I therefore now carry with me a digital recorder at all times, so I am available and equipped.

4.9.2 Although I have chosen not to teach that it is a biblical requirement to record prophecy, I do take my prophetic gift very seriously and expect those I serve to do the same. How you can honestly believe that you can remember accurately what was said with even a short prophecy – and I am not short – is beyond me. I have often proven the point by reading out a one-minute-only prophecy, asked people to write it down immediately afterwards, and then let them compare the two. End of argument.

4.9.3 We used Sony cassette tape recorders in the early years, which were so much easier. You recorded any personal prophetic ministry and handed the cassette tape over to the recipient, job done. I did learn the terror of the 'blank' tape or the unfortunate failure of the sound desk we were relying on, so I carried spare batteries with me. This sometimes meant you were faced with the question, "Please can you do it again?" shortly afterwards or even sometime later.

4.9.4 Inevitably, the time came when people started saying they did not have a cassette player; could I email it to them? Nightmare. I found that digital recorders at that time were manufacturer-exclusive, needed specific software to play and usually only worked on Microsoft Windows-based computers. I now carry with me an Olympus MP3 digital recorder, which works wonderfully easily with Microsoft and Apple products, without any additional software, connects by USB and can be easily emailed if I don't go on for too long!

4.9.5 Fortunately, many people now receiving prophecy have smartphones with the capability to record it for themselves. Mind you, this means I have become quite proficient at explaining how the voice recorder on an Apple and Samsung mobile works, as frequently people have never used it before. Furthermore, many mobile phones have a good voice recorder app, which allows you to email it immediately from your phone to the recipient.

4.9.6 Mistakes, failure and harsh discipline have ended many ministries better than mine. I have faced personal, public and aggressive criticism on a few occasions, and given there are well over 1,000 recordings of mine out there, I would be surprised otherwise. However, because I record prophecy, those involved have been invited to review their prophecy with me and listen carefully to what was said. This has proven an absolute lifesaver on those occasions because the review usually revealed I had not said what they thought I had; they had misunderstood it or misinterpreted it.

School for Prophecy

4.10   Frequently Asked Questions

4.10.1   How is a prophecy different from a word of knowledge?

4.10.2   They are both listed in the traditional nine gifts of the Spirit. The Bible says they come from the same source, have the same purpose but operate differently. I believe the Bible teaches that words of knowledge are exactly that: the gift to be able to know something through your spirit and not any of your five senses.[114] It is a gift based on facts, knowledge and information; while prophecy is God speaking to us for our strengthening, encouragement and comfort [4.3.2].

4.10.3   I feel more comfortable prophesying in the first person; why is that wrong?

4.10.4   I am not teaching that it is wrong; you need to follow your leadership. However, I am pointing out that phrases like "thus says the Lord" give the impression that you are an Old Testament prophet speaking with Old Covenant authority, which you do not have. It also undermines those listening as they will not realize they need to test, be in faith and act on the word following biblical principles. I encourage my students to say, "I believe," "I feel," or, "I sense," which better reflects our biblical gift [5.4.2].

4.10.5   Lots of people say I am prophetic; does that mean I have a ministry?

4.10.6   It appears you are already moving in the gift of prophecy. To have the potential for a level two ministry [4.6.4] usually means other people recognize the gift of prophecy as a significant part of you and its anointing on you. This appears to be the case. The good news is that with practice, training and experience it can be grown significantly in accuracy, detail and frequency with the potential to develop into a mature prophetic ministry.

4.10.7   If a prophet has said it, why do I have to test it?

4.10.8   It is important we appreciate that we are not under the Old Covenant anymore. While God still speaks through prophets and the gift of prophecy, we do not speak the exact words of God [6.3.1] and therefore testing is a biblical principle for quality control [5.7.1]. Even in the Old Covenant, prophets had to be tested in case they were false, and if so the penalty was being stoned to death. We need to come to a place where we know what we believe God has said to us so we can then have a living faith in it.

4.10.9   Surely if I now have a prophecy, all I have to do is wait?

4.10.10   Unfortunately, this is a common and fatal mistake. We now live by faith and not by sight. Consequently, I teach that a prophecy is not alive in our lives until we have an active faith in it [5.8.2]. Faith is fundamental to the fulfilment of prophecy, while on occasions subject to the amazing grace of God. Furthermore, the Bible teaches us that faith without action is dead! So, considering the implications of the word, how we position ourselves for fulfilment and any training or character development necessary is important.

114. Mark 2:8

Study Notes

5

NEW AND OLD COVENANT PROPHECY

Study Notes

5.0   Chapter Summary

5.0.1   *Introduction – Prophetic Foundations* are a set of core principles that, very much like the foundations of a building, are what all our other teaching, understanding and experience of the gift are based upon. The second subject will explain the crucial differences between New and Old Covenant prophecy and reveal a biblical pathway for a confused church and a deceived world.

5.0.2   *Fundamental Reorientation* – The biblical principle we need to grasp is that prophecy has fundamentally changed between the Old Covenant and the New Covenant, in ways that have changed its purpose, operation and environment, but not its supernatural source, nature or anointing.

5.0.3   *Role of a Prophet* – In the New Covenant, Jesus promised that we would know God's Spirit; he would live with us and live in us. The Holy Spirit dwelling within us has a role to guide us into all truth, being the Spirit of Truth. In the New Covenant we no longer need to rely on a prophet to tell us what God is saying, because we can simply ask him ourselves.

5.0.4   *Final Authority* – One of the common obstacles to prophecy I have encountered has been a fear that it undermines the authority of the Bible by setting itself up as an equivalent inspired authority. In the New Covenant, the Bible, or more formally the Canon of Scripture, is now our final authority, because the authority of the spoken word has moved to the written word between the Covenants.

5.0.5   *Everyone Can Prophesy* – One of the most significant changes foretold in the Old Covenant about the New Covenant is by the prophet Joel, who prophesied that God would pour out his Spirit on all people, both men and women, young and old, master and servants. I believe that there is ample evidence in the Bible to teach that anyone who wants to can prophesy.

5.0.6   *Conditionality* – The biblical conditions in prophecy inevitably reflect the core principles of salvation under the New Covenant, those which have triggered the changes in prophecy between the covenants. In order of occurrence, but not necessarily in order of priority, they are *Interpretation, Testing, Faith, Implementation* and *Timing*.

5.0.7   *Testing Prophecy* – It is a significant contrast between the New Covenant and the Old Covenant that prophecy is required to be tested as one of the above conditions, while Old Covenant prophecy mainly involved obedience to any requirements to guarantee fulfilment. The role of testing is to bring you to a place where you are confident enough about what you believe God is saying.

5.0.8   *Faith in Action* – The New Covenant has heralded in a completely new way of relating to God that is based on faith. The testing of prophecy practically enables us to decide what specifically God is saying to us, which then allows us, through the confidence of the testing process, to come to a position of faith in what we believe.

5.1 Introduction

5.1.1   Following the previous chapter on *Understanding Biblical Prophecy* [4], the next *Prophetic Foundation* I want to examine, and in some detail, is the difference between *New and Old Covenant Prophecy*. *Prophetic Foundations* are a set of core teachings that, very much like the foundations of a building, are what all our other teaching, understanding and experience of the gift are based upon. The second *Prophetic Foundations* subject will explain the crucial differences between New and Old Covenant prophecy, and reveal a biblical pathway for a confused church and a deceived world.

5.1.2   There are three main areas of misunderstanding about the gift of prophecy by the wider church, and this is the most significant of them. It is not an exaggeration to say that the majority of misunderstanding, misuse and malpractice in the operation of the gift can be directly attributed to a lack of appreciation, ignorance or confusion about the change in the gift of prophecy between the covenants. I could use the terminology New and Old Testament instead because it nearly fits the timescales, but it is the change in covenants that is the foundational principle that we need be grasp, not the Testaments.

5.1.3   If *Understanding Biblical Prophecy* [4] represents the quality of the mix of the concrete in our foundations [4.1.4], then this chapter represents the accuracy of the surface, dimensions and edges of our foundations. Once the foundations are in place, everything inevitably reflects their accuracy, or lack of it, in the rest of the building. The taller, or more prominent the building, the more obvious any errors in the level and accuracy of the foundations will be. In fact, at some height such errors can make the building unsafe for its occupants and those around it, not to put too fine a point on it.

5.1.4   This chapter is completely different from all the others because its sole purpose is to correct the disturbingly widespread error of bringing Old Covenant principles and practices into the expression of New Covenant prophecy. While the Old Covenant attractively imbues prophecy with more authority, perpetuates superstar personalities and provides easy solutions to those unsure of their decisions, the New Covenant is fundamentally different through the impact of salvation, the indwelling Spirit and the body of Christ.

5.1.5   There is a considerable beneficial side effect from correctly understanding the differences between New and Old Covenant prophecy. As you re-educate your understanding of the covenants, your appreciation and experience of your salvation and relationship with God will inevitably deepen – not an insignificant side effect, and possibly one more important than even the gift of prophecy itself. Given that I believe the majority of our weaknesses and problems as Christians come from a poor, or lack of, understanding of what salvation means for us and what Jesus truly achieved on the cross, you will appreciate my enthusiasm.

 **School** for **Prophecy**

5.2 Fundamental Reorientation

5.2.1   This chapter on *New and Old Covenant Prophecy* could involve a major reorientation of your appreciation of biblical prophecy. Too much of our understanding stands on what we have seen others do, assumptions about how prophecy works and our experience of far too many apparently Old Testament style prophets still alive today. The biblical principle we need to grasp is that prophecy has fundamentally changed between the Old Covenant and the New Covenant, in ways that have changed its purpose, operation and environment but not its supernatural source, nature or anointing.

5.2.2   The inauguration of the New Covenant by Jesus,[115] the introduction of salvation by faith, has inevitably changed the purpose, operation and environment of the gift of prophecy. There are many ways that our lives are very different from the Old Covenant that we realize, understand and accept quite naturally. No one would be at all happy if we started teaching salvation by the Law, resting on the Sabbath, celebrating every Jewish festival, or not being allowed to talk to God except through a priest etc. The list is endless. We accept that we are in a New Covenant and not under the Law, praise God.

5.2.3   Salvation by faith means we are no longer reliant on a prophet, priest or king for our relationship with God. Jesus fulfils all these primary roles in our lives, and we have unlimited, unhindered and unrestricted access to God through him. *Amen.* We are no longer reliant on a prophet to hear from God, a priest to enter the presence of God or a king to lead us. We now have the Holy Spirit living with us and in us[116] as our counsellor, teacher and supernatural power. This revolutionary change impacts the operation of prophecy.

5.2.4   This change in salvation between the covenants affects the operation and purpose of all the gifts of the Spirit, some more than others. Those like healing and miracles have many similarities between the covenants, while there are New Covenant gifts of tongues and interpretation. There are similar ministries like pastor (shepherd) and teacher in both covenants, while there are New Covenant ministries of apostle and evangelist. The nature of the change in salvation between the covenants has a direct impact on the purpose and operation of the gift of prophecy more than any other of the gifts of the Spirit.

5.2.5   To be fully effective, the gift of prophecy needs to make the same transition that other gifts have and as is reflected in our salvation. This transition means that the purpose of prophecy has fundamentally changed, as we are no longer reliant on a prophet to be the very mouthpiece of God because now we can ask him for ourselves! Perhaps more significantly, the outpouring of the Holy Spirit is available to everyone who believes, not just the anointed few. The change in salvation between the covenants requires us to embrace the same change in the purpose, operation and environment of the gift of prophecy.

5.2.6   Prophecy will never achieve its full potential until it is allowed to change covenant.

115. Luke 22:20 | 116. John 14:16-17

5.3   Role of a Prophet

5.3.1   In the Old Covenant, prophets of God were rare, handpicked and powerfully anointed individuals, often with odd characters, who appeared out of nowhere to change the history of God's people. Their life stories and prophecies provide the majority of what we now call the Old Testament in our Bibles. God said to Jeremiah that he had been selected before he was born to be a prophet to the nations.[117]

5.3.2   In the Old Covenant, God explained to Moses that he would raise up prophets like him from among the Israelites, and he would speak through them.[118] What the prophet said was to be acted on as though it were from God, and it had the same disobedience consequences as if it were from God. Consequently, the penalty for being a false prophet was to be put to death, which is understandable given the circumstances.

5.3.3   In the Old Covenant, the significance of prophets was that they spoke the exact words of God. When God commissioned Ezekiel, he told him to eat the scroll of words provided for him.[119] It is a clear image of God's word being given to him for delivery. Prophets became, supernaturally, the very mouthpiece of God. Consequently, their prophecies have become part of our Bible to recognize their authority as the word of God.

5.3.4   In the New Covenant, prophecy is not just for an anointed few. Joel prophesied that in the New Covenant God will pour out his Spirit on all people and they will prophesy, dream and have visions as a result.[120] This changed prophecy from being a sign of a significant appointment to becoming the gift for all people, in this way changing the role of the Old Covenant prophet forever.

5.3.5   In the New Covenant, the need for prophets to be the only mouthpiece of God has been removed, symbolized by the tearing of the Temple curtain in two[121] on Jesus' death. It represents our ability to access the Holy of Holies, a place in the Temple where only the high priest could enter, and only on certain feasts. Jesus' victory now gives us unrestricted, unhindered and unlimited access to an intimate relationship with our heavenly Father, forever!

5.3.6   In the New Covenant, Jesus promised that we would know God's Spirit; he would live with us and live in us.[122] In the New Covenant, we no longer need to rely on a prophet to tell us what God is saying, because we can simply ask him ourselves. Jesus is now our prophet, priest and king. The Holy Spirit dwelling within us has a role to guide us into all truth,[123] being the Spirit of Truth.

5.3.7   A New Covenant prophet brings oversight, insight, foresight and anti-parasite.

117. Jeremiah 1:4-5 | 118. Deuteronomy 18:18-22 | 119. Ezekiel 3:1-4 | 120. Joel 2:28-29
121. Matthew 27:51a | 122. John 14:16-17 | 123. John 16:13-15

School for **Prophecy**

5.4 Final Authority

5.4.1 One of the common obstacles to prophecy I have encountered, particularly amongst leaders, has been a fear that it undermines the authority of the Bible by setting itself up as an equivalent inspired authority. This is easy to understand if you believe prophecy still operates in an Old Covenant environment of calling, anointing and authority. Hence the fear that prophecy could be held up to be equal in authority to the Bible, being God's word itself, with all the obvious consequences and pastoral complications.

5.4.2 However, this is an unnecessary fear because there has been a significant change between the covenants that has clarified this issue for us. The Bible teaches that the prophecies recorded in it were by men speaking from God as led by the Holy Spirit.[124] To put it more simply, the prophets in the Old Covenant were speaking the word of God, and as a result this has now been written down for us in our Bibles. In the New Covenant, the authority of the spoken word in the Old Covenant (prophet speaking the Bible) has now moved to the written word (Bible record of the prophecy).

5.4.3 In the New Covenant, the Bible, or more formally the Canon of Scripture, is now our final authority, in all areas of life, such as decisions, direction and discernment. The Bible's authority is not just the written words, principles, values and morals, but also its spirit and heart. To understand the full authority of the Bible, and use it in our lives, we need to embrace the facts, flavour and framework in the Bible, not just the written content. This is an ongoing journey for us as we consider new issues not specified in the Bible but covered by its values and guidelines, such as social media.

5.4.4 Furthermore, the Bible is now recognized as complete, so that nothing can be added to it, i.e. a prophecy also claiming to be God's word. At the end of John's vision in the book of Revelation, he gives a sobering warning that if anyone adds something to his book or takes anything away from it, God will add to them the terrible curses described in his vision.[125] Being the last book in the Bible, it helpfully symbolizes that the Bible is a complete and closed work, and cannot be added to by additional prophecy, whatever it may claim to be.

5.4.5 This fear that prophecy could be held up to be equal in authority to the Bible, unfortunately, hides the fact that the Bible is the greatest exponent and proponent of prophecy. Throughout the Bible, it is a clear *exponent* of the gift of prophecy; it unequivocally supports the gift and tries to persuade us of its benefits. It is also a strong *proponent* of the gift of prophecy and encourages us on many occasions to use it. The requirement to obey the word of God inevitably requires us to recognize the significance of the gift of prophecy and seek to move in it!

5.4.6 The Bible is now our plumb line for all decisions, direction and desires.

124. 2 Peter 1:19-21 | 125. Revelation 22:18-19

5.5   Everyone Can Prophesy

5.5.1   One of the most significant changes foretold in the Old Covenant about the New Covenant is by the prophet Joel, who prophesied that God would pour out his Spirit on all people, both men and women, young and old, masters and servants.[126] The significance of this cannot be overstated as it is the foundational change on which the New Covenant is built. Having the Spirit of God in us enables us through grace to have a loving, personal and intimate relationship with our heavenly Father. One of the key manifestations of this was to be the release of the gift of prophecy to everyone.

5.5.2   I believe, and it is also my experience, that there is sufficient evidence in the Bible to teach that anyone who wants to can prophesy. I believe and teach that the gift of prophecy is available to everyone. This is not wishful thinking but based on the following biblical teaching.

5.5.3   The prophecy in Joel above specifies the gift of prophecy as a manifestation of the outpouring of the Spirit in the New Covenant, on both sexes, all ages and regardless of status. This is then referred to by both Jesus and the apostles in confirmation of its fulfilment.

5.5.4   The Bible encourages us to desire spiritual gifts eagerly, especially prophecy.[127] I do not see why the Bible would encourage the church family to desire something they could not have. Some believe that this was added to promote prophecy, but fortunately for us, it is in the original text!

5.5.5   While contrasting the value of speaking in tongues with prophesying, Paul tells the Corinthians that he wants them all to speak in tongues, but even more to prophesy[128]. This biblical statement clearly implies that prophecy is available to everyone.

5.5.6   Finally, while discussing the issue of order when bringing prophecy in public meetings, Paul says to the Corinthians that that we can all prophesy in turn so that everyone may be encouraged.[129] The capability for everyone to prophesy in turn further confirms that prophecy is available to all those who want it.

5.5.7   This does not mean that everyone will have the same anointing, calling and experience in the gift of prophecy. As explained in *Levels of Gifting* [4.7.1], I have found three ranges of gifting defined in the Bible which act as a guide. In recognition of these different levels in the Bible, this manual is designed and written to teach all those in level one [4.7.3] about the gift of prophecy, and to bring them to a biblical, grounded and fruitful understanding of the operation of the gift.

5.5.8   Prophecy is not something for the anointed few, but for the powerful many.

126. Joel 2:28-32 | 127. 1 Corinthians 14:1 | 128. 1 Corinthians 14:5 | 129. 1 Corinthians 14:31

School for
Prophecy

5.6   Conditionality

5.6.1   The lack of appreciation that all New Covenant prophecy is conditional causes many to end up with unfulfilled prophecy in their lives. This leads to disappointment and the inevitable relational fallout with God because they perceive that it is not their fault and therefore must be his. This problem fundamentally reflects a lack of understanding of the differences between Old and New Covenant prophecy. While I recognize that there will be occasions when God moves sovereignly by his grace, biblically and for daily practical application, New Covenant prophecy is conditional.

5.6.2   The misunderstanding of this principle means recipients of prophecy, in the misguided belief that it is unconditional, do nothing and inevitably undermine or negate the timely or intended fulfilment of their prophecy. They believe that because the prophet has said it, God will be faithful to fulfil his word for them. This Old Covenant type of approach is far more common than we realize due to the lack of teaching and training in the prophetic, mainly because churches are either unsure how safe the gift is or rely on celebrities to do it for them.

5.6.3   However, Jesus emphasized that his word is eternal,[130] and consequently, under the New Covenant, the Bible has become the automatic 'small print' to any prophecy, whether specified or not. Anyone who has had to review a finance agreement back page will understand what I mean. All finance agreements, and often others, have a back page of seriously small print that tends to cover all the situations when something goes wrong. The principles in the Bible are now applicable in any prophecy because it is the eternal word of God. Put simply, it applies in all circumstances.

5.6.4   The biblical conditions in prophecy inevitably reflect the core principles of salvation under the New Covenant, those which have triggered the changes in prophecy between the covenants. In order of occurrence, but not necessarily in order of priority, there are five practical biblical conditions in prophecy to consider. They are *Interpretation* [11.4.1], *Testing* [5.7.1], *Faith* [5.8.4], *Implementation* [11.7.2] and *Timing* [8.4.1]. The fulfilment of New Covenant prophecy is conditional on the correct application of these five areas, although some will be more important than others depending on the particular circumstances. That is assuming there are no other specified conditions, i.e. requirements, in the prophecy.

5.6.5   Hidden within most prophecies is a journey for our character to equip us to engage with God's destiny fully, and it will frequently involve prior preparation and proper placement [8.4.5] before we can enter it. It is never part of our heavenly Father's plan to fulfil his promises in our lives so early that our enemy can kill, steal or destroy them because we were unable to acquire, occupy and defend them properly. If this involves setting us free from prisons in our past, as it often will, this will seriously catch our attention.

5.6.6   Prophecy is no longer a 'one arm bandit' route to blessing, but an act of faith.

130. Matthew 5:18

5.7 Testing Prophecy

5.7.1   It is a significant contrast between the New Covenant and the Old Covenant that prophecy is required to be tested as one of the above conditions [5.6.4], while Old Covenant prophecy mainly involved obedience to any requirements to guarantee fulfilment. In my opinion, the requirement to test prophecy is the second biggest area of misunderstanding, mishandling and misuse of prophecy in the church today. While it is helpful to cover the principles involved here, it is such an important subject I have included a complete chapter [7] where I cover this subject in considerable and practical detail.

5.7.2   While the supernatural gift of prophecy is now available to us all, following the New Covenant outpouring of God's Spirit, we do not possess the ability of Old Covenant prophets to speak the exact words of God. The Bible teaches that in the same way that we can only partially know God, we can only prophesy incompletely.[131] On Christ's return, when prophecy will no longer be needed, then we will know him completely. In the same way that the authority has moved from the spoken word in the Old Covenant to the written word in the New Covenant, the authority in prophecy has moved from the giver in the Old Covenant [God's prophets] to the recipient in the New Covenant [the tester].

5.7.3   The key principle is explained helpfully by the Bible in a short but specific teaching on testing prophecy.[132] In particular, it says not to ignore prophecy, to test everything and then to hold on to what is good. This is the biblical balance in prophecy, of not ignoring anything or accepting everything. The role of testing is to bring you to a place where you are confident enough about what you believe God is saying to you through the prophecy. Once you have done this, knowing what you believe God is saying to you, you can then stand on it with confidence and faith.

5.7.4   Testing prophecy involves applying a series of biblical tests to help you arrive at what you believe is good and hold on to it. It is a process very much like I used to see my father do in the garden when he was preparing some earth for the greenhouse. He would remove any obvious stones and rubbish from the earth [weed]. Then he would use a small grid sieve to remove any small impurities and seeds [sieve]. Then, finally, he would use his finest grid to remove impurities in the soil under close examination [weigh].

5.7.5   Fortunately, testing is one of those areas where we can significantly develop our ability, insight and accuracy with practice.[133] While testing may seem a daunting task at first, the more you do it, the easier it becomes. It reminds me very much of when I first started learning to drive. The impossible task of managing three pedals, steering the car, changing gear without stalling and still looking in the rear-view mirror left me a sweaty mess for many lessons. However, having mastered this process, it all feels more natural to me now.

5.7.6   Testing prophecy is the way of the wise, and the mistake of the many.

131. 1 Corinthians 13:9 | **132.** 1 Thessalonians 5:19-22 | **133.** Hebrews 5:14

School for **Prophecy**

5.8   Faith in Action

5.8.1   One of the considerable benefits of learning to test prophecy is that it inevitably leads us to a place of much greater clarity, understanding and insight into what we believe God is saying to us. This brings us naturally to the next key process in New Covenant prophecy, a position of faith. The testing of prophecy practically enables us to decide what specifically God is saying to us, which then allows us, through the confidence of the testing process, to come to a position of faith in what we believe.

5.8.2   The New Covenant has heralded in a completely new way of relating to God, one based on faith. Faith is the spiritual air that we breathe, and in the same way that a lack of physical air will eventually lead to death, so will a lack of faith. The Bible teaches this key principle,[134] and while it is a very short sentence, it has huge significance: "We live by faith, not by sight." The correct biblical response to any prophecy, once it has been tested, is to have faith in it. Our faith enables us to treat the tested prophetic word with the same significance as if God had said it to us directly.

5.8.3   The Bible highlights this point when it identifies two categories of people.[135] While both groups had the real gospel preached to them, it was of no benefit to one of the groups because they did not add, i.e. combine it with, faith. Hearing the truth is not enough on its own; we need to add faith to it for it to be of benefit in our lives. While the writer is not speaking specifically about prophecy, he is laying down a New Covenant principle which also applies when responding to prophecy. New Covenant prophecy requires faith in action.

5.8.4   One of the powerful impacts of faith is that it can take the invisible [what is in heaven] and make it visible [what is on earth]. It can bring what God intends for us in heaven into actual reality in our earthly lives. Faith releases the invisible – prophecy – into our lives. A prophecy is not alive, active or accomplishing in our lives until we have real faith in it. The false belief that 'the prophet has said it, so we just wait for it to happen' is an Old Covenant model which can lead to confusion, disappointment and deception.

5.8.5   This particular error undermines the effectiveness, inheritance and fulfilment of prophecy because it neutralizes the need for our participation in the process. James is famous for his teaching that faith, if not accompanied by action [deeds], is ineffective [dead].[136] A living faith means that we will act on what we believe and that inevitably leads to action: 'faith in action'. While I am certainly not teaching that we should make our prophecy happen, as in birthing an Ishmael,[137] we do need to become co-workers with Christ in our lives and act in faith on what we believe he has said to us.

5.8.6   A prophecy is not alive in our lives until we have an active faith in it.

134. 2 Corinthians 5:7 | 135. Hebrews 4:2 | 136. James 2:14-17 | 137. Genesis 16:1-4

5.9   Personal Testimony

5.9.1   There is no doubt in my mind that the primary cause for the continued ineffectiveness of prophecy is the distressing lack of biblical understanding about the differences between New Covenant and Old Covenant prophecy. The Old Covenant model of prophecy is demonstrably visible in the Church. There is a predominance of rare, powerfully anointed, celebrity status, itinerant prophetic ministries, and church leaderships continue to struggle in their relationships with prophetic people over authority, accountability and accuracy.

5.9.2   There is considerable material in the Old Testament, and enough role models in the public arena, to propagate and reinforce a model based on the prediction of the future, provision of guidance and the judgment of our failings. The church's continued lack of expectation, encouragement and example in this area only exacerbates the problem. This has created a culture of commercial professionalism, entertainment and celebrity status, leaving the vast majority of the church clearly not equipped, encouraged or empowered by the gift of prophecy in their day-to-day lives.

5.9.3   A simple example would be the continued use of "thus says the Lord" prophecy. This claims a level of revelation, accuracy and authority that is just not true in the New Covenant. I understand that it is not easy when our language moves on; I did not find leaving behind my favourite RSV Bible verses easy either. But much of the time this Old Covenant rhetoric is someone thinking they are more anointed than they are. It implies that the more religious the wording, the more reliable it is and leaves you facing confrontation if you do not accept everything that was said.

5.9.4   The Internet is full of prophetic websites declaring global predictions, vitriolic judgment and promises of unbelievable favour. Too many people in the Church and the world still patently believe prophecy is based on an Old Covenant model, and, as a result, it inevitably reflects a gospel of judgement and not one of grace. Old Covenant prophecy was full of prophetic direction and judgement, and I have New Covenant authority concerns with both.

5.9.5   Firstly, claiming to bring accurate direction for others has serious implications. It claims a level of accuracy that may be wrong, with inevitable consequences. It effectively puts us in a position of a priest, between people and Jesus, and even more so if in people's weakness they seek this out. It also creates the opportunity for control and manipulation through prophecy, the main tool of false prophets, as it requires unquestioning acceptance.

5.9.6   Secondly, an unhealthy emphasis on judgement creates a focus on failure and punishment that does not reflect the gospel of grace. I believe a better term for correction is *discipline,* particularly as this is one of the hallmarks of our salvation.[138] The need for correction is too often understood and implemented as punishment, instead of improvement – whereas the purpose of discipline is the loving intervention by our heavenly Father to bring us into full maturity.[139]

138. Hebrews 12:8-9 | 139. Hebrews 12:10-11

 School for Prophecy

5.10 Frequently Asked Questions

5.10.1 There is a lot of prophecy in the Old Testament. Why can't I use it as a guide?

5.10.2 You are actually answering your own question. There are many things that are in the Old Testament, i.e. Old Covenant, that are not applicable today. In the same way that it would not occur to you to follow the Mosaic Law, the operation of the gift of the prophecy has changed in the New Covenant. While it is still a gift and ministry in the New Covenant, salvation and the indwelling of the Holy Spirit have changed its operation significantly [5.2.2].

5.10.3 We have a prophet in our church; isn't he there to tell us what God is saying?

5.10.4 The role of the prophet is different in the New Covenant, because now you can, and should, ask and hear God for yourself. We no longer have to rely on prophets as the mouthpiece of God, because we have a personal relationship as sons and daughters through Christ [4.7.5]. Apostles and prophets are now the foundation layers of church; the prophet is one part of a body, i.e. team ministry, and his primary role is equipping others, not doing it for them.

5.10.5 Isn't prophecy more interesting and relevant than the Bible?

5.10.6 While prophecy is important and appears more relevant at times, we do need to recognize that the Bible is the final authority and is always applicable [5.4.3]. We need to be clear that any prophecy which contradicts the letter or spirit of the Bible is a false prophecy. Prophecy, being supernatural, often feels more 'exciting', and may speak into specific situations in our lives. However, it can never replace or amend the 'manual of life', which contains everything we need to follow Jesus.

5.10.7 Are you sure I can prophesy? Not many people in my church can.

5.10.8 A very understandable question, and one this manual is trying to correct! Bottom line: there is sufficient evidence in the Bible that everyone who wants to can prophesy, and even more than that, it encourages us to personally seek after the gift of prophecy [5.5.2]. The truth is that it is not that people cannot prophesy, they just don't realize that they can and God intended them to. Training in prophecy is rare compared to other more common gifts, so it tends to only be the 'creative' few who take the first step into the unknown.

5.10.9 Surely, I can only act on a prophecy when I know what it means?

5.10.10 Reviewing and testing prophecy will bring you to a place where you know what you believe God is saying to you, but not necessarily clarity on every detail. Prophecy is a journey for your faith, what you believe after testing [5.8.1]. Testing will involve confirmation – independent, hopefully – and the wisdom of those you trust. So, while you are unlikely to have 'writing in the sky', you will have enough to consider the implications of the prophecy and ideas on how you might implement them.

Study Notes

89

6

BIBLICAL PROPHETIC CULTURE

Study Notes

6.0   Chapter Summary

6.0.1   *Introduction – Prophetic Foundations* are a set of core principles that, very much like the foundations of a building, are what all our other teaching, understanding and experience of the gift are based upon. The final *Prophetic Foundations* subject identifies core values, principles and practices that are essential to the correct and complete operation of the gift of prophecy.

6.0.2   *Maintaining Motivation* – The Bible teaches a powerful principle in the now famous exposé chapter on love. It states that if we have a gift that can fathom all mysteries and all knowledge, without love we are wasting our time. Prophecy not motivated by love is futile. Love is the currency of the kingdom and the primary motivation for biblical prophecy.

6.0.3   *An Art, Not a Science* – The next principle that we need to establish is that the gift of prophecy is an art, not a science. It is not an exact science, but a creative environment more like art. One key part of this understanding is that, as the Bible teaches, we only know in part and consequently prophesy in part. We are working on limited information, in part, not with full knowledge.

6.0.4   *The Battle with Fear* – Fear is the main weapon our enemy uses to stop us prophesying. Despite our experience of moving in the prophetic ministry, he still stands at the threshold of any ministry telling us that it is all going to go wrong. Whether you are afraid of getting it wrong, of hurting somebody or of what others might say, it is fear trying to stop you prophesying.

6.0.5   *Self-Control* – One of the key frameworks that have an immediate impact on the assumed, traditional or copied operation of the gift of prophecy is the biblical principle that prophets, and those moving in prophecy, have self-control. The Bible teaches that the spirits of the prophets are subject to the control of the prophets.

6.0.6   *Discerning the Body* – The next framework reflects yet another of the significant changes between the Old Covenant and the New Covenant. We are now all part of one body, one building and one family, so the gift of prophecy now needs to function in a body context. The prophetic ministry can only work biblically if it is an integral, living and active part of the church.

6.0.7   *Limited Liability* – The next biblical framework for the gift of prophecy is the issue of responsibility. The critical principle is that our responsibility ends with our delivery. If our only body role is to bring a prophecy, our responsibility ends there, and consequently any authority ends there too.

6.0.8   *Your Inner Well* – The final biblical framework we are going to look at in this chapter is to recognize that we have an 'inner well' and how it operates with respect to prophecy. Jesus taught an important principle when he said that once we had received the Holy Spirit, "streams of living water" would flow from within us.

6.1 Introduction

6.1.1   The final *Prophetic Foundations* topic I want to cover after *Understanding Biblical Prophecy* [4] and *New and Old Covenant Prophecy* [5] is *Biblical Prophetic Culture*. *Prophetic Foundations* are a set of core teachings that, very much like the foundations of a building, are what all our other teaching, understanding and experience of the gift are based upon. These three subjects together will ensure biblical alignment, stability and growth in your gift. The final *Prophetic Foundations* subject identifies core values, principles and practices that are essential to the correct and complete operation of the gift of prophecy.

6.1.2   This chapter's principles are important in helping us to understand how biblical prophecy should operate, as opposed to just prophecy which is the result of Old Testament patterns, denominational traditions and exposure to poor public ministry practice. They define the biblical context that the gift of prophecy is a part of, the correct biblical environment that prophecy is designed to operate in, and provide a clear biblical purpose that aligns with the kingdom of God. They are not complicated; they are easy to apply and in many cases are well known.

6.1.3   Continuing my construction illustration [5.1.3], *Biblical Prophetic Culture* is represented by the steel framework of a skyscraper being erected, like some strange skeleton, before it vanishes behind the external linings. While the accuracy and reliability of our foundations inevitably put limits on the accuracy, maturity and anointing of our gift, the steel framework of the building defines the shape, access and capacity of our gift. It very much represents the operational aspects of our gift – the how and why – that others will encounter whenever we move in prophecy.

6.1.4   The previous two foundations chapters have focussed on 'un-teaching' what people have learned or assume is biblical and then laying secure biblical foundations. This chapter is more about introducing biblical principles into areas of operational assumptions, style-copying and old traditions. Due to the lack of teaching in this area, many naturally follow the principle, "We have always done it this way," which only reinforces bad practice and creates the potential for even unhealthier variations. This chapter takes well-known biblical values and applies them, to bring our practice, where necessary, back into alignment with the Bible.

6.1.5   The obvious benefit of learning and applying a biblical framework into the operation of prophecy is that the majority of them equally apply to many other areas of our Christian walk. While we are applying key biblical principles to the practice and operation of prophecy to establish secure foundations, by definition, they are key biblical principles that apply equally elsewhere in our lives. By bringing the operation of the prophecy into the living 'river' of truth, we are, by definition, benefiting from being in the river. *Biblical Prophetic Culture* naturally reinforces the core truths that we are meant to be living.

 **School** for **Prophecy**

6.2 Maintaining Motivation

6.2.1   Jesus regularly talked about the importance of what is inside a man, rather than what is outside that we see. It could equally be said about the gift of prophecy. In the area of our motivation, the reason why are we moving in prophecy, it is even more significant. The Bible teaches a powerful principle in the now famous exposé chapter on love.[140] It states that if we have a gift that can fathom all mysteries and all knowledge, which everyone is going to say a big amen to, without love we are wasting our time. Prophecy not motivated by love is futile. This changes everything.

6.2.2   This is compatible with, and extends the principle in, the first and second most important commandments[141]. Biblical prophecy is therefore meant to operate in an environment of, and reflect the principles in, these commandments. The motivation for biblical prophecy is to share, out of our love for God and our love for our neighbour, with the person receiving our ministry. Love is the currency of the kingdom and the primary motivation for biblical prophecy – not pride, recognition, self-worth, showmanship, supernatural drug, 'keep up with the Joneses' or better meetings.

6.2.3   I have found the principle in the second most important commandment a practical and pragmatic guide when considering where, when and how to bring a prophecy. The alternative version[142] is even more obvious in its application and was simplified further into, "Do as you would be done by," in *The Water Babies* by Charles Kingsley. It makes you think about how you would like to receive the prophecy and has multiple applications throughout the use of prophecy. My prophetic mentor insisted we should always consider when, where and how we prophesy, and this principle has become my day-to-day guide.

6.2.4   A motivation of love has the significant effect of taking the spotlight off us and putting it on to those receiving. Our ministry focus then becomes considering what is best for them, rather than what is best for us. We become servant-hearted and not ministry-focused. Jesus drew out this key principle with his disciples[143] when they were arguing about who would get the best seats in the house! The overriding principle as followers of Jesus is that to become great, you must become a servant, just as he came and gave the ultimate service, his life.

6.2.5   Our motivation has an overriding impact on the effectiveness of our gift, quite simply because it determines our goal. If our motivation is to look good, impress others of our anointing or confirm our opinions, then what we will do and how we will act will completely reflect this. On the other hand, if our motivation is servant-hearted love, then what we do and how we act will be very different indeed. We should not deceive ourselves either because those around us can tell the difference between the two quite accurately.

6.2.6   Your motivation defines your goal, and your goal reveals your motivation.

140. 1 Corinthians 13:1-3 | 141. Matthew 22:37-40 | 142. Luke 6:31 | 143. Matthew 20:25-28

6.3   An Art, Not a Science

6.3.1   The next principle that we need to establish is that the gift of prophecy is an art, not a science. It is not an exact science, but a creative environment more like art. One key part of this understanding is, as the Bible teaches,[144] we only know in part and consequently prophesy in part. We are working on limited information, in part, not with full knowledge. It very much reflects the creative nature of prophecy. There is a danger that if we do not accept this we will make assumptions about any gaps in our knowledge or, even worse, act like we know everything.

6.3.2   A good example of this is the prophecy by a recognized prophet, Agabus, who foretold Paul's arrest and imprisonment when he was going to Jerusalem.[145] He prophesied that the Jews of Jerusalem would bind Paul's hands and feet and hand him over to the Gentiles. Most people would accept that the prophecy was then fulfilled if we assume the two chains used were for his hands and feet, which seems very likely. However, if we examine the exact details when he was first arrested,[146] or later on when he was handed over to the Governor,[147] it was the Gentiles who bound Paul, not the Jews. Paul was told what he needed to know, the art, and the discrepancy is insignificant to the outcome.

6.3.3   The point I am making is that we do not know enough to come to any conclusions, yet it is tempting to do so based on what we do know and let it affect our message, delivery and purpose. When we prophesy, we are only a postman delivering an open letter. We don't know the reason for the letter, the whole correspondence to date, the significance of its timing, the current circumstances of the recipient or their personal history to this point. Even if it is somebody we do know, we may think that we know enough to make decisions, but we still only have limited information.

6.3.4   God works on a need-to-know basis, and as we are usually not part of the problem or the solution, we don't need to know. The fact that we know in part and prophesy in part enables the Holy Spirit to say a lot of specific and meaningful things through us because they only mean something to the recipient. They know a lot of the information we do not know, so that phrases like 'a blue ball', 'school cap' or 'great aunt' mean something very specific to them and absolutely nothing to us.

6.3.5   In estate agent parlance, the key ingredient is 'location, location, location'. The prophetic equivalent of this is 'timing, timing, timing'. My experience is that despite all the effort we put into the quality, accuracy and significance of the prophecy, timing is often the most powerful aspect. I have lost count of the times that forgotten, lost, half-done and incomplete prophetic words have been finally finished, only for me to be told that they arrived exactly on the day needed. Timing is in the hands of our loving heavenly Father, for we know in part and prophesy in part.

6.3.6   "Art is not what you see, but what you make others see." – Edgar Degas

144. 1 Corinthians 13:9-12 | **145.** Acts 21:10-14 | **146.** Acts 21:33-34 | **147.** Acts 23:31-33

School for Prophecy

6.4   The Battle with Fear

6.4.1   Fear is the main weapon our enemy uses to stop us prophesying. Despite our experiences of moving in the prophetic ministry, he still stands at the threshold of any ministry telling us that it is all going to go wrong. Whether you are afraid of getting it wrong, afraid of hurting somebody or afraid of what others might say, it is fear trying to stop you prophesying. Fear is the most common reason why the majority of people don't prophesy. "How do you know it's from God?" is the favourite 'handbrake' in our enemy's armoury.

6.4.2   I came across a humorous book title some years ago: *Edge of the Cliff* by Hugo First [you-go first]. I have found prophesying to be like standing on the edge of a high cliff overlooking a canyon which is so deep you cannot see the ground. Then the Father's voice from below says, "Jump and I will catch you." I respond, "Come up a little higher so I can see you, then I will jump." This argument goes on for some time. In the end, I always jump, thinking this could get messy if he does not catch me. To my complete relief and joy, he safely and gently catches me. Then suddenly I am back on the edge of the cliff again, and his voice from below is saying...

6.4.3   Another aspect of fear that we encounter, because we are now in a more public environment, is the pressure of the 'fear of man'. This fear imprisons many people, and its presence may become more obvious as we move more and more in prophecy. There is a short but meaningful account of an example of the effect of the fear of man on some Pharisees during Jesus' ministry.[148] They came to be believers in Jesus but would not confess their faith because of fear of man. It poignantly says, "They loved human praise more than praise from God," i.e. what men said was more important than what God said.

6.4.4   I have not found the same level of fear in any of the other gifts and ministries I move in. When I am teaching on a Sunday, I am often nervous for the first five minutes, but once I get rolling, with my notes in front of me, and little chance of any interruption from a U.K. audience, I am often quite peaceful and very focused from then on. Not so with prophecy. Two actions are required to combat and overcome fear in prophecy: first, we must learn to move clearly in faith, recognizing that we live by faith and not sight;[149] and second, we must learn to trust our gift, which is a supernatural equipping from God.

6.4.5   Fear is one of the hallmarks of the work of our enemy in our lives, and we need to be alert to them. While I understand the 'fear of the Lord' [overwhelming awe] is biblical, I do not believe that disabling, disempowering or self-destructive fear is ever given to us by our heavenly Father. My mentoring is based on the firm belief that any decision based on fear is a bad decision. It might be the right decision, but it will eventually fail because it has the wrong motive. For your reference, our enemy's hallmarks and the godly alternatives are anxiety [faith]; confusion [conviction]; impotence [hope]; and condemnation [endorsement].

6.4.6   "The only thing we have to fear is fear itself." – Franklin D. Roosevelt

148. John 12:42-43 | 149. 2 Corinthians 5:7

6.5　Self-Control

6.5.1　One of the key principles that have an immediate impact on the assumed, traditional or copied operation of the gift of prophecy is the biblical principle that prophets, and those moving in prophecy, have self-control. The Bible teaches that the spirits of the prophets are subject to the control of the prophets.[150] Simply put, they are not under the control of another spirit, which would be a hallmark of the work of our enemy, but they are in control of their own spirits. Being out of control is not biblical prophecy, nor a blessing to others.

6.5.2　This is in direct contrast to the behaviour in some meetings where the overly enthusiastic, immature or pushy, feeling the urgency of their anointing, consequently seek to interrupt whatever the Spirit is doing at that moment. One of the hidden errors that were birthed in the Charismatic renewal of the 70s was that spontaneous contributions are more spiritual than organized ones. It is very much like the use of dynamite. Put thoughtlessly up against an object it can do a lot of damage, but when placed in the foundations, weak point or strategically, it can have ten times the impact.

6.5.3　The Bible teaches the church that order is important in meetings so that everyone benefits,[151] not just the ministering few. It is specifically referring to times of the moving of the Holy Spirit in supernatural gifts, and that as a result God is not a God of disorder but peace. Put simply, meetings should be run in an orderly way: one thing at a time; there is room for everyone, pre-prepared or spontaneous. It is down to our leaders to translate these principles into practice, but the underlying principle is that prophecy is under the control of those bringing it, not some overwhelming, immediate or pushy urgency.

6.5.4　This principle is further reinforced by the contents of the fruit of the Spirit, as described in the Bible.[152] I am sure many, like me, have read off the list of the fruit of the Spirit easily, only to find the final one, self-control, causes us to falter. But self-control is there, and is a fruit of the Spirit whether you prophesy or not. It is part of our born-again DNA, a manifestation of the Holy Spirit and a significant part of our journey to maturity through self-awareness. As we all know, having the gifts of the Spirit without the fruit of the Spirit is a dangerous place to be.

6.5.5　Finally, the Bible stipulates, when specifically mentioning prophecy, to recognize that we all have different levels of gift and should use them in proportion to our faith.[153] I am not sure why, but my experience is that many try to prophesy way beyond their anointing and experience, with no track record or wisdom, into subjects like national events, judgement on nations and predictions of revivals. We need to recognize our current level of anointing and experience, and by all means take one more step, but minister in proportion to our faith; not in accordance with our hope, ambition or presumption.

6.5.6　Self-control is the most significant fruit for those developing their gift.

150. 1 Corinthians 14:32 | 151. 1 Corinthians 14:26-33 | 152. Galatians 5:22-23 | 153. Romans 12:6

School for
Prophecy

6.6 Discerning the Body

6.6.1 The next principle reflects yet another of the significant changes between the Old Covenant and the New Covenant. We are now all part of one body, one building and one family, so that the gift of prophecy now needs to function in a body context. The prophetic ministry can only work biblically if it is an integral, living and active part of the Church family, i.e. body of Christ. The days of isolated, independent and in-your-face prophetic characters are no longer part of biblical prophecy. One of the primary functions of prophecy is to build up the Church family.[154]

6.6.2 This is naturally and inevitably reflected in the biblical role of the prophet. The Bible explains in the over-quoted description of the 'five-fold ministry' that the purpose of these gifts given by God is to train and equip the church family in their calling and ministry until we all reach full maturity like Jesus[155] – a tall order if there ever was one! Bottom line: prophecy is a gift to the body, as a body ministry, to build up the body to maturity. Not only that but it is meant to function as part of a team of ministries, all with the same function and goal.

6.6.3 The Bible takes time to emphasize this point in three black-and-white statements with the Corinthians. Firstly, it says no one can say they don't belong because they are not like everyone else.[156] Secondly, it says no one can say they don't belong because they don't need anyone else.[157] Finally, as if that is not enough, it confirms that everyone is part of the Church family.[158] Forcefully put, not recognizing the body context is effectively a form of amputation, with the same terrible and tragic consequences!

6.6.4 A direct consequence of being in a body is that the authority naturally rests in 'the head', that is, Christ, and is then delegated locally to our leaders. The writer to the Hebrews calls us to recognize the authority of our appointed leaders, follow their leadership and not to make it a hard job for them.[159] I am not referring to following those leaders who, whether due to weakness or deception, lead us into unbiblical acts, seek to control and manipulate us, or effectively set themselves up as priests between Jesus and us.

6.6.5 Those with the gift of prophecy frequently come from the creative and artistic end of the spectrum, are very committed to their gift and are passionate about the kingdom of God. Given the character challenges that prophecy, more than any other gift, inevitably creates, they can benefit considerably from having the stabilising influence of wise and experienced people in their lives. Whatever you call it, having independent, godly and loving advisors in our lives can help us avoid considerable pain and suffering, as well as substantially accelerate our growth and maturity.

6.6.6 Not recognizing the body is, effectively, self-harming.

154. 1 Corinthians 14:1-4 | 155. Ephesians 4:11-13 | 156. 1 Corinthians 12:16 | 157. 1 Corinthians 12:21
158. 1 Corinthians 12:27 | 159. Hebrews 13:17

School for **Prophecy**

6.7   Limited Liability

6.7.1   The next biblical framework we are going to look at is the issue of responsibility. Alongside the inability to say no, I have found the lack of recognition of boundaries in people one of the most common weaknesses in their maturity. The passion, enthusiasm and commitment of many prophetic people make this a very important area in their lives, and the lives of those they interact with! The foundational principle is that our responsibility ends with our delivery. If our only body role is to bring a prophecy, our responsibility ends there, and consequently any authority too.

6.7.2   We have a responsibility to deliver it as best as we can, to the person it is meant for, at an appropriate time. A simple but practical guideline I use for this is 'no more, no less'. Our job is to share no more than God gives us and no less than he tells us to share. Initially it feels like the 'no more' guideline is the hardest, particularly when we come under a heavy anointing during delivery. However, those experienced will recognize that the guideline 'no less' is much harder, because it is common practice to withhold 10% just in case.

6.7.3   The principle within the well-known second most important commandment has considerable application, and this is another of them. Under the requirement to love our neighbour as ourselves, we clearly have a biblical responsibility to them when bringing prophecy. When Jesus quotes my preferred version, "Do to others what you would have them do to you,"[160] he is laying down a clear biblical guideline for the operation of prophecy. This overriding principle causes us to imagine we are on the receiving end of the prophecy we are about to deliver. Knowing the content, we can ask ourselves how, where and when we would like to receive it.

6.7.4   The Bible also teaches that we should only share what is helpful for building others up, according to their needs and for their benefit.[161] We are not only responsible for *how* we share, but *what* we share, unsurprisingly. It specifies three very pragmatic criteria which, while they may seem obvious, are often missed under the guise of ministry, revelation and pride. What we share should [1] be designed to build others up, [2] be relevant to their current needs and circumstances and [3] be specifically for their benefit. These are actually three very exacting requirements and often the source of much consideration.

6.7.5   I am fundamentally of the opinion that no-one should ever prophesy when someone is going to have a baby, going to get married or going to die [hatch, match or dispatch]. Even if you have a recognized successful track record in any of these areas – and most people who prophesy on these occasions, disturbingly, do not – I am convinced that the pastoral damage of the one you get wrong, including the potential loss of faith through painful disappointment, far outweighs any benefits from when you were accurate. Please feel free to disagree, as long as you are willing to be responsible for the consequences.

6.7.6   What is often a question of responsibility is really a question of authority.

160. Matthew 7:12 | **161.** Ephesians 4:29

6.8   Your Inner Well

6.8.1   The last biblical framework we are going to look at in this chapter is to recognize that we have an 'inner well' and how it operates with respect to prophecy. Jesus taught an important principle when he said that once we had received the Holy Spirit, "streams of living water"[162] would flow from within us. This establishes that there is a source of the Spirit within us, which I refer to as our 'inner well', out of which it flows. The significance of this is that it is a permanent feature, and not necessarily dependent on our feelings or external surroundings.

6.8.2   While it is natural for those young in the gift to easily draw inspiration from the things around them and in front of them, the long-term goal is to move their source of inspiration to the well within and not the experience without. While the Holy Spirit can speak to us through the colour of people's clothing, their names, pictures in the room and the view outside, the true, objective and unlimited source of our revelation is our inner well. Those who don't realize this miss out on a greater consistency, depth of revelation and maturity in their gift.

6.8.3   Furthermore, recognizing this and the resulting lifestyle moves our focus on to the Holy Spirit within us, and gives us greater access to one of the key aspects of the Holy Spirit's ministry to us. Jesus explained to his disciples that it was better for them that he left them [which was going to take some selling] because as a result the Counsellor would come and indwell them. Furthermore, Jesus promised that the Holy Spirit would then "guide [us] into all the truth"[163]. The Holy Spirit has become an inner well of spiritual truth dwelling within us, which we can draw on anytime and anywhere.

6.8.4   Drawing from the inner well means that we are no longer reliant on being in the moment, needing visual inspiration around us or feeling in the mood. The difficulty of drawing our inspiration from around us is that it also works in reverse, and can seem to neutralize our gift. However, when we rely on the inner well, we are fully capable of prophesying whether we feel like it or not, and whether it's a good atmosphere or not. We can then grow in confidence, experience and anointing through our unchanging source of revelation.

6.8.5   One of the ways I have found helpful in developing our inner well is to imagine it is like a pool of water within us. This pool is the inner well of revelation we look into when we seek to prophesy. If there is movement inside, for example from anxiety, busyness and stress, this movement will cause ripples on the surface of the pool and blur the image due to its interference. The more internal 'noise', the worse the picture. However, as we learn to be able to bring the pool of water to stillness, through learning to rest, the picture takes on an HD quality image for us, with obvious impact on our revelation.

6.8.6   Our inner well is a doorway into the invisible, inspired and impossible.

162. John 7:37-39 | 163. John 16:13

6.9 Personal Testimony

6.9.1   My personal testimony is that I have been very fortunate to have had regular access to expectation, encouragement and example in my journey. These three elements are critical for growth in any environment [12.6.5] and have enabled my gift to develop significantly over the years. I have also been privileged to grow up in a strongly Charismatic church[164]. I then had access to years of training, practice and experience with an internationally recognized prophetic mentor[165] who started my journey.

6.9.2   The most important words in my journey above are 'training', 'practice' and 'experience'. Interestingly 'practice' is the one word I use more in this manual than 'testing'; that is how important it is. I was able to learn, establish and develop the framework taught in this chapter by practising it, but my concern is that this is not generally available in the church today. Practice is an essential means of growth through which we can learn from our mistakes and not be buried by them [12.6.4].

6.9.3   This is the main reason that workshops are such an important part of my school courses; they provide an opportunity to "practice"[166]. My meeting briefings describe my workshops as "easy, relaxed and guided times to help you practice moving in the gift of prophecy in a safe and structured environment". Interestingly, this is one of the times that I feel the American term 'activation' is actually a better description of what they are.

6.9.4   The challenge of learning to prophesy is that it involves testing, which this manual is a great proponent of. However, without the opportunity to learn through practice, the resulting fall-out, burn-out and cast-out rates are simply too high. Too many young gifts die on the cross of misunderstanding, mistake or mistiming, by deciding they will 'never do that again' or being disciplined into too much fear or discouragement with the same result. I do appreciate that some gifted people can learn to drive without driving lessons and the assistance of dual-controls, but they are few and far between.

6.9.5   The fact that the wider church recognizes the need for training and experience in teaching, pastoring and evangelism but not for prophecy continues to distress me. Unfortunately, too often we expect people to leap from no experience and training in the gift of prophecy to a fully matured ministry, with painful consequences for everyone involved. This is at the heart of this manual, to provide training resources for prophecy where they are not readily available.

6.9.6   I appreciate that many churches simply do not have the experience to develop the gift of prophecy, but the problem simply does not go away. Unfortunately, without training or practice opportunities the prophetic environment tends to then develop elements of combat, conferences and celebrities. There is an urgent need for the wider church to create and develop learning and practice opportunities for those seeking to grow in the gift of prophecy, for the safety of everyone involved.

164. Community Church, Southampton | **165.** Graham Cooke | **166.** Hebrews 5:14

6.10 Frequently Asked Questions

6.10.1 Why can't I share the prophecy when I feel like it? God did give it to me!

6.10.2 Ignoring the issue of your leadership and your ownership [6.6.1], the main reason is that the purpose of prophecy is to help somebody else, not ourselves. The consideration of where, when and how depends on them and the purpose of the prophecy, not on your feelings [6.2.2]. In a sense, the decision is still yours, but the consideration is all about others, not you. Prophecy should come from a servant's heart to be able to reach its full potential, power and penetration.

6.10.3 Surely a prophecy is false if it is not completely accurate?

6.10.4 This is a common misconception, based on an understanding of Old Covenant prophecy. In the New Covenant, today, we now only know a part and prophesy in part, hence the need for testing by the recipient. Most prophecy is neither completely right nor completely wrong [5.7.4]. Hold on to what you feel God is saying to you through prophecy. The Bible calls this holding on to what is good, and the rest can be discarded or put on the shelf for later consideration.

6.10.5 I am still struggling with prophecy. How do I know if it's from God?

6.10.6 The Bible repeatedly teaches prophecy is a supernatural gift of the Holy Spirit, and we are told to eagerly desire it to build others up [5.5.4]. After that, it is an issue of simple trust, i.e. faith. Jesus said that he was more generous than any of our earthly fathers, and he will give us what we ask for, and not something harmful.[167] The person receiving is required to test everything [5.7.3], so I would encourage you to share what you have that satisfies biblical conditions unless you have a reason to withhold it.

6.10.7 The anointing is so strong; why won't they let me just share my prophecy?

6.10.8 In the early days of prophecy, it can feel like this. I hope you understand why 'they' need it to fit in with everything else that God is doing [6.6.4]. Otherwise, you will just give it to the next person, and not the necessarily the right person. Prophecy is not like a grenade where you pull the pin and have three seconds to get rid of it [6.5.2]. You will learn to channel the pressure of the anointing, which is often worse because it is 'turbo-charged' by our own anxiety, and use it at the point of ministry.

6.10.9 Why don't I fit in? There is nobody else prophetic and I feel odd.

6.10.10 The fact that you feel odd actually makes you special. Those organs in our body we only have one of are very important and we take great care of them. God is very creative and he has actually made everyone different, it's just that prophecy tends to label us more in the eyes of others [6.6.3]. Develop good lines of communication with your leaders, look for ways to serve others and don't act weird or spooky [6.6.5]. It will change over time. People need time to learn to trust you before they will open up to you.

167. Matthew 7:7-11

Study Notes

7

THE PRINCIPLES OF TESTING PROPHECY

Study Notes

7.0   Chapter Summary

7.0.1   *Introduction – Prophetic Protocols* are the biblical procedures and guidelines that govern the operation of the gift of prophecy and are fundamental to the safe, satisfactory and successful operation of the gift. The first prophetic protocol covers testing prophecy, the fourth of the 7 I's of prophecy.

7.0.2   *Why Test Prophecy?* – Many churches down the years have found understanding, implementing and managing the testing of prophecy a challenging and difficult task. It is a fundamental requirement in the Bible to test prophecy. This principle is birthed in the changes between the covenants as a direct result of our salvation and the indwelling of the Holy Spirit.

7.0.3   *Practical Application* – The Bible teaches that the mature have trained themselves by constant use, or practice, which is colloquially referred to as 'practice makes perfect'. Learning to test prophecy is an area where there are considerable benefits from practice and experience, making it easier to apply, yield more accurate results from, and develop a greater understanding of the message.

7.0.4   *Types of Tests* – The series of tests I have developed from biblical principles includes three types of tests, with two detailed tests in each type. There are six biblical tests available to use in total. The first type are *Authenticity* tests [burglar alarms]; the second type are *Alignment* tests [fire alarms] and the final type are *Alert* tests [carbon monoxide alarms].

7.0.5   *Authenticity Tests* – The first authenticity test is what I call 'the inner witness'. The inner witness is also sometimes called having an inner peace, or the opposite, 'dis-peace', about decisions and direction. The second authenticity test is 'independent confirmation' and works by providing such confirmation from an objective source outside of ourselves.

7.0.6   *Alignment Tests* – The first alignment test is confirmation by agreement with the Bible, or what some refer to as the word of God. The prophecy needs to be in alignment or compliance with both the word and the spirit of the Bible. The second alignment test checks compliance with a 'Jesus-centred focus'. What we are seeking to test is that the prophetic word complies with Jesus as the source, author and centre of the message.

7.0.7   *Alert Tests* – Alert tests are not checking for what is there but for what should not be there. The first alert test is designed to examine whose kingdom a prophecy is building. The second is designed to check for the correct 'flavour of freedom'. While the first test seeks to examine the kingdom direction of the prophetic word, the second looks at the results or impact on our freedom.

7.0.8   *Benefits of Testing* – As well as the obvious biblical quality assurance benefit of testing prophecy, there are other not-so-obvious but significant benefits to consider. Testing prophecy is a process, and the careful examination, consideration and review will help to ensure a correct understanding of the prophecy.

7.1   Introduction

7.1.1   I have explained the concepts and practices involved in successful *Prophetic Engagements,* and then covered the necessary biblical teaching in our *Prophetic Foundations.* We will now look at the essential *Prophetic Protocols* required when moving in the gift of prophecy. I am obviously teaching the gift of prophecy in stages. It is important to understand that *Prophetic Protocols* only function effectively if the previous topics on *Prophetic Engagements* and *Prophetic Foundations* are understood as core values and are being put into practice to the best of our ability.

7.1.2   In the third teaching topic of the manual we will cover the three core subjects of *Prophetic Protocols: The Principles of Testing Prophecy* [this chapter], *The Principles of Interpreting Prophecy* [8] and *The Principles of Responding to Prophecy* [9]. *Prophetic Protocols* are the biblical guidelines that govern the operation of the gift of prophecy and are fundamental to the safe, satisfactory and successful operation of the gift. The first prophetic protocol covers the fourth of the 7 I's of prophecy, *Investigation,* i.e. how to test prophecy. It addresses the second major area of misuse, misunderstanding and manipulation in the Church.

7.1.3   This chapter looks in detail at the biblical principles of how to test prophecy, and in particular their practical application. If you have not realized that I consider testing prophecy to be important, where have you been? I have already introduced the subject in the chapter *Understanding Biblical Prophecy* [4.8] and highlighted its significance in the chapter *New and Old Covenant Prophecy* [5.7]. The testing of prophecy is the equivalent of commercial quality assurance procedures that ensure there are no hidden additives, impurities or poor-quality materials in the product.

7.1.4   Continuing my illustration of the skyscraper from the previous chapter [6.1.3], the alarm system installed within the skyscraper is a good illustration of the reason for, and practice of, testing prophecy. While it is usually silent, it is always active and will trigger in dangerous situations. Furthermore, there are a variety of types of alarm installed, as described in this chapter, including motion sensors to detect intruders, fire alarms to detect flames and carbon monoxide alarms to detect invisible killers. They may be unobtrusive and often forgotten, but they are strategically located and essential for our safety.

7.1.5   My prophetic mentor had many famous quotes, but there was one that many overlooked, and in time I realized it was crucial if you wanted to develop your prophetic gift: "How you administer [or use] your gift is just as important as having a gift in the first place."[168] If you are a 'one-shot wonder', then this is not applicable. However, when considering maturity, body ministry and longevity, this area becomes very important. *Prophetic Protocols* are pivotal in creating a biblical environment for prophecy, in determining the effectiveness of prophecy and for the long-term survival of those moving in prophecy.

168. Graham Cooke

School for
Prophecy

7.2 Why Test Prophecy?

7.2.1 Many churches down the years have found understanding, implementing and managing the testing *[Investigation]* of prophecy a challenging and difficult task. Unfortunately, this has resulted in the emergence of two extreme historical versions of the testing of prophecy, both unhelpful and unbiblical. While they stunt any growth and development of the gift, they are much easier to operate and manage. The first approach restricts or ignores prophecy, wherever possible avoiding confrontation, thereby removing any risk of damage through error. The second approach is to allow and enjoy the experience of prophecy, but never take it seriously or act on it, so that there can never be any harm done.

7.2.2 While the middle ground between these two is, as is so often the case, the more difficult ground to occupy, it is the biblical place. It is a fundamental requirement in the Bible to test prophecy. This principle is birthed in the changes between the covenants [5.7] as a direct result of our salvation and the indwelling of the Holy Spirit. While testing prophecy does take time, and requires maturity and wisdom, quality assurance is vital. When you grasp the *Prophetic Protocol,* i.e. biblical principles involved, it is not difficult. With practice and patience, it will become quite natural and normal over time.

7.2.3 The key principle is helpfully explained by the Bible in a short but specific teaching on testing prophecy.[169] For a four-verse passage, it certainly packs a powerful punch of truth. Unpacking the principle, it says: [v.19] "Do not quench the Spirit." = do not resist the gift of prophecy; [v.20] "Do not treat prophecies with contempt…" = do not ignore all prophecy; [v.21a] "…but test them all…" = do not accept all prophecy; [v.21b] "…hold on to what is good…" = be selective; [v.22] "…reject every kind of evil." = do not allow control and manipulation.

7.2.4 Testing is the process where we examine the delivered prophecy through a series of biblical tests to arrive at what we believe God is saying to us. It enables us to receive confirmation and remove any impurities, and it protects us from control. It will remove any elements of human intervention, detect any deception by our enemy, correct any unbiblical elements, put aside unclear ideas for later review and identify poor quality revelation. Through this process, we will arrive at what we confidently believe is the truth so that we can have an active faith in it.

7.2.5 While only a side effect, one of the great benefits of testing prophecy is that you can only realistically grow and develop in the gift when testing is operational. Without testing as part of the process you get what I call 'candyfloss' prophecy. It tastes really nice, everyone wants one, and they are not hard to produce, but they always leave you feeling hungry afterwards! It would be like learning to run a race but never having anyone timing you. You will certainly get fitter, but it is virtually impossible to measure your progress, set yourself goals or be competitive without knowing how well you are doing.

7.2.6 Testing enables us to tease out temptation while tackling the truth.

169. 1 Thessalonians 5:19-22

7.3 Practical Application

7.3.1 Before we get into the detail of the tests to apply, an obvious item to consider is the biblical definition of prophecy[170] [4.3]. Obviously if the prophecy concerned falls outside the definition of biblical prophecy, then it has already failed the test. While not going into the detail of any particular prophecy, the definition is helpful because it describes the objective of any biblical prophecy, which I refer to as the 'essential flavour'. All prophecy is given for our encouragement, strengthening and comfort. Given this is an all-inclusive definition, every prophecy must have this essential flavour to be biblical.

7.3.2 I have found on my journey with Jesus – and it has become core teaching in my mentoring – that there are some obvious hallmarks of our enemy's work in our lives that will never come from God. Similarly, if they are present in a prophecy, or their taste is, then those elements need to be rejected or amended. God will never give us anxiety, confusion, impotence or condemnation; these do not come from God. He will give us faith, conviction, hope and endorsement, which all reflect his character. Much of our misunderstanding in this area is a wrong view of our heavenly Father, his love for us and our sonship [3.2].

7.3.3 In my *Essential Health and Safety* introduction to this manual I emphasized the need for ongoing learning through practice. The Bible teaches that the mature have trained themselves by constant use,[171] i.e. practice, which is colloquially referred to as 'practice makes perfect'. Learning to test prophecy is an area where there are considerable benefits from practice and experience, making it easier to apply, yield more accurate results and develop a greater understanding of the message. My example of learning to drive a car [5.7.5] being similar to learning to test prophecy does make the point nicely.

7.3.4 It is important to understand that testing *[Investigation]* is not a one-size-fits-all process that tells us if anything is wrong. This would be similar to how garages test our cars these days. They plug into our car's onboard computer and out come the test results. Testing prophecy is more like going to your doctor, who will employ a series of tests to try to identify if anything is wrong with you. Some problems can be identified by just one of the tests. However, it is more common that a combination of tests will highlight issues and, on occasions, more specialized tests may also have to be applied.

7.3.5 Finally, give yourself time. There is no pleasure in being under time pressure to come up with a decision on a prophecy. People create pressure, and pressure creates mistakes. Taking time is quite important when applying tests to any prophecy, particularly when it is a creative process. I take encouragement from how Mary reacted[172] to some mind-blowing news about giving birth to God's son. She pondered on these things! You cannot rush pondering; it needs time and space. I have developed a personal guideline to take a minimum of seven days to test any prophetic word, so I don't feel rushed.

7.3.6 Your best teacher is your last mistake.

170. 1 Corinthians 14:3 | 171. Hebrews 5:14 | 172. Luke 2:19

School for **Prophecy**

7.4 Types of Tests

7.4.1 The series of tests I have developed from biblical principles includes three types of tests, with two detailed tests in each type. There are six biblical tests available to use in total. The first type are *Authenticity Tests* [burglar alarms]; the second type are *Alignment Tests* [fire alarms] and the final type are *Alert Tests* [carbon monoxide alarms]. Depending on the circumstances, some tests may be easier to apply than others and some tests will feel more relevant than others. However, they should all be considered in the process, however briefly, to ensure there is full coverage.

7.4.2 It will help you a lot if you are familiar with the tests and their purpose, so you understand what the particular test is trying to find out for you. I have listed below a summary of the tests as a simple, and hopefully helpful, introduction to the considerable detailed analyses over the next few pages.

7.4.3 *Authenticity Tests* [burglar alarms] seek to confirm the genuine nature and source of the word. The two tests include the confirmation of the prophetic word by our own inner witness, the Holy Spirit, and confirmation of the prophetic word from an independent source outside of ourselves, for example a God-incidence. This is like a burglar alarm being alert to any outside interference and is the main alarm for your tests.

7.4.4 *Alignment Tests* [fire alarms] seek to confirm that the contents and purpose of the word comply with, i.e. match, other established and reliable sources. The two tests include the compliance of the prophetic word with the Bible, in both word and spirit, and compliance of the prophetic word with a Jesus-centred focus. This test is illustrated by a fire alarm; it warns you when there is danger within so you can beware.

7.4.5 *Alert Tests* [carbon monoxide alarms] seek to warn us about any deceptive or devious elements in the prophecy. The two tests include any caution arising from whose kingdom the prophetic word is building, and any caution generated by the lack of a flavour of freedom in the prophetic word. Like a carbon monoxide alarm these tests are looking for something invisible but still deadly. These rarely go off, but when they do, action is required.

7.4.6 One final nuance I would like to clarify before we jump into the tests is the difference between poor and bad prophecy. This is all about motivation, but the danger is the guillotine can unnecessarily fall on poor prophecy when it should be falling on the bad prophecy. Infrequently we will receive prophecy from 'players'; for example, false prophets, political spirits or people with an agenda.

7.4.7 We may also receive weak prophecy from the inexperienced, 'only just started' and the 'quite nervous'. The difference is important, because the bad prophecy can sound a lot more accurate than the poor prophecy. Poor prophecy is a weak message coming from a good heart, whereas bad prophecy sounds like a strong message but comes from a bad motivation.

7.4.8 "Only one word of advice: avoid the steaming divot." – *Pretty Woman*[173]

173. *Pretty Woman;* dir. Larry Smith; Touchstone Pictures [1990 Film]

7.5   Authenticity Tests

7.5.1   The first authenticity test is what I call the 'inner witness'. The inner witness is sometimes called having an inner peace, or the opposite 'dis-peace', about decisions and direction. It can give us a slightly positive to a very confident feeling about the word; a little uncomfortable to a negative feeling about the word; or no discernible reaction either way. This test works independently of our logical minds and is therefore quite capable of guiding us in the opposite direction to our personal preferences. It frequently becomes clearer with time and often becomes magnified once we have made our decision.

7.5.2   Jesus explained that the Father would give us another counsellor, the Spirit of Truth, who would live with us and live in us.[174] This enables us to test prophecy by using the discernment of the Holy Spirit within us. Later Jesus emphasized this important principle by specifying that the Holy Spirit [inside us] would guide us into all truth.[175] This promise gives us great confidence that the Holy Spirit will guide us to the correct evaluation of the prophetic word, using the inner witness as a primary resource.

7.5.3   The second authenticity test is independent confirmation, which works by providing independent confirmation from an objective source outside of ourselves. It protects us from our subjectivity and agendas; limitations in our understanding and expectations; and vulnerability to our emotions. For example, a similar prophecy from a different source; identical thoughts from our daily Bible readings; our circumstances changing to match the word; or something like an advertising hoarding having an amazingly matching statement. God-incidences are simply relevant and timely coincidences.

7.5.4   This test utilizes a fundamental principle repeated throughout the Bible and is therefore particularly helpful when testing prophecy. I am aware of six references in the Bible to the principle of 'independent confirmation by two or three witnesses', particularly with important decisions. Moses' Law states that one witness is not enough to convict anyone accused of a crime;[177] it must be established by two or three witnesses. Paul tells Timothy not to consider an accusation against a leader that does not satisfy this principle.[178]

7.5.5   The authenticity tests are the primary tests, and the ones you will most frequently use. In fact, on the majority of occasions their application will be sufficient to help you reach a decision about the authenticity of the prophecy. They provide both an internal and an external confirmation and produce a powerful and Holy Spirit based foundation for decision-making. It is well worth prioritising, practising and pursuing the two authenticity tests as they will be the most effective weapons in your testing armoury. The Alignment and Alert types of tests will only ever be needed if the authenticity test inconclusive.

7.5.6   Authenticity ensures compatibility with reliability.

174. John 14:16-17 | 175. John 16:13 | 176. 1 Kings 19:11-12 | 177. Deuteronomy 19:15
178. 1 Timothy 5:19

School for Prophecy

7.6   Alignment Tests

7.6.1   The first alignment test is confirmation by agreement with the Bible. The Bible is now the final authority in all matters of life, and consequently a natural resource for testing prophecy. Therefore, compliance with the Bible is an obvious key alignment process in testing prophecy. Paul emphasizes the importance of the Bible to Timothy[179] and encourages him to continue in what he has learned from an early age from the Bible, and that it is able to make him wise in all matters of life. He then states the Bible is inspired, God-breathed and can equip 'everybody for everything'.

7.6.2   It is at this point I need to expand on what alignment, i.e. compliance, with the Bible means in practice. The prophecy needs to be in alignment with both the word and the spirit of the Bible. First, it needs to comply with the word, i.e. facts, of the biblical values, principles and practices as specified. Second, it needs to comply with the spirit of the Bible and apply the values and principles to subjects not specifically covered by the Bible, e.g. television, social media, employment.

7.6.3   The second alignment test checks compliance with a Jesus-centred focus. What we are seeking to test is that the prophetic word complies with Jesus as the source, author and centre of the message. I often explain that prophecy comes from the same heavenly Father that people have come to know in their quiet place so, allowing for cultural differences, the two should sound a lot like each other! My frequent prayer is that people will hear Jesus' words and heart through my voice and vocabulary – is this something that Jesus would say?

7.6.4   The Bible warns us not to believe every spirit but to test the spirits.[180] The 'litmus test' is whether they acknowledge Jesus as the Christ. Also, during his end times vision, John describes an encounter with an angel that usefully demonstrates this principle and its practice. Overawed, John kneels down to worship the angel, who firmly rebukes him and tells him not to because he is a fellow servant of Jesus. However, the angel then says, "For it is the Spirit of prophecy who bears testimony to Jesus."[181] Prophecy is all about testifying about Jesus.

7.6.5   Compliance tests are not as decisive as authenticity tests, because they are more a matter of degrees, grades and judgement. So, remembering the "hold on to what is good" principle, they help us to discern what to hold on to, what to defer for later consideration and what does not seem right. This test is looking not only at *what* is said but *how* it is said and *why* it is said. This test allows us to review the prophecy from the perspective of the character of God. It needs to comply with the 'heart' of Jesus, reflect that he is a God of love and seek to give him all the honour and glory. Is Jesus the centre?

7.6.6   Alignment enables refinement of our assignment.

179. 2 Timothy 3:14-17 | 180. 1 John 4:1-3 | 181. Revelation 19:10

7.7   Alert Tests

7.7.1   The first alert test is designed to examine whose kingdom a prophecy is building. Jesus taught a core principle that we are to seek to build his kingdom first, above everything else.[182] Consequently, anything which is building something else fails this test. For example, one of the strongest features of the kingdom of God is that it is servant-hearted. Jesus frequently taught his disciples this principle,[183] and strikingly contrasted it with the officials and authorities around them. This test is not looking at the facts of the word, but checking the flavour and focus of the prophetic word against its kingdom goal.

7.7.2   This test is particularly important in protecting us from control and manipulation through the prophetic ministry or by those using the prophetic word out of context. These could include human empires, dominating public ministries and cult leadership for example. Unfortunately, due to the directional nature of prophecy, it can be easily used as a form of authority over us by those with another agenda. Their prophecies sound genuine initially, but on closer examination have a different purpose and agenda. Identifying whose kingdom is being built will protect us from this abuse.

7.7.3   The second alert test is designed to check for the correct 'flavour of freedom'. While the previous test seeks to examine the kingdom direction of the prophetic word, this test looks at the results and impact on our freedom. This test is checking for any influences diluting, undermining or destroying our freedom in Christ. It is being alert for any elements in the prophecy which seek to reduce our biblical freedom through the unhealthy presence of such items as works, legalism and control. When present, all of these will impact our freedom in Christ and seek to move us away from the truth.

7.7.4   This test is built on the fundamental truth pronounced by the Bible that, "It is for freedom that Christ has set us free."[184] This verse powerfully explains that freedom is not a means to an end, but the objective itself. Freedom is fundamental in our relationship with God, our salvation and our inheritance. The Bible also teaches that receiving the Spirit does not make us slaves to fear, but adoption as free sons and daughters of God.[185] Finally, this is exemplified in what became the battle cry of the late 70s' Charismatic renewal: "Where the Spirit of the Lord is, there is freedom."[186]

7.7.5   Alert tests, by their nature, are very different in their operation from authenticity and alignment tests. They have no impact at all if there is nothing unhealthy in the prophetic word, and only have significance when they detect something wrong. They are like a carbon monoxide alarm, which may sit quietly for years and only goes off when things are dangerous for us. This test is checking to make sure we do not allow ourselves, through false prophetic inspiration, to come under any other gospel than that of grace.

7.7.6   Alarm equips us to disarm any potential harm.

182. Matthew 6:33-34 | 183. Mark 10:42-45 | 184. Galatians 5:1-6 | 185. Romans 8:15
186. 2 Corinthians 3:7

School for Prophecy

7.8   Benefits of Testing

7.8.1   As well as the obvious biblical quality assurance benefit of testing prophecy, there are other not-so-obvious but significant benefits to consider. One which may sound strange, but is often a considerable benefit, is that testing ensures you hear what was said – not what you thought was said, what others tell you was said or what you can remember was said. Testing prophecy is a process, and the careful examination, consideration and review will help to ensure a correct understanding of the prophecy. It ensures you don't act on what was not said, or miss anything that was said which is important.

7.8.2   Testing takes time. This naturally leads us to, and makes more opportunity for, prayerful consideration. The process of testing tends to lead us into prayer, as we seek a heavenly perspective for the truth within. Prayer opens us up to the invisible and spiritual aspects of the prophetic word, brings much greater clarity into our thinking and points our dependency clearly at our heavenly Father. Prayer specifically helps us review the prophecy from a position in heaven [from above it] rather than a position on earth [from under it]. Prayer encourages peace and rest into the testing process, which puts us in a much better place to hear the whole truth.

7.8.3   One of the significant aspects of responding to prophecy is that we often receive more revelation than is in the prophecy because of our knowledge of our circumstances, journey to date and other previous guidance. The testing process brings us into a place where this can naturally occur. I call this 'hearing between the lines' as opposed to 'reading between the lines'. This neatly identifies that once the prophetic word has been written out as a record, and for judgement, we are often able to hear more than was actually said, through the release of additional truth by the Holy Spirit.

7.8.4   The presence and operation of testing prophecy effectively creates a barrier, i.e. defence, against ungodly forces and influences in our lives. Anyone who travels is now very familiar with, and understands the necessity of, the security procedures at airports. They are an active deterrent for smuggling, illegal substances and terrorists. The existence of testing prophecy, similarly, acts as a deterrent to anyone or anything trying to deceive or harm us. While the alarm tests check for specific forms of personal harm, the actual existence and operation of testing prophecy impacts the wider environment we live in.

7.8.5   Finally, testing prophecy brings us to a detailed knowledge and understanding of the prophetic word, and consequently helps us to consider the *Implication* [11.6] and *Implementation* [11.7] of the word as well. Taking time to test our prophecy means we are much more likely to be able to recognize any prior preparation and proper placement [8.4.5] that the fulfilment of the word will require. While these are both particular stages in the prophetic process, the results of testing inevitably lay a foundation for both of these due to the helpful *Investigation* of the word's contents.

7.8.6   Testing increases the insight into the integrity, ideas and impact of prophecy.

7.9   Personal Testimony

7.9.1   One of the most important prophecies I have been given to test was a major prophetic word that came at one of the most challenging times in the history of a large church in Southampton. It was received shortly after the two most significant statesmen in the church had left under difficult circumstances, and the church was in shock and great distress as a result – particularly as one of them had been the founding father of the church. While I am not going to cover the detail of what became known as the 'train and tunnel' prophecy, it does helpfully reinforce many of the principles of this chapter.

7.9.2   Testing this prophecy formalized much of my understanding of the process. The first one I immediately encountered was the need to take time [7.3.5]. Straight away I felt under considerable time pressure, due to the urgency of the situation and the significance of the contents. I am sure I was not the only one reviewing the prophecy, but it was interesting how this pressure blurred my insight. This was the birth of my seven-day rule, which gave me the personal space to fully access my gift and evaluate the prophecy.

7.9.3   The next lesson I clarified was to identify under the authenticity test what was and was not prophecy. The prophecy had been transcribed on to two full pages, and I felt the beginning of both pages, while godly wisdom, was not revelatory prophecy. This did not mean we ignored it, just that it was not God's supernatural wisdom and did not carry the same authority as prophecy [3.6.5]. In my opinion, this moved the focus from the historical interpretation to our future guidance, which I felt was significant.

7.9.4   The prophecy contained significant guidance and some very strong images. However, one of them did not sit comfortably with me, and I applied my 'be selective' principle under the *Alignment Tests* [7.6.6]. The train entered a significant mountain called 'sin' on its journey, and while I responded to the image, the name did not witness to me. Altering the name to 'holiness' was a small change with a big impact. It changed the atmosphere, flavour and purpose of the prophecy. Not done lightly, but with a strong witness.

7.9.5   The final principle I crystallized was my 'hearing between the lines' ability to hear more revelation than is in the prophecy because I am the recipient [7.8.3]. On top of the significant guidance and promise in the prophecy, there were many areas where more revelation was available to us. However, there was none more significant than the clear message that we were in 'the right place at the right time'. Given our recent circumstances, this was an incredibly powerful truth to hear and absorb as we journeyed together. It challenged the majority view of our situation head-on, and spoke powerfully of hope!

7.9.6   Like many prophecies, the 'train and tunnel' prophecy cleared the significant tests comfortably and became a source of great encouragement, promise and guidance for the church at a crucial time. The last lesson that became clear to me during the review of this prophecy was how the testing process naturally leads you to a place of faith in what you believe God has said [5.8.1]. Wrestling with what is the truth inevitably gives you a strong grip on it when you find it!

7.10 Frequently Asked Questions

7.10.1   I know I should test my prophecy, but I am not sure how to do it.

7.10.2   It may seem hard to start with, but I can promise you, with practice and experience it will become much easier [7.4.1]. Primarily, all you are trying to do is get enough confirmation that you are confident it is from God [7.2.4]. Then you are checking the content to make sure there are no dubious or unbiblical elements. Finally, you need to check the feel of the word in case there are any hidden agendas within it. If you are doing your best, the grace and love of God will cover anything you miss. Just be open to more wisdom.

7.10.3   Why do I need confirmation? It seems to fit and is exactly what I want.

7.10.4   Confirmation is important because it makes sure it is God's agenda, and not ours or somebody else's [7.5.3]. Without any confirmation, we are vulnerable to words of hope not prophecy, the kindness but not revelation of friends, and our reinterpretation of what God is saying. Through confirmation, we are ensuring that we don't set our faith, hope or heart on something that is not from God and will lead to discouragement and disappointment. I am also naturally cautious when the prophetic word promises us exactly what we want.

7.10.5   Why does prophecy have to be limited to what the Bible says?

7.10.6   Prophecy is a wonderful gift and resource, but it is still vulnerable to our human weaknesses and is therefore never perfect [5.4.3]. On the other hand, the Bible is a recognized, established and completely inspired word of God. This makes the Bible a better source of reference, i.e. the final authority. Furthermore, prophecy is not limited by the Bible because the Bible covers every possible aspect of our lives. Prophecy could be described as the one verse out of all the sixty-six books of the Bible that you need today!

7.10.7   My friend often shares a prophecy to confirm his teaching. Is that normal?

7.10.8   If this is innocent, it is simply misguided and unwise. While this may be produced by an overenthusiastic and overexcited atmosphere, it is extremely dangerous because of the high risk of subjectivity, prejudice and lack of accountability. Unfortunately, this deception could be intentional and, if so, looks like control and manipulation [7.4.5]. It puts you in a position where you feel you cannot question what is taught because it is confirmed by prophecy [7.8.4]. Prophesying confirmation of your own thoughts, teaching or vision is one of the symptoms of control.

7.10.9   I have rather a personal prophetic word. Should I get advice about it?

7.10.10 I would certainly recommend that you do, while at the same time taking into account the confidential nature of its contents [3.6.4]. Advice from others gives you access to three sources of wisdom not available within yourself [8.6.1]. First, an honest counsellor will ensure you get an objective perspective. Second, talking to those whom you love and know you well will allow you to see yourself through others' eyes. Finally, you can access wisdom from those who are more mature and experienced in these matters than you are.

Study Notes

8

THE PRINCIPLES OF INTERPRETING PROPHECY

Study Notes

8.0 Chapter Summary

8.0.1   *Introduction – Prophetic Protocols* are the biblical procedures and guidelines that govern the operation of the gift of prophecy and are fundamental to the safe, satisfactory and successful operation of the gift. The second *Prophetic Protocol* provides biblical, practical and experienced guidance on the challenging and important area of interpreting prophecy.

8.0.2   *Seeing the Unseen* – There are many areas where learning to see with the eyes of your heart is important, but of all these, interpreting prophecies is one of the most significant. It involves using the eyes of our heart to see into the core revelation and interpret the meaning of the background, activity and detail.

8.0.3   *Understanding God's Ways* – Interpreting prophecy requires an understanding of who God is, how he works and why he speaks; i.e. seeing through God's eyes, understanding his ways and learning to recognize his voice.

8.0.4   *Timing in Prophecy* – The timing of a prophecy is an important area in the interpretation of prophecy. It is important for the person sharing the prophecy to be accurate about the timescale, and it is also crucial for the person or organisation receiving the prophecy to get the right timing.

8.0.5   *Prophetic Symbolism* – Another significant area in the interpretation of prophecy is the use and understanding of images and symbols within a prophecy. Symbolism, images, pictures and objects are frequently a significant part of a prophecy, and therefore the interpretation of symbolism is important in accessing the full meaning of a prophetic word.

8.0.6   *Maintaining Objectivity* – Learning to be objective is an important element in the mature, impartial and independent interpretation of prophecy. Objectivity protects us from our past experiences, personal agendas and particular preferences, which can impact the accuracy of our interpretation.

8.0.7   *Taking Time* – Interpretation works best at identifying the full wisdom and revelation of God in a prophecy without the pressure of time. It is important to give yourself enough time so you do not feel under stress, whether you are giving or receiving a prophecy.

8.0.8   *Dissecting Prophecy* – When faced with the task of interpreting a prophecy, it is normal to feel a little overwhelmed because you are trying to take it all in at once. The technique of dissecting prophecy enables you to do this and break your prophecy up into manageable pieces. I will explain several key steps I have found helpful in dissecting prophecy.

8.1 Introduction

8.1.1 Following the previous chapter on *The Principles of Testing Prophecy* [7], the second subject in the *Prophetic Protocols* topic is its well-known partner *The Principles of Interpreting Prophecy*. *Prophetic Protocols* are the biblical guidelines that govern the operation of the gift of prophecy and are fundamental to the safe, satisfactory and successful operation of the gift. The second *Prophetic Protocol* provides biblical, practical and experienced guidance on the challenging and important area of interpreting prophecy.

8.1.2 The principles of interpretation utilize, more than most, all the areas of *Prophetic Engagements: Battle for Your Mind* [1], *Seeing the Bigger Picture* [2] and *Hearing Your Father's Voice* [3]. It is very much an art, not a science, and relies a lot on our creativity through images, impressions and insight. I should point out that I am not an advocate of the picture and image dictionaries that are available, both for dreams and interpretation. While I recognize that some images are frequently associated with specific meanings, I believe our God is far too creative for them to have only one primary meaning.

8.1.3 Continuing my illustration of the skyscraper from the previous chapter [7.1.4], as a way of describing the gift of prophecy, the interpretation is represented by the floor plan of the building. It is an essential part of finding your way around and specifically shows you where you are and how to get to your destination. It provides detailed information about entrance and exit points, stairwells you need to use to go up a floor, and any obstacles or dead ends to avoid. Like a floor plan, *Interpretation* helpfully provides perspective, route-planning and details of the journey to where God wants to take us.

8.1.4 A common error is having a prescriptive approach to who should bring the interpretation. It is frequently an activity for both the deliverer and receiver of prophecy, although there are cases when it is only the deliverer or only the receiver. *Interpretation* is the only one of the 7 I's of prophecy [11.2] that applies to both the deliverer and the receiver. Inevitably, the receiver knows their history, current circumstances and latest wisdom so much more than the deliverer, so it would be surprising if they were not involved in developing the *Interpretation* further. The deliverer engages in *Interpretation* for *Initiation* [11.5], while the receiver engages in *Interpretation* to identify the *Implication* [11.6].

8.1.5 One of the major beneficial side effects of growth in the art of interpreting prophecy is a heightened awareness of the invisible, i.e. unseen, spiritual dimension around us. This awareness creates new opportunities, even through the simple day-to-day images we encounter. It directly impacts our walk with our heavenly Father and makes us much more aware of the evidence of his footsteps in our lives. One simple benefit from learning to see all the detail in a prophecy is that we learn to look and see what is actually around us. Interestingly, many witnesses in court are of no real use because they did not 'see' what was right in front of them.

8.2   Seeing the Unseen

8.2.1   There are many areas where learning to see with the eyes of your heart [2.3] is important, but of all these, interpreting prophecies is one of the most significant. Interpreting prophecy requires an understanding of who God is, how he works and why he speaks; i.e. seeing through God's eyes, understanding God's ways and learning to recognize his voice. *Interpretation* is a key element in the operation of the gift of prophecy, and the development of your gift will significantly depend on you learning to grow in the art of interpretation.

8.2.2   *Interpretation* is that part of our gift that can unpack the concentrated 'seed' of a message and then deliver the full grown 'tree' as a prophecy. To put it simply, this requires us to see the bigger picture from the detail. *Interpretation* naturally leads on to the next stage of *Initiation,* i.e. the delivery of the prophetic word, which is frequently the end of the process for many of us. Interestingly, after receiving a prophetic word, interpretation is just as important to the recipient, who now has to unpack the word and consider its implication. In contrast, but in symmetry, this requires us to see the detail within the bigger picture.

8.2.3   During a workshop I ran many years ago, one of those attending shared a prophecy about waves hitting the beach and leaving patterns in the sand. I remember the surprise on their face when I asked, "What patterns?" Fright initially set in, but after a moment they relaxed and sought to 'see' more. Sure enough, after a few moments they confidently shared that there were three pictures: a castle, a rose and a dove. Thinking they were off the hook, a smile grew on their face. "What do the pictures mean?" came my reply. Consternation quickly turned to more waiting and seeing. Then, in a relieved tone, they shared they represented strongholds, hope and freedom.

8.2.4   *Interpretation* enables us to 'unwrap and unpack' the full meaning of the inspiration we have received from the Holy Spirit. It involves using the eyes of our heart to see into the core revelation and interpret the meaning of the background, activity and detail. We are looking for the invisible that is linked to the inspiration we have received. "I see a windmill on the shores of a fork in the river," is just the start. The Bible explains this very helpfully within a life principle. It says we should focus not on what is seen but on what is unseen, because what is unseen is eternal.[187] *Interpretation* looks for the unseen.

8.2.5   With any revelation using images, our initial task is to sense whether it is an object, a door or a recipe! The first case is where the object is the prophecy, so it is a matter of interpreting the detail, uses and location of the object. The next possibility is where the object, by way of association, is a key to the prophecy. It will 'unlock' a train of thought, memory or situation which is the actual source of our prophecy, not just the key. Finally, is our image part of a recipe, or one of a group of related objects, people or places that lead us to other involved elements related to its location, function or design?

8.2.6   Interpretation enables the manifestation of realisation.

187. 2 Corinthians 4:17-18

8.3 Understanding God's Ways

8.3.1 The first principle to grasp is the flavour, purpose and objective of freedom in all areas of our lives [7.7.4]. Freedom is the means and the end of Jesus' ministry,[188] and therefore will be reflected in the purpose, fabric and often detail of any prophetic word. We need to understand that freedom is a priority to our Lord, and breaking, destroying and undermining bondages are part of this process. God is not looking for a compromise, adaptation or counterbalance. He is releasing freedom to fulfil his promises and our inheritance.

8.3.2 Next, our heavenly Father is wise and will only build on rock, and not on sand.[189] God will not build on inadequate foundations. This wisdom means he will dig down through any unsatisfactory material until he reaches rock he can build on. Given this material usually represents our character, you might want to meditate on the significance of that principle. It has two aspects. Firstly, prophecy will reflect this principle in removing inadequate foundations before it starts to build. Secondly, God builds our foundations so they reflect the size of our calling and destiny, not just our short-term needs.

8.3.3 Samuel was a prophet of great gifting, yet he learned a foundational principle while anointing the next king of Israel after Saul. God explained to Samuel that man [us] looks at the outward appearance, but God looks at the heart [inside].[190] This approach is an important lesson for us when considering interpreting prophecy. Prophecy will inevitably reflect what God sees on the inside, in a man's heart, while we can be affected, deflected and conflicted by the unreality of the outward appearance. Prophecy is often speaking into what you cannot see, have no knowledge of and have no reason to suspect.

8.3.4 Perhaps the most obviously challenging interpretation principle is that God does not make decisions based on finance. Materialism, one of the gods of this world, is in fundamental opposition to how God works. We are taught to seek treasure in heaven and not on earth,[191] which will naturally become a standard and flavour in many of our prophecies. God is looking to grow our faith, not our finances, and our complete dependence on him, not on money. God has enough money for anything he wants to do, so, as the saying goes, "If it's God's will, it is God's bill."

8.3.5 Finally, something our time-obsessed generation finds hard to grasp is that God is more interested in the journey than the destination. This is often a very different mindset to ours and is important when interpreting prophecy. God's relational nature emphasizes the importance of our time together rather than how quickly we reach the destination. We tend to draw straight lines between us and our destination, accept the quickest route in the satnav and measure success in speed. Not so with God. Relationships are measured in our time spent together, what we talk about and the experiences we share.

8.3.6 If God is the chef, we had better follow the recipe.

188. Galatians 5:1 | 189. Matthew 7:24-27 | 190. 1 Samuel 16:7 | 191. Matthew 6:19-21

School for
Prophecy

8.4   Timing in Prophecy

8.4.1   The timing of a prophecy is obviously an important area in the interpretation of prophecy. It is important for the person sharing the prophecy to be accurate about the timescale, and it is also crucial for the person or organisation receiving the prophecy to know the right timing. Prophecies are often given without any reference to timescale, and it can be an easy mistake to assume that this means it is a word for today. While considerable effort is often expended on the meaning and significance of a prophecy, understanding the timing of any prophecy is equally as important.

8.4.2   The primary principle here is to match your current level of anointing with the level of detail you are delivering in your prophecies, and not any more. Too many prophecies have caused unnecessary controversy because, while they did happen, it was not on the day or date that had been predicted. Declaring a level of predictive capacity well beyond our gift is actually another form of pride. It was for this reason that in the mid-90s, during the Toronto[192] phenomenon, they developed the prophetic guideline "no dates and no mates" to deal with this issue.

8.4.3   The story of Abraham contains a good example of how a lack of appreciation about the timing of a prophecy can lead to disaster in our lives. God had promised Abraham an inheritance though his own son,[193] yet under the pressure that nothing seemed to be happening, he slept with his wife's servant and had a son called Ishmael. This was not God's purpose, which was later fulfilled in the birth of Isaac, and had serious consequences for his inheritance. It created the phrase 'giving birth to an Ishmael', the consequences of making something happen outside of God's promise.

8.4.4   We also need to understand the difference between spiritual timing and physical timing. Prophecy is sometimes talking about the change in spiritual reality in heaven, that may take some time to be revealed in our physical reality on Earth. Samuel declared to Saul that "now" and "today"[194] his kingdom had been taken from him and given to another, well before it actually happened. Similarly, Samuel anointed David as king of Israel,[195] but he did not become king until much later. Yet when Samuel finally declared to Saul that "tomorrow"[196] he and his sons would be dead, the two timings coincided.

8.4.5   There are two aspects to the fulfilment of prophecy that can often help us to interpret the proper timing in the process of a prophecy. The first is prior preparation. This is where the fulfilment of the prophecy is dependent on some form of preceding preparation, training or equipping to take effect. The second is proper placement. This is where the commencement of the prophecy is dependent on us being relocated in an area, like our occupation, location or gifting, so that the prophecy can be fulfilled.

8.4.6   God is never in a hurry and always on time.

192. Toronto Airport Christian Fellowship | 193. Genesis 15:4 | 194. 1 Samuel 13:14; 15:28
195. 1 Samuel 16:13 | 196. 1 Samuel 28:19

8.5   Prophetic Symbolism

8.5.1   Another significant area in the interpretation of prophecy is the use and understanding of images and symbols within a prophecy. Symbolism, images, pictures and objects are frequently a significant part of a prophecy, and therefore the interpretation of symbolism is important in accessing the full meaning of a prophetic word. Fortunately, this can be learned and developed with both time and experience. While I do not believe in the image-specific dictionaries [8.1.2] that populate this area, I do recognize that there are often common meanings, themes and symbolism associated with many images.

8.5.2   The Bible is full of imagery and symbolism, a natural reflection of our creative God. A good example is when Elijah came to Horeb[197] and God said to him to come out of his cave and stand in his presence. He then used four common symbols all associated with his presence. On the mountain, Elijah experienced a powerful wind, an earthquake, a fire, and then a "gentle whisper" [earlier versions use "still small voice"]. These are all powerful images commonly used to represent the presence of God, and yet he was not in the first three, but only in the still small voice.

8.5.3   An important lesson to learn about the interpretation of images is that it is not only about identifying the specific symbolism of an image, but also what the image may be communicating to us, 'hearing between the lines'. A good example that illustrates this is that of Jeremiah's first two lessons [4.5.5] in prophecy.[198] While the first lesson involves the interpretation of symbolism in a picture, the second lesson starts with the same symbolism principle but then moves into greater inspiration [revelation], than is initially available in the picture. This demonstrates how *Interpretation* can involve layers of revelation [7.8.3].

8.5.4   An alternative to this principle of peeling back layers of revelation, reading between the lines, is the accessing of more information through the revealing of increasing levels of detail in the picture. I call this 'the more you look, the more you see'. Ezekiel's prophetic vision of the river flowing east from the Temple[199] is a very good example of how more and more detail was revealed to him and to some considerable extent: from the detail of the river, then into its surroundings and finally to when it reaches the sea. Increasing levels of detail can take us far from where our interpretation first started.

8.5.5   Images are a very powerful part of the communication of a prophecy, but they are also significantly helpful in its interpretation. They create the possibility of a variety of applications, while helping us focus on the heart of the issue being communicated. Furthermore, they greatly assist our memory by providing what I call a 'hook to hang it on'. The power of the image is that it helps us to remember the original picture, which can then trigger our recollection of its meaning. This can simply be demonstrated by the number of prophecies that people refer to by their image, e.g. the 'train and tunnel' prophecy [7.9].

8.5.6   "A picture is worth a thousand words." – Anon.

197. 1 Kings 19:8-13 | 198. Jeremiah 1:11-16 | 199. Ezekiel 47:1-12

School for Prophecy

8.6   Maintaining Objectivity

8.6.1   Learning to be objective is an important element in the mature, impartial and independent interpretation of prophecy. Objectivity protects us from our past experiences, personal agendas and particular preferences affecting the accuracy of our interpretation. Objectivity stops the delivery vehicle from 'discolouring' the message, by being aware of our own subjectivity. It's humbling but very helpful. We need to know ourselves[200] and recognize when a prophetic interpretation moves into an area where we are likely to be subjective. Objectivity protects us from assumption in its many forms, and I am going to look at the key ones next.

8.6.2   Firstly, objectivity protects us from consumption, the immature urgency to proceed, causing a lack of proper consideration of the interpretation. A classic example of this would be the unfortunate prophetic habit of assuming everything we hear is a prophecy for someone else. It is also a common prophetic trait to find yourself under emotional pressure or urgency to deliver your prophecy. This can be caused by many factors: inexperience in the gift; unsettling levels of anxiety through fear of man; a prophecy with a higher level of anointing than you are used to; and the need to contribute during worship.

8.6.3   Next, maintaining objectivity will protect us from presumption, the jumping to conclusions based only on the presenting information at hand. It is in this area of guarding against presumption that we need to be particularly aware of any subjectivity created by our past experiences or prejudices. A simple example of presumption would be, if the current prophetic image has had a powerful meaning on a previous occasion then the same interpretation must apply this time. Not so. Similarly, while the recipient may have a specific need, it does not necessarily mean that the interpretation will be about it.

8.6.4   Furthermore, maintaining our objectivity will protect us from precipitation, the assumption that the prophecy is a 'now' message for today and without proper consideration of the timing. It is so much easier if you do not have to consider the timing of a word, so I can understand the pressure, but it is a grave mistake for the unwary. We simply need to be honest about what revelation we have about timing, and also stay within the level of grace and faith of our gift. While we should not assume a word is for today, neither should we be under any pressure to predict when, if we have not been told.

8.6.5   Finally, guarding our objectivity will protect from consummation, the assumption that the prophecy has no specific conditions or any process before fulfilment. I have previously mentioned [8.4.5] the frequently important process of prior preparation and proper placement in responding to prophecy, and we should be conscious of this principle when considering the interpretation. Appreciating how our heavenly Father works [8.3] will guide us in interpreting if there are any conditions, process or requirements for fulfilment.

8.6.6   Objectivity prevents our personality, prejudices and past obscuring our view.

200. James 1:23-25

8.7 Taking Time

8.7.1 *Interpretation* works best at identifying the full wisdom and revelation of God in a prophecy without the pressure of time. It is important to give yourself enough time so you do not feel under stress, whether you are giving or receiving a prophecy. The Holy Spirit works from a place of 'rest'[201] and we should do the same. I have previously mentioned my seven-day rule for testing prophecy [7.3.5], and the same applies for interpreting prophecy. Unless I am in a prophetic ministry situation which requires immediate delivery, for which I will have prepared, I will take the time I need to get a real 'feel' for a prophecy.

8.7.2 Taking time allows you to find the right environment to meditate on the prophecy, and move in a stillness that heightens your sensitivity to the Holy Spirit's instructions. Frequently, *Interpretation* involves 'peeling' back a layer of initial revelation to reveal another one, and then another etc. Time allows you to pursue this process of revealing to access the full depth of meaning. Sometimes our first interpretation initially gets us through the 'front door' of the house, i.e. the message, and then exploring all the rooms accessible to you will produce much more detail and significance [8.2.3].

8.7.3 Prayer is a wonderfully powerful way to help the process of interpretation, whether giving or receiving. Prayer helps us clearly bring our focus and attention on the source of the prophecy, and releases intimate communion through the Holy Spirit. As is often the case with sharing, it is quite remarkable how talking about your thoughts and ideas with the Holy Spirit brings clarity and new revelation that was not there before. Prayer soaking enhances insight. Talking with the Holy Spirit brings our thoughts more into alignment with his and this often helps us see things from a very different perspective.

8.7.4 Taking time also makes space for contemplation, deep reflective thought, which is particularly important when the fast pace of our noisy world works against this. I have often found that contemplation is much like trying to chew the Quality Street toffees left in the bottom of the tin after Christmas. They are like chewing a bullet initially, but with patience they gradually become soft and then release a remarkable amount of flavour over an extended period of time. Contemplation enables us to 'chew' the interpretation so that over time we can release the full depth of its meaning.

8.7.5 Finally, time provides a buffer during those times when nothing is happening and we start to feel under pressure to get results. Having 'enough' time should help protect us from the stress of performance and the barrage of doom from our enemy. We need to move from rest, i.e. trust in our heavenly Father. We must put our confidence in the Holy Spirit [3.3.3], whose ministry is to lead us into all truth,[202] which certainly includes the interpretation of our prophecy! We are putting our confidence and our faith in his ability to communicate with us, not our ability to communicate with him.

8.7.6 Taking time will break anxiety, increase accuracy and release anointing.

201. 1 John 3:19 | 202. John 16:13-15

8.8 Dissecting Prophecy

8.8.1 When faced with the task of interpreting a prophecy, it is normal to feel a little overwhelmed because you are trying to take it all in at once. I have found that the best approach is the same way that you eat an elephant. One bite at a time! The technique of dissecting prophecy[203] enables you to do this and break your prophecy up into manageable pieces. I have listed below several key steps I have found helpful in dissecting prophecy. When dissecting prophecy, like testing prophecy [5.7.5], practice will significantly improve your ease of application, yield more accurate results and develop greater insight.

8.8.2 The first step is seeing the bigger picture without getting lost in the detail. It is natural to be initially drawn to the detail, images and phrases in a prophecy. But what is its strategy, its overall purpose? What is your heavenly Father seeking to achieve through this prophecy? Is it about freedom, bondage, inner healing, calling, identity, etc.? The detail of any car journey is much easier to understand once you have decided on the destination. The depth of our understanding of God's ways [2.6.1] comes into play in this area, which may trigger the need to refer to wise counsellors. Understand the strategy.

8.8.3 Secondly, identify any promises in your prophecy. They are a significant and common part of any prophecy. Promises are what your heavenly Father is going to do for you or through you. Promises in a prophecy cover a wide range of possible topics, such as new gifts, anointings, impartations, abilities, opportunities and blessings. This is when an accurate recording of the prophecy [4.9] is essential and enables you to be clear and positive about accessing what is being promised. It is important to take practical ownership of any promises and actively seek ways to claim and press into them. Stand on your promises.

8.8.4 Next, identify any conditions in your prophecy. Conditions are what I call 'pivotal points', and while they are not always present, they are very significant when they are. Conditions are changes specified in the prophecy that are crucial to its activation, development or fulfilment. Two examples of these I have previously referred to as prior preparation and proper placement [8.4.5]. They can involve changing location, a different role, training requirements, inner healing, character development, change of season, etc. It is important to develop an action plan, or road map, where possible, to fulfil any conditions. Engage with your conditions.

8.8.5 Lastly, identify any Kingdom identity revelation. The Holy Spirit is on a mission to make us like Jesus, so this will inevitably spill over into our prophecies. Like the previous two steps, Kingdom identity revelation covers a wide range of topics. It reveals more of our true identity to us, specifics about our journey, and our final destiny. It can involve clarifying our calling, new authority, our assignments, breaking bondages, forgiveness and mindset changes. All these are designed to bring us into alignment with Christ's character and deliver the freedom of the cross into our experience. Embrace your identity.

8.8.6 *Interpretation* is a journey into insight, intuition and intimacy with the Holy Spirit.

203. Ivan & Isabel Allum, Your Destiny, [USA, 2008]

127

8.9   Personal Testimony

8.9.1   One of the most challenging interpretations I have had to do started in the most innocuous of ways. I was away leading a course and because it was so busy, I had parked on the edge of the car park under the trees. Going home, in the space of time it took me to get into the car, a hand-sized maple leaf floated in across my lap and settled on the passenger seat. That seriously got my attention! It certainly meant something, but I did not have a clue what it was. Next morning, I opened my daily notes to find the story of Jesus cursing the fig tree[204] because it was all leaf and no fruit. Well, that's not good news!

8.9.2   After I had pulled myself out of discouragement and confessed that God is good, I stopped jumping to the worst conclusions [1.2.2] and began to search for the truth. As I meditated on the Bible story, without fear, the first clear revelation I received was that this was all about pruning[205]. This was good news, but probably not going to feel like it to start with. Non-fruit-bearing branches would be cut off and fruit-bearing ones pruned to grow more.

8.9.3   The next question was, what area of my life did this apply to? While I pondered and considered many options, the first and easiest application proved to be the right one: my church ministry. I admitted to myself that I had already recognized that my workload had reached capacity and had been quietly wondering where to go from here. It was time for a refresh, otherwise I would be guilty of doing it 'this way' because "I have always done it this way".

8.9.4   My next consideration was, how does it apply? This abruptly came through a friend who said, "That's easy. It applies to those you are in partnership with; it landed on their seat and not yours!" I was uncomfortable with this at first, as it felt like I was avoiding the issue, but in time this was strongly confirmed to me. I am in relational ministry with all my church friends. It was not going to be easy to be cut off from some and prune my involvement with others, let alone decide who!

8.9.5   The deep challenge in these issues forced me to consider why I was doing this work in the first place. *Bam!* This brought abrupt clarity and focus for me. I was here to build the kingdom of God – not my ministry network, or support man's empires. It became clear I needed to re-examine all my church ministry to make sure it satisfied the criteria of my calling, my gifting and building God's kingdom. This was going to require considerable honesty on my part.

8.9.6   While this summary genuinely covers my *Interpretation* and *Implication,* little did I know God had already planned and started the *Implementation*. The above revelation had changed me. I saw goals more clearly, I challenged circumstances more openly and I was much more decisive about choices. Over the next term, doors closed and doors opened spontaneously. Interestingly, I was invited to a number of new churches over this period.

8.9.7   "Though no one can go back and make a brand-new start, anyone can start from now and make a brand-new ending." – Carl Bard

---

204. Matthew 21:18-22 | **205.** John 15:1-2

School for **Prophecy**

8.10 Frequently Asked Questions

8.10.1 Surely, all I have to do is look up what each of the images means?

8.10.2 Assuming there are images in your prophecy, I believe God and the Bible are far too creative for any one image to only have one meaning [8.1.2]. While an image may have a more common interpretation, not only do images have the capability of multiple meanings, but these can also be dependent on the context in which they are used. The advantage of images is that while they are memorable, they are also incredibly flexible in communication. To limit any image to only one meaning, I believe, is profoundly legalistic and short-sighted.

8.10.3 The prophecy seems relatively straightforward. Do I really need to interpret it?

8.10.4 Absolutely not. Please do not make interpretation any more complicated than it needs to be. If it says what it means and means what it says, end of story. Also, you may perceive the interpretation immediately or feel you appreciate its application straight away. My only word of caution is that you should be aware that the Holy Spirit can say to you more than is said in the message [8.5.4]. The particular timing and use of words can have a very personal application, and often open up new doors or avenues of revelation to you.

8.10.5 I am confused by some very different pictures and themes. Can you help?

8.10.6 The inclusion of multiple images or themes can make interpretation quite difficult. It is a version of 'mixed metaphors'. It is usually easier to treat multiple images as different layers of revelation within the word and, consequently, break the message down into more easily digestible parts [8.5.2]. Alternatively, it may be better to consider the stronger images or themes as different prophetic messages altogether, rather than as one cohesive whole. They may build on one another like stages or be reinforcing the same point from different angles.

8.10.7 There is a large amount of detail in the prophecy to interpret. Where do I start?

8.10.8 I have tried to provide detailed guidance in this area in the section on dissecting prophecy [8.8], and the specific advice on being able to see the bigger picture [8.8.2] is very applicable here. It is often easy to be get overwhelmed by the length, detail and images in a prophecy, and miss the overall purpose, which is far more important. Therefore, I recommend starting with the bigger picture and then drilling down to more and more detail as and when required. Getting a feel for the heart of the prophecy will considerably help in its interpretation.

8.10.9 The prophecy contains a lot of Old Testament language and images, which are hard to understand.

8.10.10 It is unfortunate that the prophecy is from someone who feels the King James Bible's religious language is more appropriate for prophecy. I suggest that you convert it into modern English first before you start to interpret it. However, the Old Testament images are good news. They will be strong symbols, well documented in the Bible and have a number of recognized interpretations and backgrounds. This should be very helpful in unpacking their full meaning.

Study Notes

9

THE PRINCIPLES OF RESPONDING TO PROPHECY

Study Notes

9.0 Chapter Summary

9.0.1   *Introduction – Prophetic Protocols* are the biblical procedures and guidelines that govern the operation of the gift of prophecy and are fundamental to the safe, satisfactory and successful operation of the gift. The final *Prophetic Protocols* subject explains the importance, process and stages of how to respond to prophecy, from the often-ignored recipient's viewpoint.

9.0.2   *Essential* – To have a complete understanding of the gift of prophecy we need to understand the principles and process involved in both the giving and receiving of prophecy. It should be obvious to us all that the vast majority of people, unfortunately, are only ever likely to see it from the responding perspective.

9.0.3   *Proof* – The first of the 6 P's represents testing or investigation, an element of prophecy I have previously covered in *The Principles of Testing Prophecy* [7], the first of the *Prophetic Protocols* we covered. It is a New Testament requirement that all prophecy must be tested before it is trusted.

9.0.4   *Participation* – While not the most important of the 6 P's in this chapter, it is the most critical because it is the most common mistake people receiving prophecy make. *Participation* is our faith-filled response to the prophecy we have received.

9.0.5   *Perspective* – Seeing the prophecy from God's viewpoint, or, as the Bible teaches, being seated in heavenly places, releases *Perspective*. *Perspective* requires us to grasp where God sees us starting from, what the journey from here to there involves, and what growth we may need to occupy the new territory fully.

9.0.6   *Patience* – An important element in responding to prophecy is patience, because it brings balance to our *Participation* and prevents us from any manipulation to meet human expectations. *Patience* helps us make sure that we allow the process of transition to come to its proper completion.

9.0.7   *Perseverance* – The principle we need to grasp is that our heavenly Father uses testing or trials to check and ensure we have properly established new territory in our lives. *Perseverance* is the 'response' he is looking for to ensure we have real, radical and reliable faith for what he is doing in and through us.

9.0.8   *Prayer* – The privilege of *Prayer* brings us into a deliberate, conscious and active, not passive, conversation with the Holy Spirit. This is obviously of considerable benefit in helping us with the fulfilment of our prophecy, by increasing our understanding of the meaning, journey and destination.

9.1   Introduction

9.1.1   We have covered two of the more traditional *Prophetic Protocols, The Principles of Testing Prophecy* [7] and *The Principles of Interpreting Prophecy* [8]. We now need to cover the less well known of the trio, *The Principles of Responding to Prophecy. Prophetic Protocols* are the biblical guidelines that govern the operation of the gift of prophecy and are fundamental to the safe, satisfactory and successful operation of the gift. The final prophetic protocol explains the importance, process and stages of how to respond to prophecy, from the often-ignored recipient's viewpoint.

9.1.2   This chapter is very different from all the others because it views the prophetic process purely from the standpoint of the person receiving the prophecy, and not the person delivering the prophecy. It is not a subject I have often met elsewhere, which is disappointing. It is the third area of major misunderstanding, misuse and malpractice after *New and Old Covenant Prophecy* [5] and *The Principles of Testing Prophecy* [7]. It is particularly important in helping those who desire to move in prophecy to have an all-round perspective and understanding of the complete process, not just the delivery.

9.1.3   The significance of this subject can best be demonstrated using the unlikely example of 'golf lessons'. I was once fortunate enough to have some golf lessons with my local club's professional. I was surprised that he never watched where the golf ball went but always seemed to know where to look! On asking him how he did this, he explained that my follow-through [my actions after hitting the ball] told him exactly where the ball had gone. I believe this principle is equally applicable to the fulfilment of prophecy. It is important for the person receiving the prophecy to understand the principles of responding correctly [following through properly] so that the prophecy [the golf ball] goes where it was intended to [by the pin].

9.1.4   One of the major areas of error in this subject is that a distressing number of people still believe that if 'God has said it', it will happen, regardless. This is not even a correct understanding of Old Covenant prophecy, let alone that of the New Covenant. While I recognize the grace of God, this 'one arm bandit' approach to prophecy usually leads to disappointment, disorientation and then distress. As a direct result of being people who move in the prophetic gift, we need to be active ambassadors and promoters of the key principles of how to respond to prophecy.

9.1.5   There are clear benefits to a solid understanding of the biblical principles of this subject. Responding to prophecy is the other side of the coin to delivering prophecy, and will give us a much better understanding and perspective of the gift. It will inevitably affect how we move in prophecy, not only in content but also in seeking to dovetail with a healthy responding environment. Last, but not least, it makes us very alert to the need of the recipients to 'follow through' properly, and support such people in this area as we become more experienced.

9.2   Essential

9.2.1   It has fascinated me down the years that what I consider a core element of my teaching in my *School for Prophecy,* I rarely find included in the many other prophecy training meetings I have attended. It is just not there. While the teaching included in *The Principles of Responding to Prophecy* may not seem essential in the journey of delivering a prophetic word, the same core biblical principles are there, just expressed very differently. So, I think I can provocatively declare that if you do not know and understand the biblical principles involved in responding to prophecy, you do not fully understand biblical prophecy!

9.2.2   To have a complete understanding of the gift of prophecy we need to understand the principles and process involved in both the giving and receiving of prophecy. It should be obvious to us all that the vast majority of people, unfortunately, are only ever likely to see it from the responding perspective. As a direct result, when I am planning with a church leadership to do a school, training or ministry, one of my strong suggestions is the opportunity to teach the wider church how to receive prophecy. Otherwise, we are potentially making problems for ourselves.

9.2.3   It is natural and right to thoroughly cover the biblical principles and processes of how we are to move in the gift of prophecy. This would include *Inspiration* [11.3], *Interpretation* [11.4] and *Initiation* [delivery] [11.5]. I also recognize and teach that we are spiritual 'postmen', and once our 'mail' is correctly delivered, our responsibility ends there. However, I would argue it is just as important to understand 'the other side of the coin', which includes *Investigation* [testing] [7], *Implication* [11.6] and *Implementation* [11.7]. All of the elements of 'both sides of the coin' are needed to bring a prophetic word to fulfilment.

9.2.4   Perhaps the strongest argument for the importance of teaching on how to respond to prophecy is the number of people with unfulfilled prophecy in their lives, and the destructive effect it has on their relationship with God. It is a familiar journey. We receive a prophecy promising something very significant, or that we desperately want, but it does not happen even after some time. It must be somebody's fault, surely? It can't be mine, so it must be God's fault. The journey of disappointment then leads to discouragement, which eventually results in distress. In fact, the potential harm to our relationship with God can [and has, in my experience] lead to fatal damage.

9.2.5   I have organized the teaching on *The Principles of Responding to Prophecy* under 6 P's, to provide keys for our memory and assist you and me in coaching others into a biblical pattern. The key biblical principles in how to respond to prophecy are *Proof, Participation, Perspective, Patience, Perseverance* and *Prayer.* I hope you find this helpful so you too can be an active ambassador of these biblical principles. We will now go through them systematically, explain their significance, and examine their interaction and their role in the fulfilment of prophecy.

9.2.6   It is prudent to be proactive in promoting these principles.

9.3   Proof

9.3.1   The first of our 6 P's is *Proof*. It is the responsibility of every recipient to test all prophecy to give them the confidence that it is from God and in the accuracy of what is being said to them. While our testing will be affected by the anointing, track record and maturity of the person delivering the prophecy, this can in no way detract from our responsibility to test the prophecy. Given that we need to put our faith in the prophecy, and consequently act on it, we first need to make sure we have the same confidence in what we believe God is saying to us as we do with the Bible.

9.3.2   *Proof* represents *Investigation,* i.e. testing, an element of prophecy I have previously covered in *The Principles of Testing Prophecy* [7], the first of the *Prophetic Protocols* we covered. It is a New Testament requirement that all prophecy must be tested before it is trusted. The key principle is laid down by the Bible,[206] in a short but very specific teaching on testing prophecy. For only a four-verse passage, it contains a large harvest of truth. It simply says not to treat prophecies with contempt, to test everything and to hold on to what is good, i.e. be selective.

9.3.3   There are three topics of tests, and two tests in each topic, described in detail in an earlier chapter [7]. The first topic is *Authenticity Tests,* which seek to confirm the genuine nature and source of the word. The second topic is *Alignment Tests,* which seek to confirm that the contents and purpose of the word comply with, or match, other established and reliable sources. The final topic is *Alert Tests,* which seek to caution, i.e. warn us, about any deceptive or devious elements of the word. They work together as a group of health checks, which provide a solid foundation for our testing.

9.3.4   The two authenticity tests are core principles as they always apply during testing, unlike the other tests. They are the confirmation of a prophecy by our own inner witness, the Holy Spirit, and independent confirmation of the prophetic word from a source outside of us, for example, a God-incidence. They work by using objective points of reference to provide objective confirmation, and the more there are, the more confidence we can have. This relies on the biblical principle of independent confirmation by two or three witnesses, particularly for important decisions [7.5.5].

9.3.5   Effectively, what happens when we do not test prophecy is that we are unwittingly moving in presumption. Alternatively, we are relying on the person delivering the prophecy, effectively having faith in them instead of God. This completely opens us up to inaccurate, hope-driven or manipulative prophecy, with the obvious consequences. This is very likely to lead to the lethal sequence of events of disappointment, then disorientation and finally developing into relational damage. *Proof* enables us to be confident and peaceful about precisely what God is saying to us.

9.3.6   *Proof* is about being sure of the ground you are standing on.

206. 1 Thessalonians 5:19-22

9.4   Participation

9.4.1   *Participation* is not the most important of the 6 P's in this chapter, but because it is the most common mistake people make with prophecy, it is the most critical. Quite simply, the majority of people receiving prophecy do not realize that their participation, to one degree or another, is critical to the fulfilment of the prophecy they have received. This disturbing state of affairs means we are assuming we are already at the 'starting gate' of the prophecy, require no training or equipping, already mature enough to reach our destination, and God will take care of everything else. Heavens!

9.4.2   The correct New Testament response to a prophecy, as with everything in our lives, is to respond with faith. *Participation* is our faith-filled response to the prophecy we have received. This is another reason why testing prophecy is a prior requirement. It ensures that what we are about to commit ourselves to is what we believe God is saying to us. *If we have the wrong map, we are unlikely to reach the correct destination.* At an early stage, I developed the personal value that "prophecy is not alive in your life until you have an active faith in it". I added the word 'active' to reflect the importance of *Participation.*

9.4.3   There is a clear pattern of principles in the Bible regarding participation. The Bible teaches the fundamental truth that everything we do should be from and in faith.[207] The writer to the Hebrews explains this point when he points out that while two different groups received the same message, it was of no benefit to one group because they did not add faith to it.[208] The 'coup de grace' comes from James' teaching on faith when he makes it abundantly clear that faith, if not accompanied by action, is dead.[209] Faith is the spiritual equivalent of the oxygen our bodies need to survive – there is no life without it.

9.4.4   *Passivity, instead of participation, is a lethal form of presumption.* My unfortunate experience is that it consistently leads to unfulfilled prophecy and the heartache that follows. I am certainly not advocating action that makes a prophecy happen, often referred to as 'making an Ishmael[210]', as this then moves us to the other extreme of presumption. *Participation* is about us actively playing our part in the fulfilment of God's word, engaging with the process and recognizing the need for change. Prophecy is undoubtedly a gift from God, but it is like the gift of a bicycle that he wants us to learn to ride.

9.4.5   *Participation* is a key element in all four of the recipient's 7 I's of prophecy: *Investigation, Implication, Implementation* and *Investment.* All of these need our active involvement to be able to move on to the next one and reach our goal. The journey with unpacking the implication of our prophecy requires our active participation, particularly as it will frequently involve character development at some point [11.7.4]. Similarly, the implementation of our prophecy will simply not happen without our participation, bar the intervention by our heavenly Father.

9.4.6   *Participation* is about being part of the solution, and not part of the problem.

207. Romans 14:22-23 | 208. Hebrews 4:1-2 | 209. James 2:14-17 | 210. Genesis 16:1-2

9.5   Perspective

9.5.1   *Perspective* involves seeing the prophecy from God's viewpoint or, as the Bible teaches, seated in heavenly places.[211] This is difference between looking down at our problems from above, i.e. a heavenly perspective, and looking up from underneath them, i.e. an earthly perspective. *Perspective* requires us to grasp where God sees us starting from, what the journey from here to there involves and what growth we may need to fully occupy the new territory at our destination. One area often overlooked is the need for character development, particularly to obtain, maintain and sustain the prophetic goal.

9.5.2   The deep truth is that sometimes "you can't get there from here"[212]. Many people seem to assume that their prophecy inexorably begins where they are, which is frequently not the case. Imagine the prophecy was like an aeroplane ticket to Italy. Amazing! But first, you have to get to London Gatwick, before you can catch the plane. In reality there are two journeys. Trying to catch a plane from here, where there is no airport, is going to get very frustrating. This first shorter journey is often critical in providing essential preparation, such as breaking anchors in our lives, which could stop us completing the journey.

9.5.3   Another area where *Perspective* is important is the destination and the journey. Frequently, all we see in the destination is what we can acquire or rid ourselves of. We understand the journey as the shortest distance between two places. To understand the destination, we need wisdom about what God is achieving in us through the journey. Our appreciation of the journey is considerably dependent on our grasp of the purpose of the destination. Using a heavenly GPS for directions may give you some very unexpected results, the Israelites' forty years in the wilderness being a good example.

9.5.4   *Perspective* involves understanding how God works, to be able to see our situation from his perspective. An area of frequent contrast between our heavenly Father and us is his commitment to long-term strategies and our preference for short-term fixes. His goal is not to develop us as quickly as possible, as ours often is. He is interested in establishing his kingdom in us with permanent effect. The quote I often think of here is that "God is more interested in the journey than the destination". He is quite happy taking time to make thorough changes that last, in contrast to our obsession with today.

9.5.5   A lack of heavenly perspective frequently, and unfortunately, leads us to unreal expectations and pre-emptive actions. This can again trigger the lethal sequence of events that cause disappointment, disorientation and then distress. To put it another way, "You can have a bicycle long before you have learned to ride it, but you can't ride it until you do." God is only interested in building on secure foundations so that his work is permanent, and he is willing to invest the time and patience to achieve this. He understands the difference between head knowledge and heart knowledge.

9.5.6   *Perspective* is about engaging with God's journey, and not just the destination.

211. Ephesians 2:6 | 212. Graham Cooke

9.6   Patience

9.6.1   A helpful quote to consider is, "Prophecy releases a process of transition."[213] While it is a small quote, it includes three deeply meaningful words: 'releases', 'process' and 'transition'. Two of these may require considerable patience. The Bible is full of stories of faithful servants who had to exercise patience before they entered their promised inheritance. *Patience* is a key element in responding to prophecy, and contrasts with the increasing pace of life we live within these days. It focuses our attention on the progress of our journey, how far we have come, and not the distance to our destination.

9.6.2   *Patience* is an important element in responding to prophecy, because it brings balance to our *Participation* and prevents us from any manipulation to meet human expectations. *Patience* helps us make sure that we allow the process of transition to come to its proper completion. Abraham was a man of great faith and patience, and yet in a time of doubt[214] he initially missed God's best through manipulation. Firstly, note that God waited until his promise was not physically possible so there could be no doubt it was his power. Secondly, Abraham's intervention had consequences for everyone, still to this day.

9.6.3   One area that can help us to learn patience is to appreciate that during the process released by prophecy, we move in 'progressive revelation'. This simply means that we understand more at the completion than at the beginning. We learn more about the prophecy during the journey and we don't know everything we need to know at the start but find out gradually. This specifically means we must not jump to conclusions. Prophecy frequently works on a 'need to know' basis to protect us from incorrectly predicting the destination until we have a better grasp of the true purpose.

9.6.4   *Patience* is essential because it combats the biggest prophetic killer: frustration. Prophetic people not only hear prophecy, but they can smell it, see it and taste it, yet still can't have it. This commonly leads to frustration and even conflict with leadership. If you have travelled on the London Underground, you will have heard the phrase "mind the gap" many times. We need patience to manage the frustration that results from minding the gap. Frustration is energy, and if it does not find positive outward expression, it can go inward and become poisonous.

9.6.5   Finally, I would like to introduce a maxim I have heard a number of times: "Man measures time, but God values growth." In this area, patience protects us from operating with human time values, and enables us to engage with God's growth objective. The world we live in is very time-obsessed. It measures success in terms of time and often seeks to control our lives with it. Our heavenly Father's goal in us is maturity, and this is relationally-based, not time-driven. Our understanding of time is definitely one area where God's ways[215] are not our ways.

9.6.6   *Patience* is about being strong when nothing seems to be happening.

213. Graham Cooke | 214. Genesis 16:1-4 | 215. Isaiah 55:8

9.7   Perseverance

9.7.1   The next P is *Perseverance*. While I have found that many prophetic people tend to find *Patience* harder than average, due to their character type, I have also found them much better at keeping going when things get tough, i.e. persevering – a bit stereotypical, I admit, but often true. The principle we need to grasp is that our heavenly Father uses trials to check and ensure we have properly established new territory in our lives. Perseverance is the 'response' he is looking for to ensure we have real, radical and reliable faith for what he is doing in and through us.

9.7.2   He understands that there is a difference between receiving and possessing new territory in our lives. James explains that the process of perseverance in us brings us to full maturity.[216] Our heavenly Father uses trials in our lives to produce perseverance in us. As we hold on through the storm, it transforms the reality of our faith into much greater strength and authority. This is similar to the way that during the production of steel, it is initially hard but brittle; however, after being tempered it becomes much stronger and able to take knocks without breaking.

9.7.3   *Perseverance* causes us to hang on and not let go of the truth in our prophecy. The power of perseverance is that having once possessed territory, it will refuse to let go of it. Too many people have received the fulfilment of their prophecy [*Implementation* 11.7] but do not realize they need to occupy it [*Investment* 11.8]. As a result, they are ill-equipped to defend their new territory, and our enemy soon returns and takes back their newly won inheritance. *Perseverance* is frequently the required biblical response to our enemy trying to take back recently gained territory. *Perseverance* says, "Oh no, you don't!"

9.7.4   There is a powerful moment early in Jesus' life when he receives publicity most itinerant ministries would 'give their left arm for'. At his baptism,[217] the audible voice of God announces his status, relationship and success to all those present. Today that would be on the front pages of all the newspapers the next day, viral on the Internet, and the initiator of a million pilgrimages to Israel. Did this launch his public ministry? No. He was led into the desert, prepared by forty days of fasting and then tested. Only when it was finished did his public ministry begin. Proper preparation produces powerful people.

9.7.5   Sometimes on receipt of a genuine and powerful prophetic word, our circumstances immediately move in totally the opposite direction. This shock is enough to make many give up straight away. We must choose whether to accept the authority of our prophecy or be controlled by our circumstances. The principle here is still the same, although the perseverance required is much more immediate and demanding. We forget God has to get us out of what we are in, to get us into what he has for us.

9.7.6   *Perseverance* is about keeping going when things turn against you.

216. James 1:2-5 | **217.** Matthew 3:16-4:3

School for **Prophecy**

9.8   Prayer

9.8.1   *Prayer* is the sixth and final P in this chapter and probably a subject most of you are already familiar with. I will therefore be specifically looking at prayer in terms of its impact on our responding to prophecy. *Prayer* brings us into a deliberate, conscious and active, not passive, conversation with the Holy Spirit. Jesus taught that our advocate, the Spirit of Truth, would guide us into all truth and tell us what is yet to come.[218] This is obviously of considerable benefit in helping us with the fulfilment of our prophecy, by increasing our understanding of the meaning, journey and destination.

9.8.2   Bringing our prophecy to our heavenly Father in prayer puts it on a specific agenda, and helps us see it from heaven's viewpoint and find clarity within it. It keeps the prophecy alive in our heads and heart. *Prayer* keeps it in our thoughts, as we meditate on it and consider what the Holy Spirit has said to us. It helps us carry it in our heart, where our sense of direction and confidence can grow over time. Lastly, as well as during the times of prayer, we are much more open to hear further revelation, explanation and confirmation as we walk out our word.

9.8.3   Fundamentally, *Prayer* opens a direct line to heaven, and consciously seeks the Holy Spirit's wisdom, guidance and faith for our prophecy. A good illustration of what we participate in during prayer is the story of Jacob and his dream at Bethel.[219] He saw a stairway to heaven (not the song!), with angels ascending and descending on it. God effectively prophesies to Jacob about his future, although prophecy from God is very different. *Prayer* helps us to access heaven and engage in two-way communication about our prophecy, and consequently releases the other two 'P's: *Patience* and *Perspective*.

9.8.4   One area where *Prayer* is particularly helpful is in the *Interpretation* [11.4] and *Implication* [11.6] aspects of responding to prophecy. *Prayer* is a real-time conversation with God and tends to create a 'greenhouse' effect on our prophecy that inevitably reveals more clarity and insight. *Prayer* causes us to take time to actively seek, clarify and develop the implications of our prophecy, in an atmosphere of rest and not stress. Both *Interpretation* and *Implication* benefit through *Prayer* from progressive revelation, so that as we learn more about our prophecy we are in a position to develop it further.

9.8.5   Last but not least, *Prayer* creates a healthy atmosphere to engage with the change prophecy brings, the process of transition, and also embrace positively the challenges we will encounter. An active prayer conversation provides heavenly points of reference to help us navigate the changes that our prophecy will instigate. *Prayer* keeps us close to our heavenly Father, so that we have a robust relationship for the challenging times we will inevitably encounter as we press in towards our prophecy's fulfilment. Both change and challenge can have significant impacts on our relationship with our heavenly Father, and *Prayer* is a considerable stabilising influence in this area.

9.8.6   *Prayer* is about sending and receiving regular progress reports.

218. John 16:13-15 | 219. Genesis 28:10-19

9.9 Personal Testimony

9.9.1 Alongside the principle of always recording prophecy [4.9], was the sister practice of giving every recipient of a personal prophecy the *Guidelines for Responding to Personal Prophecy*. In the 'good old days', the prophetic team all had handheld recorders and a supply of cassette tapes [Google it, if you're too young] to record the personal prophecy and hand it to the person receiving prophecy afterwards.

9.9.2 The cassette tapes usually came with pre-printed covers, and ours had room to write the name of the recipient and the date it was recorded. After 2005, they had a P.R.I.S.M. [Prophetic Resources Inspiring Spiritual Maturity] ministry tape. The clever element was that the inside of the cassette tape cover, not visible until the tape was removed, had the guidelines for responding to prophecy printed on it for future reference. It read:

9.9.3 "Everyone who receives a prophetic word should [1] Immediately write out the prophecy and meditate on it; [2] Review the prophecy with Church Leadership; [3] Judge and weigh the word according to biblical principles; [4] Do not move on the word without confirmation and counsel; [5] Remember that personal prophecies are always conditional."

9.9.4 This was not meant to be a complete summary of this chapter, given the limited amount of space available on the cassette tape cover. However, as you can see from the above reproduction, it does cover many of the major considerations and should easily lead people to review the critical elements of *The Principles of Responding to Prophecy* covered in this chapter. With the demise of the cassette tape and the heralding of the digital era, life became complicated because I wanted to continue this well-established convention as best practice.

9.9.5 I initially used 'playing card' sized paper to print the guidelines for responding to prophecy on, but eventually I started to print them on the back of my business cards instead. This has proved very successful and become a permanent feature, even with the use of people's own smartphones to record their prophecy. The print is a bit small, I will admit, but I can still get all five points [slightly modernized] on it, I always have a good supply with me and my contact details are on them if they or their leadership need to contact me.

9.9.6 While this practice may be new to you, or not suit your style, I do feel that by not recording prophecy we are missing an opportunity to assist in the proper fulfilment of prophecy. Telling someone after a prophetic ministry session is unlikely to help. A documented set of simple instructions, permanently available to an individual, is going to take some beating. Please consider your practice and follow me until you find something better.

9.9.7 Hindsight is a wonderful thing, and it has taught me after twenty-plus years in prophetic ministry that providing an accurate and timely record of prophecy is a major step in encouraging and assisting the proper response. It fundamentally points people in the right direction for the fulfilment of their prophecy. It is profoundly encouraging when someone enthusiastically tells you how their prophecy has transformed their life.

9.10 Frequently Asked Questions

9.10.1   I have fully tested the prophecy, but I am not sure what to do next...

9.10.2   You are now in a position to have faith in the prophecy and should be considering what action to do next under the heading *Implication* [9.4.4]. What does the prophecy *imply* you need to do or plan in preparation? Take time to consider the practical journey between where you are now and where you see the prophecy leading you. We are not looking to make something happen, but on the other hand, do not ignore the role you need to play in preparation, readiness and training, for example.

9.10.3   The prophecy seems straightforward, but I am not sure where it gets me...

9.10.4   I think what is needed here is for you to try to see the prophecy from God's perspective, i.e. seated in heavenly places [9.5.1]. As it is God's message, you need to consider what his goals and objectives are through the prophecy, as an extension of the known will of God through the Bible. Prophecy is often about the journey within, rather than the journey without, and how the prophecy initiates change within us. Start thinking long-term strategy, rather than short-term goals, and look for similar patterns in your life [9.5.4].

9.10.5   It is very hard holding on to my prophecy when nothing is happening...

9.10.6   Patience may be a fruit of the Spirit, but many find it hard, especially when a prophecy has opened a door into tomorrow [9.6.4]. Patience, once you are clear what you believe in faith that our heavenly Father is saying to you, is all about trusting him to fulfil his word. Engaging in a conversation with God may bring more revelation and clarity, but even if it does not, it will bring you into a greater sense of his purposes through the prophecy. Patience itself may be the lesson for this season, resting in challenging times [9.6.5].

9.10.7   My prophecy talks of great success, but all I am experiencing is more hassle...

9.10.8   Firstly, it appears God is preparing you by testing so that you will be strong enough to receive the fulfilment of the prophecy but also to possess it, occupy it and defend it [9.7.5]. This is therefore essential preparation, and as you engage with it positively, it will bring you to a place of readiness for fulfilment. Secondly, you appear to be in a faith gymnasium, a direct challenge to your faith in what you believe God has said to you. It is a time to step up in faith, not fall back in fear.

9.10.9   I know I should pray about my prophecy, but I am just not getting anywhere...

9.10.10 It sounds like you need to relax and start resting in God first. You may have expectations that are not happening and need to get back to a place of openness. Prayer is about having a two-way conversation and bringing your feelings and heart about your prophecy to your heavenly Father [9.8.3]. Prayer releases a healthy environment for him to speak to you further. It brings greater clarity into your understanding and brings you into an active place of faith for its fulfilment. If he has something you need to hear, you can be assured he will find a way.

Study Notes

10

PREPARING TO PROPHESY

Study Notes

10.0 Chapter Summary

10.0.1   *Introduction – Prophetic Developments* covers those areas of our anointing, training and calling that with proper investment can significantly shape and improve the consistency, maturity and longevity of our gift. The first *Prophetic Developments* subject looks at the many ways we can prepare to prophesy, the resulting benefits, and how it helps us to develop a prophetic lifestyle.

10.0.2   *Preparation is Key* – Preparation plays a key role in the process of developing your prophetic gift. Prophecy is a supernatural gift, so our level of anointing is in the hands of the Holy Spirit, and to some extent our character development. However, preparing ourselves is completely within our grasp and control, and has a direct impact on our growth.

10.0.3   *Waiting on God* – The first area of preparation I want to cover is waiting on God. It involves spending time alone with him, not necessarily being still or quiet, but in ways that bring us into an experience of his closeness, i.e. presence, and most importantly his rest. Waiting on God enables us to experience that place powerfully, rediscover it and practise living from it.

10.0.4   *Prayer Power* – Prayer is where we open our hearts, become vulnerable and faith-filled, and share completely who we are and where we are. Growth happens in an environment where there is love, encouragement and acceptance. Prayer is this place. It has its lighter moments and its slightly darker moments, but it is a safe place.

10.0.5   *Activating Our Inner Well* – I have previously explained the concept of having an inner well of revelation. There is a permanent well of revelation within us that is not dependent on our feelings or mood. This makes prophecy about the presence within and not the experience without. As part of our preparation to prophesy, we need to learn how to activate our inner well.

10.0.6   *Keeping Fit* – For the same reasons that we need to keep physically fit, we also need to keep spiritually fit, by maintaining a healthy position of rest and readiness. This involves speaking in tongues; encouraging an expectant outlook; learning the art of strengthening ourselves; guarding our tongue; and maintaining a thankful attitude.

10.0.7   *Personal Training* – As part of our preparation to prophesy, we need to encourage a lifestyle where we are our own personal trainer. This involves using our gift regularly; learning different styles and formats; moving outside of our comfort zone; travelling to different locations when possible; and broadening our experience outside our stream or denominational style.

10.0.8   *Common Hindrances* – While we have been looking at preparation practices you should encourage and build into your life, there are clearly those practices which you should be seeking to avoid: being double-minded; moving in the fear of failure; living in salvation by works; quantity instead of quality; and the 'distinct danger of daily distractions'.

10.1 Introduction

10.1.1   I have covered in the first three topics everything needed to move comfortably, confidently and correctly in the gift of prophecy. In *Prophetic Engagements,* we learned how to move in the Holy Spirit, in *Prophetic Foundations* I explained the principles of biblical prophecy and in *Prophetic Protocols* I explained the 'highway code' of prophecy. I will now cover the final topic, *Prophetic Developments,* which is only available in the extended course. The final three chapters are more advanced and will build on the first three topics to take us to the front door of my next course, *Growing a Prophetic Ministry.*

10.1.2   In this final topic of the manual we will cover the three core subjects of *Prophetic Developments: Preparing to Prophesy* [this chapter], *Unlocking the Prophetic Process* [11] and *The Character Challenges of Prophecy* [12]. *Prophetic Developments* covers those areas of our anointing, training and calling that, with proper investment, can significantly shape and improve the consistency, maturity and longevity of our gift. The first *Prophetic Developments* subject looks at the many ways we can prepare to prophesy, the resulting benefits and how it helps us to develop a prophetic lifestyle.

10.1.3   In this chapter I will introduce the subject of *Preparing to Prophesy,* which looks at the lifestyle aspect of moving in prophecy, rather than treating it as a series of events. It reflects a change in approach from just having a gift to developing a talent, and explains how we can move from an infrequent event into a consistent gift. Your studying this manual itself represents a desire to develop your gift of prophecy further in the service of our God. *Preparing to Prophesy* looks at how to use the time leading up to our moving in the gift of prophecy, and the beneficial effect this can have.

10.1.4   The significance of preparing to prophesy can helpfully be illustrated by comparing it with D.I.Y. Decorating a room involves many tasks, but you soon learn that the preparation, everything needed before you even pick up a brush, makes a huge difference to the ease and success of the task. You can just get on and do it, but there is a cost in the workload and quality of the finished product. Preparation makes everything so much easier on the day, and ensures you have all the tools you need for the job and all the surfaces are ready to be decorated. Preparation is the key to success.

10.1.5   There is no doubt that learning the art of *Preparing to Prophesy* has been very significant in helping me grow in my prophetic gift. While I don't think I can claim that my preparation has increased my prophetic anointing, it has undoubtedly provided an environment that has facilitated faster and sustained growth. I have found it helps me combat ministry fear, has increased the depth and detail of my inner well, and enables me to handle any unexpected and unhelpful environments better. However, the most significant side effect has been the growth in my intimacy and relationship with God as a result.

10.2 Preparation is Key

10.2.1 Preparation plays a key role in the process of developing your prophetic gift. Prophecy is a supernatural gift, so our level of anointing is in the hands of the Holy Spirit and, to some extent, our character development. However, preparing ourselves is completely within our grasp and control, and has a direct impact on our growth. The first impact preparation has on our prophetic gift is that it brings our spirit into alignment, perspective and readiness. We are engaging with the Holy Spirit before we even start, and reinforcing the foundations of our relationship, sonship [3.2] and our ability to see and move in the spiritual realm, i.e. supernaturally.

10.2.2 It is important to appreciate that preparation is a lifestyle and not a pastime. I am not drawing a works-style equation between time spent in preparation and anointing. Only spending time in preparation when you have to is better than none at all, but will never have the same impact. Preparation is more like a magnifying glass; it cannot create more light, but it can intensify what light we have. Therefore, preparation is a lifestyle that we engage with whether we are prophesying or not. A lifestyle of preparation keeps the well within us full [6.8], while occasional preparation throws the odd bucket of water into the well.

10.2.3 Preparation helps bring clarity about the true biblical purpose of prophecy and therefore releases our servant heart into all that we do. It is all too easy to become busy 'doing the stuff', i.e. caught up in a ministry mindset. This diverts us into being occupied with organisations, celebrities and hierarchy, and not serving. Preparation creates a healthy environment to align our focus and engage in our servant nature before we get involved in the pressures that can come with ministering. It allows us the head-space and heart-space to come into alignment with God's purpose for our prophetic gift.

10.2.4 Inevitably, and delightfully, seeking to move in prophecy causes us to seek inspiration from our heavenly Father, which brings us regularly into his presence. This is profoundly healthy because time spent with someone is a good indicator of how deep the relationship is. Everything we do as Christians, including prophecy, should come out of our relationship with the Father, Jesus and the Holy Spirit. Preparation disciplines us to start there, strengthens our relationship with God, and helps us prioritize our relationship with him above everything else. Building our relationship with God impacts our identity significantly, which is a secure platform for serving.

10.2.5 Preparation also helps us learn to enter God's rest before we get caught up in God's work. Practising stillness within will considerably help us to control the inner and outer noise we experience and keep us in the present. We tend to live our lives above the biblical speed limit. Although we may look calm on the outside, we're actually carrying a lot of unhealthy inner noise. While it is not always the case, prophetic ministry frequently involves being in environments with a lot of outer noise and distractions. This creates a real need for inner quiet to be able to minister to our best capacity. Preparation helps us to practise this.

10.2.6 The height of our anointing depends on the depth of our preparation.

10.3   Waiting on God

10.3.1   The first area of preparation I want to cover is waiting on God. It involves spending time alone with him, not necessarily being still or quiet, but in ways that bring us into an experience of his presence, i.e. closeness, and most importantly, his rest. The Bible teaches that as we seek God he will give us rest, and rest is the "fortress of the Spirit"[220]. We are called to enter God's rest and live from and in that rest. Waiting on God enables us to experience that place powerfully, rediscover it and practise living from it.

10.3.2   Waiting on God facilitates the discovery of the true power in stillness. It is a long-lost art, experienced in many monasteries but anathema in the intensity, noise and stress of our modern-day society. The Bible teaches that as we become still, we come to know him as God more fully.[221] Stillness pushes away our fears, confusion and impotence, and reveals to us God's true nature. Through being still in his presence, we come to experience him more, understand him more and recognize him more. It often facilitates and generates a complete renewal of our perspective on our lives.

10.3.3   Waiting on God also helps us learn to live vulnerably in complete dependence on him. The revelation released through stillness realigns our relationship with our heavenly Father where necessary. This is well described in the saying, "What we behold, we become." The Bible explains that as we remain [rest] in him, he will make us fruitful, using a vine branch as an example of this.[222] Waiting on God releases a greater clarity in us of 'remaining in him'. We can then learn to practise and take it with us, especially when ministering in prophecy. Resting in him maximizes our fruit-bearing potential.

10.3.4   Waiting on God is not a technique for growth and development, but the 'family time', i.e. intimacy, in our relationship with our heavenly Father. It is about being with him, beholding him and being loved by him. Regular waiting on God will deepen our experience of his love for us, and consequently our security and trust in him. The Bible teaches that we can never be separated from the love of God,[223] and our times with him build this into our DNA and minds, which erects a high barricade against doubt when we are moving in prophecy.

10.3.5   Perhaps the most profound impact of waiting on God is that it creates an ideal environment for us to receive ministry from the Holy Spirit, in a way that many do not appreciate. The Bible teaches that the Holy Spirit is our advocate, and will teach us all things and remind us of everything Jesus has taught us.[224] You might want to read that again! The resources available to us today on the Internet are remarkable, but this is a whole new dimension. In the peace and quiet of waiting on God, the Holy Spirit can give us insight, oversight and foresight about whatever we need at that time.

10.3.6   God sometimes shuts your mouth, to open your heart.

220. Matthew 11:28 | 221. Psalm 46:10-11 | 222. John 15:4-5 | 223. Romans 8:38-39 | 224. John 14:25-27

**School** for **Prophecy**

10.4 Prayer Power

10.4.1 The second area of preparation I am going to cover is our prayer conversation. I am choosing my words carefully because prayer is more than a shopping list, it is more than telling God how we feel; it is a conversation with our heavenly Father about anything and everything. Prayer is where we open our hearts, become vulnerable and faith-filled, and share completely who we are and where we are. Growth happens in an environment where there is love, encouragement and acceptance. Prayer is this place. It has its lighter moments and its dark moments, but it is a safe place.

10.4.2 In our conversations with God it is not just words that we are exchanging, but we are also receiving refreshing through the Spirit in our hopes, dreams and challenges. Looking into God's eyes, as the old hymn says, causes the things of the world to "grow strangely dim"[225]. Breathing in God's Spirit comes from recognizing we are seated in heavenly places and need to look down on our lives [heaven's perspective] rather than up through them [worldly perspective]. Breathing in the Spirit recognizes the transference that supernaturally occurs in a prayer conversation, as we receive faith, hope and love.

10.4.3 One of the pleasures that come from a clear understanding of our identity is that as 'sons and daughters' prayer is a two-way conversation with God, not just a monologue with spaces by us. Prayer is a two-directional process. This obviously means, as in any real conversation, that we should be listening as much as we are sharing. My Baptist roots remind me that with two ears and one mouth the principle is well demonstrated. However, we should go further because a two-way conversation makes way for questions, clarification and opinions. But please note, I rarely get answers to "why" or "when" queries!

10.4.4 Interestingly, using the phrase "you said" would normally be viewed as a very negative statement in everyday life. However, in a conversation with God things are very different. The Bible teaches that everything God says will achieve its purpose and not return to him unfulfilled.[226] He does say what he means and does mean what he says. Therefore, claiming God's promises in the Bible, the eternal truth, is very much part of our conversation, as in "you have said". Declaring, claiming and embracing his promises is part of our living everyday conversation with him.

10.4.5 One of the key lessons to learn about your prayer conversation is to engage fully with his presence as well as the power of change through prayer. Particularly when considering preparing to prophesy, developing a strong connection in the Spirit through prayer is very helpful. Learning about the fact and feel of his presence in a prayer conversation, with practice, is something we can replicate during a time of prophetic ministry. As we become more secure in our gift, we can engage more and more in a healthy conversation with the Holy Spirit while we are actually ministering in prophecy.

10.4.6 Prayer moves us into a position with a perspective that produces power.

225. *Turn your eyes upon Jesus;* 57 Hymnals by H.H. Lemmel [1922] | 226. Isaiah 55:10-11

10.5　Activating Our Inner Well

10.5.1　I have previously explained the concept of having an inner well of revelation [6.8]. There is a permanent well of revelation within us that is not dependent on our feelings or mood. This makes prophecy about the presence within and not the experience without. I also explained [6.8.5] that bringing the surface of our well to stillness, by controlling our inner and outer noise, has a direct impact on the clarity and detail of our prophetic revelation. As part of our preparation to prophesy, we need to learn how to activate our inner well.

10.5.2　We need to develop a lifestyle of expectation that the Holy Spirit will speak to us. Embracing the teaching of Jesus that the Holy Spirit will teach us all things and remind us of everything that he has taught us[227] will activate our inner well. This involves practising listening to the still small voice within us, recognizing his whispers during the intensity of life and being alert for those critical 'sound bites' in our thoughts. This is not just trusting God that he will speak through us, but reaching for the 'all' and 'everything' level of provision and abundance in our revelation.

10.5.3　Having a father in the Fleet Air Arm brought me into contact with another helpful illustration of our inner well: radar. Warships have passive and active radar. Passive radar is a form of only listening and does not give away your position, but is limited to line of sight. Active radar involves sending out a signal so you can see over the horizon, but will give away your position. While we can operate on passive 'listening' radar much of the time, we need to learn to turn on our active 'spiritual' radar to reach out for all the revelation God is making available. I often find it helpful to use my active radar to step into the spiritual current of the person I am prophesying to.

10.5.4　Worship, thanksgiving and praise are three key practices that powerfully activate our inner well, refresh its depth and heighten its intensity. The Bible is particularly helpful in explaining this principle.[228] It teaches us that worship and singing release the knowledge of his lordship within us, that thanksgiving brings us to his gates [close] and praise carries us into his courts [intimacy]. Regular sessions with your favourite worship, consistently expressing your thankfulness and regularly letting go in praise, will keep your inner well full and in a state of readiness.

10.5.5　Lastly, we need to develop the lessons of our forefathers who passed on the Bible by word of mouth, by reminding ourselves, "Testimony carries within it the spirit of prophecy."[229] We can activate, resonate and stimulate our inner well with regular reminders of testimonies of what God has done in our lives. Declaring to ourselves, as well as others, specific testimonies of God's faithfulness, provision and kindness releases the spirit of prophecy into our inner well. Testimonies will build our faith, crush our doubts and fill our minds with truth. Developing a lifestyle of testimony activates our inner well.

10.5.6　Outer manifestation comes from inner revelation.

227. John 14:26 | 228. Psalm 100 | 229. *Strengthen Yourself in the Lord;* Bill Johnson [Destiny Image]

School for Prophecy

10.6   Keeping Fit

10.6.1   For the same reasons that we need to keep physically fit, we also need to keep spiritually fit, by maintaining a healthy position of rest and readiness. While the gift of tongues was very controversial at the time of my salvation, during the Charismatic 70s renewal, it has been my experience that it has great value in building one up. The Bible teaches that using the spiritual gift of tongues strengthens us.[230] I have lost count of the number of times I have spent time quietly speaking in tongues before ministry. It increases our sense of the supernatural, releases God's presence and brings our spirit into focus.

10.6.2   Another way we can keep ourselves spiritually fit is to encourage and develop an expectant attitude. While I recognize the presence of God's grace in our lives, the principle that 'if you don't expect it to happen, it is very unlikely to' still applies. An expectant attitude releases a positive atmosphere around us, actively engages our faith and is a real magnet to the Holy Spirit. We all know the difference between a meeting where there is strong environment of expectation and one where there is not. If we want to develop our prophetic gift, then we need to expect it to happen!

10.6.3   To keep fit, we need to learn the art of strengthening ourselves, particularly during times of trial and hardship. The story of King David[231] includes what can only be described as probably the worst day of his life, remarkably also just before he was finally to become king! The Bible says that at that precise 'give up and die' moment, David "strengthened himself in the Lord his God". David was able to reach into the intimacy in his relationship with God and find fresh faith, hope and strength when everything around him screamed, "It's over!"

10.6.4   An important aspect of preparation that has a significant impact on our development is learning to guard our tongue, i.e. being careful about what we say. The Bible's teaching on this subject[232] is very black and white. Praise and cursing should not come out of the same mouth, just as fresh and salt water can't come from the same spring. Much of our prophecy will probably be spoken, so learning to guard our speech, quality control over what we say, is good preparation for growing in our gift. This is not an issue of holiness through works, but practising the fruit of the Spirit, self-control.

10.6.5   Finally, developing a thankful attitude is vital preparation for prophecy. The Bible repeatedly encourages us to be thankful and specifically in all circumstances.[233] Thankfulness brings our heart into alignment with the kingdom of God, protects us against the lies of the enemy and materialism of the world, and is simply another form of worship. It will highlight the context of our gift as it releases heaven's priorities into our lives and thinking, and helps us appreciate what we have instead of focussing on what we don't. It encourages us to live, breathe and speak the heavenly values of the kingdom of God.

10.6.6   If your output exceeds your input, your upkeep will be your downfall.

230. 1 Corinthians 14:4 | **231.** 1 Samuel 29; 30 [NASB] | **232.** James 3:9-12 | **233.** 1 Thessalonians 5:16-18

School for Prophecy

10.7   Personal Training

10.7.1   *"Use it or lose it."*[234] As part of our preparation to prophesy, we need to encourage a lifestyle where we are our own personal trainer. While this punchy quote is applicable for many of the gifts and abilities in our lives, it is particularly relevant when we are seeking to grow in something and do not want to lose the ground we have already gained. To help us grow in prophecy we need to make sure we are not only keeping our gift fit [10.6], but we are actively looking for ways to grow and develop it further.

10.7.2   *"To boldly go where no man has gone before."*[235] This is a famous quote and makes the point that we will never learn anything unless we go where we have not been before. Developing our prophetic gift involves learning and trying different ways, styles and formats to prophesy than we have previously experienced. It is too easy to limit prophecy to the public spoken word, and not release the full potential of our creator God. Find people who prophesy through drama, painting, crafts, singing etc. Explore new environments to prophesy in, and observe other people's styles.

10.7.3   *Get out of your comfort zone.* Healthy preparation involves leaving those things we are comfortable with and learning new experiences. When people ask me if I have any suggestions to help their prophetic gift grow, my most unpopular one is, "Follow your fear." Areas of fear can reflect our lack of confidence, poor identity and bad experiences. I have often found that the thing I am secretly afraid of, and which our enemy is trying to block with a wall of fear, is often exactly where I need to go next.

10.7.4   *Can I have a lift?* One of the ways I found that I grew the most was travelling to different locations where I had little or no background knowledge of the church or the people. This seemed to healthily push me into relying more completely on the Holy Spirit than usual, and I experienced less conflict in my mind, due to the lack of information. Being in different surroundings, with different people and with different requirements, helped my growth dramatically. I often found myself in environments where, even though the expectations about me were not based in reality, it still seemed to open windows of opportunity not normally available or achievable by me.

10.7.5   *The Twilight Zone.*[236] This was a science fiction TV series about the unusual and weird, and the world of the prophetic certainly has plenty of those worth avoiding. However, I have found it very helpful to go outside my stream or denominational style to broaden my experience and understanding of the prophetic. Prophetic conferences with reputable speakers would be a good example. You will probably encounter some things you don't like or you disagree with, but it will help challenge any 'unbiblical prison' you are living in, hopefully thoughtfully.

10.7.6   If you always do what you have always done, you will always get what you always have.

234. Hippocrates, 400 BC | 235. *Star Trek* [1966 TV Series] | 236. *The Twilight Zone* [1959 TV Series]

154

School for
Prophecy

10.8 Common Hindrances

10.8.1 While we have been looking at preparation practices that you should encourage and build into your life, there are clearly those practices which you should be seeking to avoid. Being double-minded is up there as number one. The Bible teaches that when we ask for something [a prophecy], we need to believe and not doubt, otherwise we are double-minded and it will be like being tossed around on the waves.[237] This clearly reinforces my encouragement [10.6.2] to have an expectant attitude. As I have previously said, be careful how you talk to yourself, because you are listening. [1.2.6]

10.8.2 The fear of failure is a close number two. Fear of failure is a major obstacle when moving in prophecy for so many, and the chosen weapon of our enemy [1.5.3]. I have built my faith on the specific promise of Jesus that if we ask it will be given to us[238]. He reinforces this promise by pointing out how much more generous our heavenly Father is than we are. The gift of prophecy is God's idea, and he says it is a special gift and we should pursue it. When I move in prophecy, my confidence and the answer to the challenge of my fear is that God is trustworthy to fulfil his promises. "Get out of the way, fear. I am pushing through!"

10.8.3 Another way of thinking that we need to weed out is that of treating preparation on a 'works' basis. Often our enemy will point out that our preparation is lacking or non-existent: we haven't prayed today, we avoided our daily Bible reading, we missed church last Sunday, we were late as usual, we rushed here from work etc. The problem is that we then allow the enemy to put guilt on us, a form of condemnation, which undermines everything we do, including moving in the Spirit. These things *are* important and *do* make a difference, but because we live under grace and not works, we must not act like we need to earn our grace through them.

10.8.4 The next area of thinking we need to learn to realign with the truth is 'quality, not quantity'. I hope I do not have to explain that a prayer being longer does not make it any better than a shorter one. Especially at a time when we are seeking to develop our prophetic gift, focussing on quality – the level of detail, accuracy and insight – is more important. We are seeking to increase the depth of our prophecy during a time of development, not just its width. This mindset will also protect us from many worldly criteria of success we need to avoid.

10.8.5 There is a distinct danger of daily distractions. I am sure we have all suddenly realized that we have not thought about God for at least an hour or more. What we need to practise and learn to do is keep our 'passive radar' [10.5.3] permanently on, and go to active radar when something comes up. This means keeping our spirit open to those sound bites, gentle thoughts and random coincidences which are the Holy Spirit leading us into the truth. You can learn to have your mind committed to a task, particularly at work, and still have your spirit on the lookout for something that needs your attention.

10.8.6 If you are too busy to pray, you are just too busy.

237. James 1:5-8 | **238.** Matthew 7:7-11

School for **Prophecy**

10.9 Personal Testimony

10.9.1 My journey in preparing to prophesy has definitely been about developing my inner well and bringing all my distractions under control. I started being serious about prophecy in 1993 when I was a chartered accountant and talkative extrovert. Being a chartered accountant was not a problem, although I never properly fitted the stereotypical mould, but my outgoing, noisy and extrovert nature was a disaster for my gift's development. Being quiet, at any time, simply wasn't natural to me.

10.9.2 Initially, my young gift and creativity flourished in all the inspiration around me, and my experience of church leadership was of great help. But my rapid growth in anointing soon outstripped the available sources of external inspiration, and I found it very hard to reach inside into my inner well. I found it extremely difficult to be quiet and still. I still vibrated, my mind wandered, I felt like I was going to burst, and I found it hard being in one place for any length of time.

10.9.3 I recognized I needed to practise self-control, being still on the inside and being able to focus my spirit and gift. I turned to what had always worked, my daily 'quiet time' and my 'Every Day with Jesus' CWR Bible study notes. This proved a familiar and healthy environment to develop 'inner peace', as I called it. I discovered meditation on Jesus and the Bible, which really helped. I started learning self-control of my inner man, my emotions and my thoughts.

10.9.4 The major breakthrough came when I started doing what I found hard and going to retreat locations, 'Be Still' days and walking in the New Forest. I began to be able to be comfortably quiet, to rest, and the more I relaxed, the easier it became. I began to able to be quiet on the inside regardless of the level of noise around me. Eventually I was able to move back into circulation and keep my peace and, even more significantly, maintain my inner stillness.

10.9.5 My final stepping stone involved spending time at a local monastery and being at peace in the palpable silence I often found. The profound level of stillness, quiet and rest I found there enabled me to appreciate what I was trying to achieve when the world around me was noisy. My surroundings seemed to be able to absorb the noise and activity and still reflect rest and peace. It was not just the volume of noise, it was *conquering* the noise created by the intensity of life and the emotional impact of those moving around you.

10.9.6 I realized the power of my inner well while I was visiting a famous Celtic site in Ireland called 'Cluain Mhic Nois' [Clon-mac-noyce]. I inadvertently touched a stone that had been part of the cathedral there, and in the midst of many talking and photographing tourists with children, I felt the Spirit start to speak to me. I was able to sit down and focus my spirit on this stream of revelation and realized later I had written six pages of powerful notes from what I had heard. These notes have been a great source of inspiration to me down the years.

10.9.7 It has taken many years to get to this place, a journey for my character, but I have learned, and am still learning, to bring my whole inner self and prophetic gift into focus on the Holy Spirit despite any outer noise and distractions.

10.10 Frequently Asked Questions

10.10.1 My gift is very spontaneous; why do I need an inner well?

10.10.2 There is no 'have to' in my teaching. I am gently but firmly sharing that just relying on outside inspiration will put a ceiling on your gift [6.8.4]. Spontaneous means sometimes it will work and sometimes it won't. Your inner well, the Holy Spirit's gift, is available 24/7 and does not rely on you feeling like it or being in the zone. The frequency and depth of your current gift may be all you need at present, but I am offering a biblical route to greater accuracy, detail and breadth. There are character implications to consider here as well.

10.10.3 How much preparation do I need to do before, say, a ministry time?

10.10.4 I don't feel I can specify any required amount of time because our gift is not based on input equals output [10.2.2]. Some preparation is better than none, but developing a lifestyle rather than an event-based approach is much more fruitful. We all live busy lives, so it is a matter of prioritising your time based on your needs and requirements at the time, remembering that we are all very different. Much of our preparation comes out of our relationship with our heavenly Father, so this provides a thermometer for you.

10.10.5 Declaring God's promises sounds a bit 'name it and claim it' to me...

10.10.6 That was not my intention. The faith camp draws congruence between what we declare and what will happen. I am suggesting that declaring what God has already promised in the Bible builds up our spirit, focusses our faith and lays a strong platform for serving him [10.4.4]. The fundamental difference is that I am referring you to eternal truths from his word and calling you to rely on your faith and trust in our Lord. If we are speaking his word, it will not return empty, but if we are speaking our words, they are just our words.

10.10.7 How exactly do we strengthen ourselves as you describe David did?

10.10.8 The Bible does not specify how David did this, but it must have been seriously powerful to help him completely pull out of the emotional black hole he was looking into [10.6.3]. I would suggest that you should have a spiritual 'first-aid kit' ready for such occasions. First, I would declare to myself God's wonderful love for me and that it can never be taken away. Second, I would remind myself of what God has already done repeatedly in my life to bring me to this place. Finally, I would stand on one of my favourite faith verses [Philippians 4:13] and seriously focus my faith on it.

10.10.9 I appreciate the benefits of travelling, but whom do you travel with?

10.10.10 I understand that it was easier while I was with Graham, but after he went to the USA, I had to apply myself like anyone else [10.7.4]. As with Graham, offering to do the driving took me to many places. You are not necessarily looking for an international ministry to go with, just someone who is travelling that you can learn from. A genuine servant heart, being willing and available, will touch people and should open doors of opportunity. Bottom line: it is down to seeking the Lord and relying on him to show you the way.

Study Notes

11

UNLOCKING THE PROPHETIC PROCESS

Study Notes

11.0 Chapter Summary

11.0.1 *Introduction – Prophetic Developments* covers those areas of our anointing, training and calling that with proper investment can significantly shape and improve the consistency, maturity and longevity of our gift. The second *Prophetic Developments* subject introduces the 7 I's, i.e. ingredients, of prophecy, and helps us understand the process by identifying the importance of each of the seven key elements.

11.0.2 *Ingredients* – This opens the way for us to look in more detail at individual stages in the prophetic process, helps you to identify where you are at any time in the different stages and encourages a more thoughtful and active involvement in the particular stages of the process. The 7 I's of prophecy are:

11.0.3 *Inspiration* – The very first stage in the process of prophecy is *Initiation,* if you don't count the potential investment of time in seeking words, waiting on God and daily interactions. It is that supernatural moment when the Holy Spirit releases spiritual revelation into our physical minds, hearts or emotions.

11.0.4 *Interpretation* – They next key stage in the prophetic process is *Interpretation,* where we use our gift to take all the revelation we have received and unwrap it into the complete message the Holy Spirit wants us to bring. It is fundamentally a creative process, and will involve growing in supernatural creativity, spiritual insight and knowledge of God's ways.

11.0.5 *Initiation* – This is the stage in the prophetic process where we deliver the prophecy that was birthed in *Inspiration* and gestated through *Interpretation.* It is often the last involvement that we will have in the process, remembering we will have been applying our own testing during development.

11.0.6 *Implication* – *Investigation* follows *Initiation* and is covered separately in *The Principles of Testing Prophecy* [7]. After *Investigation,* the next of the 7 I's is *Implication.* Here we allow the Holy Spirit to reveal the truth of our prophecy, and in particular what implications, repercussions, connotations or propositions it has for us.

11.0.7 *Implementation* – This is the stage in the prophetic process when we step out and put into action what we believe God is calling us to do. Having received a prophecy, tested it and come to a conclusion on what we believe God is saying to us, prayerfully and thoughtfully considering the implications, *Implementation* is where we put the conclusions of our decision-making into action.

11.0.8 *Investment* – The last of my 7 I's of prophecy is *Investment.* This is the stage that begins after reaching the fulfilment of our prophecy, and is the *Investment* in the necessary time, energy and resources to acquire all that God has for us. *Investment* is how we occupy, defend and inhabit the purpose of our prophecy.

11.1 Introduction

11.1.1 Following the previous chapter on *Preparing to Prophesy* [10] the next subject in the *Prophetic Developments* topic is *Unlocking the Prophetic Process. Prophetic Developments* covers those areas of our anointing, training and calling that with proper investment can significantly shape and improve the consistency, maturity and longevity of our gift. The second *Prophetic Developments* subject introduces the 7 I's, i.e. ingredients, of prophecy, and helps us understand the process by identifying the importance of each of the seven key elements. Being part of the extended course, this chapter is more advanced and necessarily builds on the earlier chapters.

11.1.2 This chapter on *Unlocking the Prophetic Process* will look at how all the jigsaw pieces of prophecy fit together. It is designed to explain the 7 I's of prophecy [page 18] which all, unsurprisingly, begin with the letter 'I'. This will allow us to walk through the whole process of the gift of prophecy from the very beginning to the very end, including both the people giving and those receiving the prophecy. The 7 I's are not rungs on a ladder of achievement, but geographic markers, i.e. road signs, along the journey that should help you understand where you are and in what direction you are going.

11.1.3 A good way to explain what this chapter does, and its challenge, is to imagine your car being in the dealer's garage and that they have had to take the engine apart and lay it all out on the floor in pieces. The advantage is that you can now for the first time see all the parts that go together to make the whole, and what they look like. The disadvantage is that it is now very hard to visualize it as a car engine, and you 'can't see the wood for the trees'. This is effectively what I have done in this chapter, in breaking down prophecy into seven distinct activities to consider.

11.1.4 The common mistake I believe many people make is to consider prophecy a simple two-stage process: I get it, I give it. This tends to make prophecy a very emotionally-guided, generated and evaluated process. Using driving as an example, you could say changing gear is a two-stage process too: press the clutch down, push the gear lever. However, this is an oversimplification and ignores all the other important aspects of the process, like road condition, weather, traffic, acceleration etc. It will considerably help you to develop your prophetic gift if you have a healthy appreciation of the elements of the process you are involved in.

11.1.5 There is a considerable benefit to our whole lives through developing an appreciation of the different stages of the prophetic process. Instead of having a generic prophetic gift you can use, you will acquire a prophetic toolbox, enabling you to apply specific elements of your gift in the other areas of your life. Being prophetic may help you, but understanding the process provides you with specific prophetic tools for specific purposes; for example, when you need guidance *[Inspiration]*, have dreams *[Interpretation]* and are challenged by others *[Investigation]*.

11.2 Ingredients

11.2.1   This manual seeks to establish a clear biblical framework for the full operation of the gift of prophecy. To assist this objective, I have broken the prophetic process down into its seven essential ingredients, using a system I call *The 7 I's of Prophecy*. This paves the way for us to look in more detail at individual stages in the prophetic process, helps you to identify where you are at any time in the different stages, and encourages a more thoughtful and active involvement in the particular stages of the process. *The 7 I's of Prophecy* are:

11.2.2   *Inspiration* – how revelation is received from the Holy Spirit, which will form the basis of the prophetic message. [11.3]

11.2.3   *Interpretation* – the process by which the revelation received is translated into its full meaning in a prophecy. [11.4]

11.2.4   *Initiation* – when, where and how the prophecy is delivered to the identified audience. It is lovingly fashioned, creatively presented and has a servant's heart. [11.5]

11.2.5   *Investigation* – the selective process through which the recipient tests the prophecy to discover what they believe the Holy Spirit is saying to them. This is such an important subject it has its own chapter, *The Principles of Testing Prophecy* [7].

11.2.6   *Implication* – the process that identifies the significance, purpose and timing of the prophecy for the recipient. [11.6]

11.2.7   *Implementation* – the identification of any actions required by the prophecy, and then actually following through with them. [11.7]

11.2.8   *Investment* – the process whereby we learn to occupy, implement and defend whatever new territory God has moved us into as a result of the prophecy. [11.8]

11.2.9   This may seem daunting at first, but the system is quite straightforward actually. Only the first three *[Inspiration, Interpretation* and *Initiation]* apply to the person delivering the prophecy, and are comfortably distinct stages. The *Investigation* stage, while inevitably in our minds when bringing a prophecy, is the responsibility of the recipient and happens independently. This then leaves the last three *[Implication, Implementation* and *Investment]* which apply only to the recipient and are relatively discrete stages. So, depending on where you are in the process, you are only ever considering one or two of them at any one time.

11.2.10   It is important not to get lost in the detail of the 7 I's teaching. The real purpose is to helpfully break down the prophetic process into easily manageable parts. This will assist your understanding of the process, facilitate your training and practice and help you deliver a greater level of anointing in accuracy, detail and timing. We will now go through them one at a time to help you grasp their principles and practices, excluding *Investigation,* which is covered in *The Principles of Testing Prophecy* [7].

11.2.11   Our awareness of the process enhances our effectiveness within it.

11.3 Inspiration

11.3.1 *Inspiration* is the very first stage in the process of prophecy, if you don't count the potential investment of time in seeking words, waiting on God and daily interactions. It is that supernatural moment when the Holy Spirit releases spiritual revelation into our physical minds, hearts or emotions; a process we do not understand. You cannot predict when it will happen. It can happen when you are seeking God, or not, and at the most inconvenient times, just like a mobile phone! It can come in multiple different forms: through words, impressions, songs and Bible verses to name but a few.

11.3.2 The initial revelation we receive can be a single package, one of a sequence of items or a part of the whole to be uncovered. I have found it helpful to imagine it like a 'seed' of revelation which, through our gift, we are able to grow into a 'tree' of prophecy, revealing the full truth in God's message. We need to exercise wisdom with the revelation we receive as it may not be intended for the recipient, but may be just for us to use to prepare God's message. This is particularly true if it would publicly expose someone, not in love. We are primarily guided here by the principle of the second most important commandment[239].

11.3.3 It greatly helps the prophetic process if we are able to determine the purpose, goal or objective of the prophecy. This should not be too difficult as it will be apparent in the 'heart' of the word and the 'feel' of the revelation we receive. It is particularly important as we develop the full prophetic word, as the same words can have very different meanings. The context we feel the word is speaking into should help us; whether strategic, transformation, relocation, training, seasonal etc. Having a clear idea of our God's objectives, being his messengers, will greatly assist our message.

11.3.4 Next, and perhaps most important, is to identify whom the revelation we have received is for. Who is the intended recipient? This is not always as obvious as when we are in a time of ministry for a particular person, and may need prayerful and thoughtful consideration. There are considerable options, even knowing the word. Is it a specific person, group of people, corporate body or even a whole nation? Generally, the subject of any word is part of the inspiration, and its content can be very helpful, but there are occasions when it is a challenge. The answer will come in time.

11.3.5 Unfortunately, prophetic people have a reputation for being able to hear God for everyone else except themselves. We should be careful that in our enthusiasm to prophesy, we don't project revelation that is simply meant for us into prophecies for other people. The inspiration may well be a 'mirror' and not a prophecy! *Inspiration* for ourselves is simply hearing from God. *Inspiration* for others could well be a prophecy. Maintaining objectivity is crucial in this process, and we need to be mature enough to recognize when our subjectivity compromises our ministry, and act on it.

11.3.6 *Inspiration* is the germination of revelation into the situation.

239. Matthew 22:39

11.4 Interpretation

11.4.1 After *Inspiration,* the next stage we are going to consider is *Interpretation. Interpretation* is where we use our prophetic gift to take all the revelation we have received and unwrap it into the complete message the Holy Spirit wants us to bring. This unwrapping and unpacking of the seed of revelation will usually mean the prophecy contains much more than we started with but is very much inspired by it. *Interpretation* is a key element in the operation of our prophetic gift, and while it is a spiritual activity, there is no doubt it can be developed with practice, experience and wisdom [8].

11.4.2 *Interpretation* bridges the gap between *Inspiration,* seeing in the Spirit, and *Initiation,* the delivery of the prophecy. This makes *Interpretation* a very important part of the prophetic process and, despite the attention that is frequently given to *Initiation,* is really the heart of our prophetic gift. Developing your prophetic gift will involve you seeking to specifically grow in this area, and will reflect the level of anointing you are currently able to move within. It is fundamentally a creative process, and will involve growing in supernatural creativity, spiritual insight and knowledge of the ways of God.

11.4.3 *Interpretation* enables us through our prophetic gift to take the 'seed' of revelation and grow it into the full 'tree' of God's message. This process often involves pressing into the *Inspiration* for more detail. What tree the seed is going to grow into, what fruit the tree will grow and where the tree is located are just the start. *Interpretation* is an unwrapping process, and as the layers come off, more information is revealed, leading to even more layers to take off. Consequently, I have developed a lifestyle in which I give myself a minimum of seven days to prepare or interpret a prophecy, rather than rushing what I have today.

11.4.4 A matter worth bearing in mind during interpretation arises out of the biblical principle that we only know in part and therefore only prophesy in part[240]. This means we are often interpreting a prophecy with partial information, and it would be natural to start making assumptions to make the process easier but we must be careful not to. The information the Holy Spirit provides will always be sufficient for his purposes. This means we may find ourselves with prophecies that don't make sense, will sound stupid or really don't fit the situation – but are correct. God sometimes maintains confidentiality, which will inevitably leave us in the dark.

11.4.5 One practice I have found very helpful in developing my interpretation is learning to see what you are looking at! If you have ever double-checked a mobile text, only to find afterward that it was obviously wrong, you know what I mean. We need to learn to see, hear and feel all that Holy Spirit is revealing to us through *Inspiration,* so that we can bring the full *Interpretation* in our prophecy. This does require patience, insight and creativity, but is well worth the effort. Learning to focus completely on your current inspiration is an art that will open up doors into greater detail and understanding.

11.4.6 *Interpretation* is the conduit, creativity and conscience of prophecy.

240. 1 Corinthians 13:9-12

11.5   Initiation

11.5.1   *Initiation* is the stage in the prophetic process where we deliver the prophecy that was birthed in *Inspiration* and gestated through *Interpretation*. It is often the last involvement that we will have in the process, remembering we will have been applying our own testing *[Investigation]* [7] during development. We are actually simply a postman, delivering the relevant letter to the right mailbox. However, even more than a letter from HM the Queen, this message is just a bit special. *Initiation* is a very significant stage in the prophetic process, and frequently does not receive the consideration it deserves.

11.5.2   I have previously specified that we should always decide when, where and how to deliver our prophecy [6.5.2]. This reflects the second most important commandment[241] according to Jesus, and ensures that thought is given to the process instead of acting on reflex. Under this heading I need to highlight that any directional, warning or correctional prophecies should be discussed with your leadership first. These type of prophecies, personal or corporate, cross over into the realm of leadership authority, and need to be submitted to the leadership for their consideration first.

11.5.3   A core aspect of the *Initiation* process is the timing of delivery. A UK estate agent [US realtor] will tell you the critical feature in any sale is 'location, location, location'. The prophetic ministry equivalent is 'timing, timing, timing'. Much of the power of prophecy is released through God's timing in people's lives, whilst most of our assessment is based on the content alone. We need to be prayerful and considerate about the right time to share a prophecy, which can sometimes require considerable patience. How we handle the emotional urgency and pressure of carrying a prophecy is crucial.

11.5.4   The style of delivery should be chosen to enhance the purpose of the prophecy and not just replicate the generic norm of our church. We do need to consider what the most appropriate delivery style is for the message, taking into account its content, location and objective. While I am sure everyone is familiar with the apparent 'international standard' of spoken prophecy, there are actually a remarkable number of possibilities if we get creative. I have seen prophecy through objects; painting; mime; songs; drama sketches; and even people's lives! Simply using the correct tenor of voice to match the content can make a huge difference in its presentation.

11.5.5   Delivery involves a variation of 'what you see is what you get' [2.8.5], which is, 'what you *hear* is what you get'. This sounds rather obvious, but without the proper recording of prophecy, many people are processing what they thought they heard, their best recollection of the bits that struck them or, even worse, what they *wanted* to hear. The recording of prophecy, particularly during personal ministry, is important to ensure there is an accurate record of what the prophecy said, and creates the opportunity to review and recall, as well as being the best basis for testing a prophecy.

11.5.6   Through *Initiation* comes the birth of transformation.

241. Matthew 22:39

School for
Prophecy

11.6   Implication

11.6.1   *Investigation* follows *Initiation,* and is covered separately in *The Principles of Testing Prophecy* [7]. After *Investigation,* the next ingredient is *Implication,* which is the important phase between testing a prophecy and putting it into action. Here we allow the Holy Spirit to reveal the truth of our prophecy, and in particular what implications, repercussions, connotations or propositions it has for us. Rather than jumping straight into 'what must I do' *[Implementation],* we recognize the accountability has moved from the 'postman' to the recipient, and taking on responsibility, we seek to reveal the full implications.

11.6.2   *Implication* involves more than just examining our prophecy. In addition to considering the message of our prophecy, we need to bring into this review our current life's story. We need to consider what the Holy Spirit has said to us so far; what related circumstances there are in our lives to consider; the implication or coincidence of the timing of our prophecy; what area or season of our life the prophecy is speaking into; what the objective of the prophecy is; and what character development might be required. *Implication* brings all aspects of our life to the 'party' to reveal the full significance of our prophecy.

11.6.3   A key factor in helping *Implication* release the full meaning of our prophecy is maintaining objectivity, as we are naturally subjective. While we may think we know a lot about ourselves, we certainly don't know as much as God does! God may have a completely different agenda, direction and outcome than we are currently focussed on. This is an opportunity to seek advice from honest friends we trust, our related leaders and valued advisors we have used before. Consciously maintaining our objectivity will protect us from the deviation of immediacy, prejudice and assumption.

11.6.4   However, one of our distinct advantages is that we do know a lot more about ourselves than any person bringing us a prophecy. We are therefore able to hear more than is actually said because we are able to 'read [or hear] between the lines'. How the prophecy connects with our previous history, significant events, current decision-making, important relationships and unfulfilled goals can open a whole new line of thinking than is possible with merely the detail in our prophecy. Even the terminology or images used can have an unexpected yet significant impact on the recipient's understanding of the prophecy.

11.6.5   Bottom line: give yourself time and space. *Implication* is an important stage that is not helped by being rushed. The process is considerably aided and helped by patient and prayerful listening. This protects us from feeling we have to come up with an answer to avoid the pressure, people and panic. I can recall the nightmare of being haunted by the question, "What are you going to do after university?"; the same can be true for us. I thoroughly recommend writing your prophecy out in full so it is readily available for regular review, and then trusting God that he will guide you. It is a helpful discipline.

11.6.6   *Implication* helps us find where our jigsaw piece fits into God's bigger picture.

11.7   Implementation

11.7.1   The sixth of the 7 I's is *Implementation.* This is the stage in the prophetic process when we step out and put into action what we believe God is calling us to do. Having received a prophecy and tested it to come to a conclusion on what we believe God is saying to us, prayerfully and thoughtfully considering the implications, *Implementation* is where we put the conclusions of our decision-making into action. It is 'where the rubber hits the road'. *Implementation* is the journey from where we are to where God wants us to be, actually bridging the gap, not 'minding the gap' [9.6.4].

11.7.2   Many of the aspects of *Implementation* can be found in *The Principles of Responding to Prophecy* [9]. However, a key aspect of *Implementation* is understanding the importance of participation [9.4.1]. Through passivity too many people, having an Old Covenant understanding of prophecy, have been disappointed, discouraged and then distressed by unfulfilled prophecy in their lives. Prophecy is not like some heavenly 'one arm bandit' where you pull the lever [prophecy] and out comes your winnings [inheritance]. Our participation in prophecy, not presumption, is a prerequisite of its fulfilment.

11.7.3   In the *Implementation* of our prophecy we need to have active faith in God – not the prophet, by the way – to bring it to fulfilment. The Bible teaches the thorny truth that faith without action is dead[242] [9.4.3]. This includes keeping the prophecy fresh in our hearts and minds, stepping out based on our personal convictions, overcoming circumstances turning against us, developing a faithful perspective of our journey and responding to changes in our anticipated route. Faith resulting in action comes from recognizing where God wants to move us to and starting to journey there.

11.7.4   One implication we often have to implement, before starting our journey properly, is if we recognize any skill training, character development or inner healing that we are going to need to complete the journey. This sometimes creates a spiritual 'packing list' we need to complete before we can fully start our expedition. Full understanding can also come shortly after we start our journey, when we begin to realize exactly what it involves. This falls under the heading of what I described as "you can't get there from here" [9.5.2.]; sometimes we have to journey to the 'starting gate' first.

11.7.5   Fortunately, we do not have to do *Implementation* on our own. Journeying with our friends and family is a natural part of the process and provides company, encouragement and comfort along the way. Similarly, confidentially involving trusted friends in the detail, emotion and decisions of our journey can be a great source of strength and sustenance. It is always wise to seek counsel and wisdom from those we respect, including our leaders, and seeking out access to any gifts and ministries that will help us along the way. Finally, it may well be worth your while seeking out wisdom from those who have successfully completed a similar journey to your own.

11.7.6   *Implementation* is the journey out of our comfort zone into our inheritance.

242. James 2:14-17

School for **Prophecy**

11.8 Investment

11.8.1   The last of my 7 I's of prophecy is the *Investment*. This is the stage that comes after reaching the fulfilment of our prophecy, and is the investment in the necessary time, energy and resources to acquire all that God has for us. After the *Investigation* of our prophecy to arrive at what we believe, processing the *Implications* to a conclusion, and participating in the *Implementation* of action, *Investment* is how we occupy, defend and inhabit the purpose of our prophecy. After you have filled up your wine bottle [prophecy] with new wine [fulfilment], *Investment* is screwing the top on securely!

11.8.2   After the wrong assumption that your prophecy must begin from where you currently are [9.5.2], the next biggest mistake people make is to underestimate, or even be unaware of, the need for *Investment*. Our enemy recognizes the most opportune moments to steal, kill or destroy[243] our prophecy's fulfilment, and he knows that arriving at our destination, before we have properly moved in, is one of the best. Arriving at the address of our destination is a moment for celebration, thanksgiving and testimony. However, it can also be a vulnerable moment when we are tired, relax and drop our guard.

11.8.3   *Investment* is making sure we don't stop at the 'front door' of our destination, but move in and fully occupy all that God intended. Reaching our destination and the goal of our prophecy is not sufficient; we need to occupy it and make it ours. This also involves considering the full implications of our prophecy, and not stopping short of the full fulfilment of its meaning. Given the journey is just as important as the destination [9.5.3], it is possible that our perspective will have changed and we will only grasp the full significance of the prophecy when we reach our destination.

11.8.4   Next, and just as important, we need to prepare to defend our new-found territory [gifting, role, location] from our enemy. He knows that an early attack has a better chance of success, before we become accustomed to our new surroundings. Even at this stage, his craftiness will try to place doubts in us about our interpretation of the prophecy, lie to us that this is not really us at all, or at the first sign of trouble or criticism announce we have obviously got it wrong. Digging in with our faith, holding to the prophetic promise and embracing change are important here.

11.8.5   Finally, we must commit to fully inhabiting our new-found territory. We need to invest time, energy and resources to not only occupy our prophetic fulfilment but inhabit it so that it becomes a natural part of our lives. We need to move as quickly as possible from a new acquisition to having an established experience. If it is a significant prophecy, then this will take time and may not be achieved quickly. We need to incorporate the fulfilment of our prophecy into our lives, so it is an integral part; not just leave it like a recent conservatory extension, which is a nice addition but not a real part of our home.

11.8.6   *Investment* in the prosperity of our prophecy has a high rate of return.

243. John 10:10

11.9 Personal Testimony

11.9.1   I am sure many experienced ministries may not see the importance of this chapter on *Unlocking the Prophetic Process,* as it will seem natural to them after years of practice and training. Similarly, I am sure many people new to prophecy, or young in the gift, will feel this chapter is far too complicated to ever understand it. However, I stand by my deep conviction [11.2.11] that our awareness of the process enhances our effectiveness within it.

11.9.2   My personal journey of learning the gift of prophecy, and my experience as a trainer in schools for prophecy, has convinced me of the importance of understanding the mechanics, process and key stages in prophecy. Furthermore, while a cursory knowledge may only be necessary for an infrequent gift, to mature and grow in prophecy involves handling unpleasant, unusual and unexpected situations. The dropout rate for those moving in prophecy, serving in the ministry, or being an itinerant prophet, is far too high not to take this seriously.

11.9.3   This chapter is not for beginners. It is chapter eleven of twelve and part of the extended course! However, it is an essential grounding for those seeking to grow beyond this level. Unlocking the prophetic process was birthed in my revelation about biblical prophecy, but it has taken me on some very profitable journeys of personal discovery as a result. In my learning about the gift, I have spent a lot of time unpacking, uncovering and understanding how prophecy operates in many different environments, as well as practising 'learning from your mistakes' [12.6.4].

11.9.4   The first main area understanding the process focussed me on was testing prophecy. I have spent considerable time as a result researching the subject, learning from those wiser than me and practising it extensively for others and myself. The detail and depth of *The Principles of Testing Prophecy* [7] is a testament to this. It became obvious to me early on that most people simply did not know how to do it, had not established biblical principles to follow and it had become a great hindrance towards the gift's effectiveness.

11.9.5   The next area unlocking the process launched me into was the need to understand God's ways. The importance of seeing things from God's viewpoint, as well as his objectives, soon became blindingly obvious to me. This has not been an easy subject to grasp, interestingly, but the benefits have been well worth it. While I am still not convinced you can have any real accuracy predicting how and when God will move, I have found you can learn to understand why he moves.

11.9.6   This led to new revelation about intimacy with my heavenly Father, and the resulting cascade of avenues of learning it released. I suddenly realized that my heavenly Father had brought me into prophecy so that, unwittingly, I would spend much more time with him. If he was silent, then even longer! It opened up a whole new understanding for me of my sonship. This, then, in quick succession sent me into a new understanding of my salvation, being born again, the purpose of the cross, and the ministry of the Holy Spirit as counsellor, to name a few.

School for
Prophecy

11.10 Frequently Asked Questions

11.10.1 I find getting inspiration difficult; how do I grow in this area?

11.10.2 Revisiting the chapter on *Hearing Your Father's Voice* [3] and making sure you are comfortable with the full breadth of this subject is a good start. Next, recognizing that this area gets easier with both time and practice should help you focus on improving, rather than measuring your performance. Lastly, you may need to learn to let your heart and emotions work with your spirit and mind to fully embrace this process, as it will get easier the more you learn to rest in it and not struggle with it [11.3.1].

11.10.3 Is it right that the person giving should not engage in any interpretation?

11.10.4 I teach that both the giver and receiver of a prophecy need to engage in the interpretation process, but in different ways. The giver often receives a package [the seed] of an idea, which needs *Interpretation* to reveal God's complete message, i.e. unwrapping the package [11.4.3]. This will be different every time. However, the important principle is the giver should stop 'unwrapping' when God does! The person bringing the prophecy should bring no more than God gives him or her [6.7.2].

11.10.5 Does it matter when, where or how I give a prophecy?

11.10.6 If you are more interested in where the javelin lands than how you throw it, then yes, it does! Prophecy is too often limited by emotional pressure, denominational regulations and meeting management. During the spontaneity of worship, it may not make a difference, but once a prophecy contains a decisive message, it certainly matters [11.5.2]. In my opinion, the delivery style should match the message and the context should be conducive to its fulfilment [11.5.4].

11.10.7 Should I go back to the person who prophesied if I need some advice?

11.10.8 The accountability for a prophecy ends with delivery for the giver [11.5.1], however you could and should take advice from those whom you trust, those who are wise and experienced and, if significant, your leadership. Your task is to engage in the *Implication* of the prophecy: where it fits into your life, your journey and your destiny [11.6.1]. You bring detailed knowledge of your history, current revelation and latest guidance to bear on the prophecy, which, with patient prayer, will reveal the full *Implication*.

11.10.9 Surely if my prophecy has been fulfilled, there is nothing left to do?

11.10.10 The principle of *Investment* warns us that just because we have arrived at the destination of prophecy, it does not guarantee we are equipped to occupy it and defend it [11.8.2]. The beginning and end of a prophetic journey are the most vulnerable times, for different reasons. Arriving at our prophetic destination, while moving us up to a new level, launches a new season of growth and development. Without the investment of thought, time and training in taking hold of the destination of our prophecy, we risk losing the ground we have gained, as well as the bridgehead for God's next work in our lives.

Study Notes

12

THE CHARACTER CHALLENGES OF PROPHECY

Study Notes

School for Prophecy

12.0 Chapter Summary

12.0.1 *Introduction – Prophetic Developments* covers those areas of our anointing, training and calling that with proper investment can significantly shape and improve the consistency, maturity and longevity of our gift. The final *Prophetic Developments* subject looks at the ways the operation and environment of the gift of prophecy create specific challenges and pressures for our characters.

12.0.2 *Gift and Character* – I am going to explore and explain the impact and effect of moving in prophecy on our personality type and character maturity. Too many want to receive a greater anointed gift without the work required to develop a character to manage it safely. It is not an either/or choice, but a both/and journey.

12.0.3 *Vision and Values* – When our character experiences change, pressure or challenge, the first thing that happens is our vision and values come into play. They are what we actually believe, and use, to interpret the situation we find ourselves in. You could say that our vision and values define us and reveal who we are at our core.

12.0.4 *Our Core Values* – Understanding what our core values are is critical to our growth, maturity and progress through success and failure. They are what we really believe, not what we necessarily present to others, and determine how we will tend to act in any given situation.

12.0.5 *Facing Our Fears* – Our enemy's main weapon against the gift of prophecy is fear. Prophecy is a potent source of inspiration, insight and illumination, so it is natural that he will attack it whenever possible. Facing our fears is an inevitable part of the journey in prophecy and I believe is the reason 70% of the church do not prophesy.

12.0.6 *The Learning Curve* – One of the foundational reasons why prophecy creates character challenges, and we need to face up to it, is that unlike Old Covenant prophecy, New Covenant prophecy is not perfect. We therefore face the real prospect of making well-intentioned mistakes.

12.0.7 *Finding Inner Peace* – The next character challenge we will experience when moving in prophecy is the source of our *Inspiration.* While our external environment is full of possibilities, for our gift to grow to its full potential and maturity we need to release the well within.

12.0.8 *Personal Integrity* – No chapter on character challenges would be complete without the inevitable inclusion of 'integrity'. The large majority of prophecy you will encounter will generally be spoken, which brings into play many biblical principles. The core one for me, and our greatest challenge, is one of the biblical hallmarks of maturity: "speaking the truth in love".

12.1   Introduction

12.1.1   The third and final *Prophetic Developments* subject I want to cover after *Preparing to Prophesy* [10] and *Unlocking the Prophetic Process* [11] is *The Character Challenges of Prophecy*. *Prophetic Developments* covers those areas of our anointing, training and calling that, with proper investment, can significantly shape and improve the consistency, maturity and longevity of our gift. The final *Prophetic Developments* subject looks at the ways the operation and environment of the gift of prophecy create specific challenges and pressures for our character. Being part of the extended course, this chapter is more advanced and necessarily builds on the earlier chapters.

12.1.2   Moving in the gift of prophecy, with any regularity, has a significant impact on our personality, character and maturity. It is this recognized phenomenon that continues to fuel the 'gift or character' priority debate. It is the obvious impact of this chapter which, through my prophetic training, directly spawned my journey into prophetic mentoring and then into professional mentoring. I recognized at an early stage, in both myself and those around me, that our maturity, i.e. character, creates a ceiling to our sustainable growth in prophecy.

12.1.3   I can best illustrate this with my tugboat story. The tugboat travels up and down the estuary working with the larger ships, but especially the warships which it dreams of becoming. The tugboat manages to acquire the biggest gun it is able to, a Battleship 16" canon. It then sails up and down the estuary looking completely amazing and, as a result, can spend time with the more recognized warships. However, the first time the tugboat fires the canon, its draft [character] is insufficient to handle the recoil [gift], and it turns upside down and sinks. Game over.

12.1.4   The most common mistake is to believe there is no correlation between the fruit of the Spirit[244] and the gifts of the Spirit[245], which include prophecy. We need to maintain a healthy balance between the level of our gift and the maturity of our character for growth and development in the prophetic to be sustainable. What is frequently not appreciated is that when we genuinely pray for a more anointed gift – and I am not saying we shouldn't – we are also praying for an equivalent growth in our character. "Buy one and get one free."[246]

12.1.5   Inevitably, after initially moving into the supernatural dimension with the gift of prophecy, it becomes the journey inward and not the journey outward. It is a journey of self-awareness and discovering who we are in Christ, and consequently, there are substantial benefits in our Christian walk from embracing this process. Actively seeking a healthy balance between our gifting and our character will have a beneficial impact on our intimacy with our heavenly Father, as a greater understanding of our identity impacts our experience of acceptance, belonging, forgiveness and freedom.

244. Galatians 5:22-23 | 245. 1 Corinthians 12:7-11 | 246. Josiah Wedgewood [1769]

School for
Prophecy

12.2 Gift and Character

12.2.1   I will not be examining the 'gift or character' controversy here, although I can "nail my colours to the mast"[247] and categorically say I am a character-first person. It is the accepted premise underlying this, that gift impacts character, that I want to address in this chapter. I am going to explore and explain the impact and effect of moving in prophecy on our personality, character and maturity. Too many want to receive a greater anointed gift without the work required to develop a character to manage it safely. It is not an either/or choice, but a both/and journey.

12.2.2   While I will be looking predominantly at the situation where the gift is significantly greater than character, interestingly, there are significant consequences in the opposite scenario. If a person's gift is much greater than their character, they are likely to harm themselves and those around them. The imbalance can easily create pride and an unhealthy reliance on their ministry by those involved. Similarly, if a person's character is much greater than their gift, then they are likely to be considerably disadvantaged by analytical reasoning, micromanagement and risk aversion. [1.2.2]

12.2.3   The potential consequence of a situation where a person's gift is far greater than their character was delightfully portrayed in my tugboat story [12.1.3]. I often find that by taking situations to an extreme, it is easier to see the real issues at stake, which may not be obvious initially. For example, parts of our car [character] that seem fine at 30mph [prayer] may show major signs of weakness at 70mph [prophecy], which we were completely unaware of before. The Bible teaches that there is no guarantee that significant growth in the supernatural gifts will generate similar growth in the fruits of the Spirit.[248]

12.2.4   The lack of understanding of this principle by the wider Church means that people tend to assume that public ministries have the same level of maturity, i.e. holiness, in their lives as they have an apparent anointing. It is simply not true in biblical or recent history. Jesus teaches a countercultural principle when he tells us to discern false prophets by their fruit and not their gift. "By their fruit will you recognize them."[249] He asks the question, do they practise what they preach? What is the fruit of their ministry? Not the standard publicity values of power, popularity and presentation.

12.2.5   Growing in the gift of prophecy brings both change, recognition and more responsibility, all of which test the biblical alignment, or otherwise, of our character. Growing in our anointing will test our source of security, identity in Christ, definition of success, fear of man, baggage from our past and much more. God could increase my gift tenfold overnight, but he has not, because my character would not cope with that amount of pressure and would probably melt down. He does, however, answer my prayers for growth in the gift, and discipline me through experience to grow in maturity to match it.

12.2.6   "Gift is given, but fruit is grown." – Graham Cooke

247. Jack Crawford [1797] I **248.** 1 Corinthians 3:1-4 I **249.** Matthew 7:15-20

12.3   Vision and Values

12.3.1   When our character experiences change, challenge and conflict, the first thing that happens is our vision and values come into play. They are what we actually believe and use to interpret the situation we find ourselves in. You could say that our vision and values define us,[250] and reveal who we are at our core. We therefore need to look at these first to understand how and why we respond the way we do. We need to bring our vision and values into complete alignment with the Bible, to reflect the new life we have in Jesus and set us free from the 'baggage' we may have picked up along the way.

12.3.2   Over the years, I have come to understand that our core values can be categorized into three key areas: where we get our security from, how we define our self-worth and how we measure our significance. What we truly believe about each one will significantly shape who we are. Each of these three core values is impacted by moving in prophecy. What we believe about them will naturally define our response and how 'straight and tall' we can grow. Safely handling the impact of a developing prophetic gift on our character will involve understanding and adhering to biblical values in these areas.

12.3.3   Our core values should protect and guide us through times of change, challenge and conflict. They should be there for us in the great times and the hard times. They specifically help us handle the character challenge of the 4 F's. These are fear, failure, fame and fortune. Any one of these may arise, to one degree or another, as we move out in a stronger prophetic gift, and our values are the secure foundation we need to handle them in a godly way. The more experienced among us will know that success is actually more dangerous for our characters than hardship appears to be.

12.3.4   One of the challenges of the gift of prophecy is that it tends to lead us to rely on externals [those things around us] rather than internals [our identity and the Holy Spirit]. This is particularly true while we are young in the gift, when our environment is full of easy inspiration through colours, images and songs. This makes our character particularly vulnerable to change, challenge and conflict, because externals are inconsistent, like sand, and will interfere with the reliability of our core values. Unreliable or inconsistent values will tend to keep us in an emotional 'greenhouse' where extremes are the norm.

12.3.5   While fear and failure are probably concepts you can relate to and understand, you may not relate to fame and fortune. Alternatively, you may find it helpful to ask yourself how you react to flattering compliments [success][251] and constructive criticism [hardship][252]. It can be quite revealing about our character. I am not talking about genuine encouragement [praise] or destructive criticism [assassination]. I am referring to the temptation of praise that leads to pride, which we should resist, and the wounds of a friend that lead to healing, which we should receive.

12.3.6   "If you truly want to test someone, give them success." – Bill Johnson

250. Matthew 6:19-21 | 251. Proverbs 11:1-2; 29:5 | 252. Proverbs 27:6; Psalm 141:5

12.4 Our Core Values

12.4.1 Understanding what our core values are is critical to our growth, maturity and progress through success and failure. They are what we really believe, not what we necessarily present to others, and determine how we will tend to act in any given situation. Having biblical core values is what we are all trying to achieve, but they are often shaped by our previous experience and family history. To help myself with this journey, and as a foundation of much of my mentoring, I have developed three simple and easily memorable core values that reflect the key truths in our relationship with Jesus.

12.4.2 Your security is in whom you know, and *not* what you know.

12.4.3 The first definition deals with the important subject of where we get our security from. What do we look for to keep us safe in times of trouble, or what do we use to combat our fear of tomorrow? Our security needs to come from our relationship with Jesus, in accordance with the most important commandment[253], and only from him. It should not be based on our knowledge, qualifications or expertise. That includes our understanding of financial planning, investments and pensions. Jesus is the only security that is the same yesterday, today and forever,[254] and anything else has the potential to be shifting sand.

12.4.4 Your self-worth is in who you are, and *not* what you do.

12.4.5 The second definition deals with where we look to for our self-worth. What measure do we use to assess our personal worth, status or value, and do we compare ourselves with others in our lives? Our self-worth needs to come from our status in Christ, as sons and daughters of God,[255] and from nothing else. The world's values use a very different measurement, based on wealth, power or fame. Too often we draw our personal value from what we do, our job or ministry. What happens when it comes to an end? As forgiven, redeemed and adopted children, we are now coheirs in Christ.[256]

12.4.6 Your significance is how much you give, and *not* how much you have.

12.4.7 The final definition deals with what basis we use to measure our significance. How do we measure our significance, importance or the impact we make in our families, work and communities? Our significance is measured by how much we give, serve or contribute.[257] This is profoundly countercultural, which makes it a real challenge because everyone around us thinks differently to us, and inevitably may not value what we do. It is very easy to use a worldly model to measure our church's significance in 'buildings, bucks and bodies', but Jesus' values are very different to the world's.

12.4.8 Your gift is what gets things done, but your character is what keeps you on track.

253. Matthew 22:36-38 | 254. Hebrews 13:8 | 255. Galatians 4:6-7 | 256. Romans 8:17
257. Matthew 20:25-28

12.5 Facing Our Fears

12.5.1 My experience has taught me again and again that our enemy's main weapon against the gift of prophecy is fear. Prophecy is a potent source of inspiration, insight and illumination, so it is natural that he will attack it whenever possible. Facing our fears is an inevitable part of the journey in prophecy and I believe is the reason 70% of the church do not prophesy. I have previously explained that fear is the opposite of faith [1.2.3]; it is effectively faith that it will go wrong. "There is nothing to fear but fear itself."[258]

12.5.2 One particular type of fear that is very harmful, and quite common, is the fear of man. Putting it simply, we are more concerned or afraid of what people think than what God thinks.[259] It is particularly prevalent when there are political spirits at work. Given that when we are moving in prophecy, we are God's messengers bringing his message, the consequences of the fear of man can be incredibly destructive. Fear of man plays on any poor self-worth issues and seeks to enforce a worldly view of significance contrary to the biblical principle of service and generosity [12.4.6].

12.5.3 Some time ago I bumped into a humorous book title, which led me to create a helpful illustration of how prophecy and fear interact: *Edge of the Cliff* by Hugo First. [6.4.2] Yes, I know! Prophecy is like standing on the edge of a high cliff, and the voice of God a long way below calls out, "Jump and I will catch you!" You reply, "Come up a bit higher so I can see you, and then I will jump." But the voice just keeps repeating himself until we conquer our fear and jump. We give a big sigh of relief when he catches us, and then, to our surprise, we find ourselves back on the edge of the cliff and the voice of God a long way below...

12.5.4 From the moment we start to seriously consider bringing a prophecy, our enemy will attack us with fear, anxiety and doubt [1.3.4]. We must respond with trust and stand in faith. Our heavenly Father is a good God. He only gives us good gifts, he specifically encourages us to prophesy and we are only the 'postman'. If we stick to biblical guidelines and stay within our gifting, the worst we can do is bless someone in the wrong area of their lives. Paying attention to our enemy's lies of 'doom' will make us double-minded[260] and, as a result, debilitated.

12.5.5 Furthermore, we need to be aware that when we move from an environment of personal prophecy into public prophecy, e.g. prophesying in public, the challenge of fear in our lives goes up a whole new level. Moving in prophecy in public will create character challenges that we may not experience in the usual personal ministry environment. We may well find that our fear of man is insignificant in personal ministry, but on doing exactly the same ministry in public, particularly on a stage, it may identify real issues within us we were completely unaware of.

12.5.6 Fear causes us to underestimate our ability, overestimate the risk and exaggerate the consequences.

258. Franklin D. Roosevelt | 259. John 12:42 | 260. James 1:6-8

School for **Prophecy**

12.6 The Learning Curve

12.6.1 One of the foundational reasons why prophecy creates character challenges, and we need to face up to it, is that unlike Old Covenant prophecy, New Covenant prophecy is not perfect. We therefore face the real prospect of making well-intentioned mistakes. The Bible specifically teaches that until Jesus returns we will only prophesy in part, not perfectly, like a poor reflection in a mirror.[261] The accuracy of prophecy is affected by the quality of the deliverer. It can also be impacted by the quality of our core values, the level of our current anointing and the maturity of our character.

12.6.2 We need to look at the Bible's use of the word 'part' because it has considerable significance that is not always appreciated. We often naively assume that we have enough information in the prophecy to draw conclusions, and therefore make judgement calls. First, our prophecy is only 'part' of what God is saying to someone, and furthermore it is only a 'part' of the message on the subject we are covering. Secondly, we only know 'part' of the person, their character, feelings and values. Finally, we only know 'part' of their history, experiences and journey, even if they are a close friend.

12.6.3 To move in prophecy means facing our fears and being delivered from a punishment mentality. The fear of failure, or hurting someone, results in a maintenance lifestyle, specifically not taking risks. This profoundly reduces the prospect of us ever moving in prophecy. It is fear-poisoned and not faith-propelled. It is man-motivated and not Bible-based. To grow we need to go where we have never been before, i.e. take risks. Recognizing our current level of experience, learning from others more mature and following biblical patterns, are healthy ways to create sustainable growth.

12.6.4 I need to publicly thank my dad for teaching me an enormous principle as a teenager, which has been so important in my journey with the gift of prophecy. He often reminded me, "There are *only* two kinds of people: those who learn from their mistakes and those who don't."[262] We all make mistakes; it is what we learn from them that makes the difference. Mistakes, given they will happen with the best will in the world, are therefore an opportunity to grow. It is important to learn from our mistakes and not be buried by them.

12.6.5 Having said all of this, we do have to recognize that the environment we are seeking to grow in has a big impact on our potential and may even set a ceiling on how far we can grow. The presence of expectation, encouragement and example will significantly increase our potential for growth, especially with the gift of prophecy. Unfortunately, the reverse is also painfully true. The lack of these elements within the environment we are seeking to develop our gift will proportionately diminish our potential to grow and create a 'glass ceiling' that will be hard to break through.

12.6.6 Someone who has never made a mistake has never tried to build anything.

261. 1 Corinthians 13:9-12 | 262. Harold E. Iles

12.7   Finding Inner Peace

12.7.1   The next character challenge we will experience when moving in prophecy is the source of our *Inspiration*. While our external environment is full of possibilities, for our gift to grow to its full potential and maturity, we need to release the well within. I have previously mentioned how Jesus taught that the true source of our gift is from within and not without[263] [6.8.1]. We also need to learn how to 'be still' within to draw from this well, when we live in a world of busy timetables, technological multitasking and high levels of noise.

12.7.2   To grow our gift to maturity we will need to learn inner stillness, which comes through practice and learning to enter God's rest. However, we also need to be aware that the depth of God's dealing with our inner self defines the capacity of our anointing. While I do recognize the activity of grace in our lives, and that prophecy is a supernatural gift, my experience has taught me that sustainable outward growth requires a matching inward journey. A respectable balance between our character maturity and prophetic anointing needs to be maintained, so inevitably growth in our anointing requires development of our character.

12.7.3   Learning the art of stillness, living in God's rest, practically means learning to manage both our internal and external noise. There is a dramatic scene in a film[264], with Kevin Costner playing a world-famous baseball pitcher, which profoundly demonstrates what is needed. On a specific personal command, he is able to turn off the huge noise of the vast crowd in the stadium [external noise] and then he is able to blur the area around the catcher so that the only thing in focus is the batsman [inner focus]. I appreciate it is cinematography, but it does visually demonstrate this principle remarkably well.

12.7.4   We are all different, so you will have to find what works best for you, but as my prophetic mentor would say, "Do this until you find something better."[265] I have personally found that committing regular quality time to meditation, speaking in tongues and waiting on God [now called 'being in his presence'] has considerably helped me to be able to block out external noise and bring my inner self to rest in many circumstances. Meditation has a bad reputation with some, but there are considerable benefits to be had from meditating on Jesus or his word, the Bible.

12.7.5   Similarly, in addition to internal development, we also need to develop godly wisdom about how we can manage the impact of distractions, pressure and opposition during ministry. Considering the issues of where, when and how may well avoid many of these situations, but not all or the unexpected. This is a personal journey, as we are all affected differently, and we need to consider and learn how we are going to manage these situations as well as being alert to our own personal weaknesses. Don't let the pressure of the moment push you into unwise ministry.

12.7.6   Embrace the movement of the Spirit and not the spirit of the moment.

263. John 7:37-39 | 264. *For the Love of the Game* [1989 Universal Pictures Film]
265. Maya Angelou

12.8 Personal Integrity

12.8.1 No chapter on character challenges would be complete without the inevitable inclusion of 'integrity'. The large majority of prophecy you will encounter will generally be spoken, which brings into play many biblical principles. The core one for me, and our greatest challenge, is one of the biblical hallmarks of maturity: "speaking the truth in love"[266]. When we move in prophecy, the maturity and integrity of our character will come under the judgement of this profound litmus test. It clearly applies to our daily lives, but comes into direct focus during prophecy.

12.8.2 This takes the principle of the second greatest commandment, and fashions it to the specific application of speaking, hence prophecy. As is often the case, I have encountered an apocryphal version that takes the heart of this principle and helpfully brings out its pragmatic application: "Say what you mean, mean what you say and don't be mean when you say it."[267] I have found this saying very helpful in applying the biblical principle. For me, this is one of the two biblical practices for church growth, the other being "each part playing its part"[268], which we have yet to fully experience.

12.8.3 One of the great prophetic principles of integrity, often not appreciated, is the fundamental requirement to be moving in love[269] rather than anything else [6.2.1]. If we are being self-centred, grandstanding or people-pleasing, then we are wasting our time. People are paranoid about pride in the church, and from the above principle it is clearly to be avoided. Yet the issue in church is not pride, but false humility. The 'smell' of pride is easy to spot, but it is the plague of false humility that currently undermines the church.

12.8.4 There are often pressurized situations generated by the environment of prophetic ministry that inevitably reveal the true nature of our integrity and maturity. They are hard to prepare for and therefore involve a reflex reaction, which naturally reveals our true values. There can be considerable pressure exerted on us by the expectation of others, both in private and public settings. We can also experience great pressure from the needs of individuals we are ministering to, where they act like we are the answer and not Jesus. Finally, we can find ourselves in urgent situations created by others, where we will experience emotional pressure to do something.

12.8.5 One of the lessons I have learned down the years is that leaders often respect how long I have been in the prophetic ministry much more than they do the anointing on my gift. I believe paying attention to, continually seeking to grow in and being transparent to others about my integrity is the grounds of my longevity. Put simply, 'Anointing + Integrity = Longevity'. The casualty rate in the prophetic ministry is the only one close to that of church leaders. Believing it could never happen to us is the beginning of our own demise.

12.8.6 Integrity is defined by what you do when no one is watching.

266. Ephesians 4:15 | 267. *Alice's Adventures in Wonderland* [1965 Fantasy Novel] | 268. Ephesians 4:16
269. 1 Corinthians 13:1-2

12.9   Personal Testimony

12.9.1   I can think of no better way to reinforce the principle of 'character before gift' than to refer you to my own life's story. It is a living testimony to this important value. While it is very clear in hindsight that God was going to release me into a prophetic ministry, which I have now been in since 1993, due to the 'character before gift' principle, it was not obvious for many years. While quite capable of moving in prophecy from my early years, he sent me in a very different direction until he had matured my character enough for me to be safe to be around!

12.9.2   The goal that my wife Julie and I shared, and the guidance of our church leadership, gradually moved us to growing in the pastoral ministry through midweek group leadership, regional leadership and the eldership in the church. In our early years, we learned the biblical principles and practice of the pastoral ministry from our pastoral mentor[270], and grew considerably through his encouragement and advice. This inevitably meant facing the immaturity in our character as well as the weaknesses in our identity.

12.9.3   The next season involved co-leading one of the congregations in the church as an elder, under what we then called the 'oversight of an apostle'. This was a time when I learned the principles and practices of leadership from our leadership mentor[271], and under his guidance I learned over time how to use them. Leadership is yet another environment where our maturity and character are tested and refined. I faced the fear of man, challenge to my motives, what success meant in biblical terms and discovered what type of leader I could be.

12.9.4   Having been an elder for twelve years, my prophetic gift started manifesting itself in many ways and set me on a journey that eventually led to my resignation, to see if I had a prophetic ministry and where it might lead us. It had taken God nineteen years to make me safe enough to really use me in prophecy! Character before gift or what! My resignation amazingly coincided later that year with an internationally recognized prophetic ministry[272] joining our church and moving his office there.

12.9.5   This launched a white-knuckle ride into the prophetic ministry. I travelled nationally and internationally, drove to his many schools of prophecy, learned from his considerable experience in ministry, built a large and experienced prophetic team, attended monthly training meetings, attended advanced training schools, and we spent a lot of time together. The next seven years were a steep learning curve, but with my pastoral training and leadership experience they were built on the secure foundations God had wisely prepared.

12.9.6   Graham eventually moved to California which, after a period of some heart-searching, started me on a journey to equip the wider church with a better understanding and experience of the prophetic gift. While this manual is all my own material, developed over the last ten years, its roots are well and truly planted in those rollercoaster first seven years.

270. Peter Light, Romsey, UK | 271. Martyn Dunsford, Hedge End, UK | 272. Graham Cook, USA

School for Prophecy

12.10 Frequently Asked Questions

12.10.1 If prophecy is a supernatural gift, why is my character important?

12.10.2 The key issue here is that while it is a supernatural gift, it is received, comes through and is delivered by us. While there is ample grace when we are learning to prophesy, our maturity will impact how we handle significant words, pressurized situations, public attention and emotive issues [12.2.3]. Put simply, if our compass is five degrees off true north, it can affect how we move in prophecy. It is also a key feature in our long-term survival through the inevitable challenges and puts a ceiling on our sustainable growth.

12.10.3 I consider myself quite mature; why do I still need character training?

12.10.4 The issue here is not that you are not already mature in your current environment, but that moving in the gift of prophecy brings pressure on our character in ways we have not experienced before [12.2.5]. When I was a fit young footballer, my uncle started teaching me golf and warned me I would seriously ache after the first time because golf used muscles I had never used before. He was right. Growing in prophecy is capable of challenging our core values in ways we have never experienced before.

12.10.5 Fear is a real issue for me when moving in prophecy. Any suggestions?

12.10.6 First of all, let me encourage you: you are not alone; we are all fear-challenged. It continues to be our enemy's main weapon to obstruct, hinder or stop people from prophesying. Fear is anti-faith, so growing in faith and trust in God is the key [12.5.4]. We need to trust in God because he only gives good gifts; it was his idea in the first place and he prioritizes prophecy. Learning to anticipate the consistent lies our enemy will present us with at exactly the moment of decision will also help you push through in faith regularly.

12.10.7 A recent prophecy was rejected and has made me lose my confidence…

12.10.8 This is the real challenge of New Covenant prophecy, as we are not yet perfect and inevitably will make mistakes [12.6.4]. This is a hard challenge, and one that has caused many to curse themselves with, "I will never do that again." Everyone makes mistakes, so the issue is what we learn from them and how we grow through them. We can only do our best, which is why it is the recipient's responsibility to test our prophecies. This is a test of our pride, motivation and identity, to face the issues and grow stronger through them.

12.10.9 Prophecy seems of great benefit, but I am really not sure I can do it…

12.10.10 Let me encourage you: my prophetic mentor taught me that if you can pray, you can prophesy [4.7.3]. The Bible says prophecy is a gift created by God that we are encouraged to seek after and that we can all move in. I am not saying you will be a prophet, bring words for the church or predict the next drought. By simply trusting God, you can bring real, timely and effective words of encouragement, strengthening and comfort to many people. It's not about how good we think the word is, but how much the person receiving is helped.

Study Notes

13

THE LEVEL TWO COURSE

School for **Prophecy**

Level Two Course Profile

Having a biblical prophetic ministry involves recognising that one of your primary gifts is prophecy, engaging with it in service for the Kingdom, and navigating the many changes, challenges and conflicts that 'come with the territory'. The School for Prophecy *Growing in Prophetic Ministry* level two training course will ensure you have the necessary biblical foundations for the proper function of a fruitful ministry, provide training to help you safely move in a stronger anointing, and equip you to handle the many demanding environments in which you may operate.

The *Growing in Prophetic Ministry* course is designed for those who already have experience moving in the gift of prophecy or have completed the *Discovering Prophecy* level one training course [or equivalent training and experience] and would like to develop their corporate prophecy, grow in anointing and maturity, and move in greater discernment.

It provides clear, candid and comprehensive teaching on all aspects of a biblical prophetic ministry, a comfortable and safe environment for you to practise, and experienced advice on hand to help you grow in your ministry. The simulation workshops are an essential part of the course and provide the necessary learning environment and relevant practice to turn the teaching into an ongoing experience.

The standard course comprises nine sessions covering the following topics, teaching subjects, and supporting small group simulation workshops. The extended course adds a fourth topic with three more advanced subjects and simulation workshops.

Topic 1: *Prophetic Character*

• Establishing Kingdom Core Values	Personal Prophecy 1
• Embracing a Prophetic Character	Personal Prophecy 2
• Engaging with your Strengths	Personal Prophecy 3

Topic 2: *Prophetic Ministry*

• Pursuing Prophetic Ministry	Corporate Prophecy 1
• Personal Prophetic Protocols	Corporate Prophecy 2
• Partnering with your Leaders	Corporate Prophecy 3

Topic 3: *Prophetic Practice*

• Targeting the Truth through Testing	Prophetic Ministry 1
• The Language of God	Prophetic Ministry 2
• Turning Revelation into Reality	Prophetic Ministry 3

Topic 4: *Prophetic Warfare* [Extended course only]

• Understanding and Discerning Religious Spirits	Personal Ministry 1
• Understanding and Discerning Controlling Spirits	Personal Ministry 2
• Understanding and Discerning False Prophets	Personal Ministry 3

Every meeting will include a teaching session with an on-screen presentation, student-style presentation notes, a small group simulation workshop, coaching discussions and the all-important questions and answers session.

There is a training course manual containing all the above teaching subjects, plus audio and video recordings of all teaching sessions, available on the school website. If you would like us to consider running a course near you, please use the school website's contact form.

Level Two Course Curriculum

Topic 1: Prophetic Character

Prophetic Character examines those core areas of our character and maturity, which will protect and guide us through prophetic ministry's changes, challenges and conflicts.

Chapter 1: Establishing Kingdom Core Values

The first *Prophetic Character* subject, *Establishing Kingdom Core Values*, seeks to explain, emphasise and establish the biblical value system's core principles to ensure that we have secure enough foundations for all that we do.

Chapter 2: Embracing a Prophetic Character

The second *Prophetic Character* subject, *Embracing a Prophetic Character,* develops *The Character Challenges of Prophecy* [L1:12] by assessing the impact of the presence or the absence of each of the fruit of the Spirit during prophetic ministry.

Chapter 3: Engaging with Your Strengths

The final Prophetic Character subject, *Engaging with Your Strengths*, introduces the personality profile system 'StrengthsFinder' to help you grow in self-awareness, understand your identity and recognise your personality type.

Topic 2: Prophetic Ministry

Prophetic Ministry identifies strategies, principles and practices essential for a prophetic ministry's mature, managed and maintained operation.

Chapter 4: Pursuing Prophetic Ministry

The first *Prophetic Ministry* subject, *Pursuing Prophetic Ministry*, explains the differences between moving in the gift of prophecy and having a prophetic ministry, and identifies the fundamental operational principles and practices of ministry.

Chapter 5: Personal Prophetic Protocols

The second *Prophetic Ministry* subject, *Personal Prophetic Protocols*, instructs and advises on developing personal prophetic guidelines to ensure we engage, endure and excel through the challenges of prophetic ministry.

Chapter 6: Partnering with Our Leaders

The final *Prophetic Ministry* subject, *Partnering with our Leaders*, examines the principles and practices of being in partnership with our leaders and the resulting dynamics of team ministry, specifically in a prophetic context.

Topic 3: Prophetic Practice

Prophetic Practice covers the biblical guidelines and procedures fundamental to a fruitful prophetic ministry's safe, secure and successful operation.

Chapter 7: Targeting the Truth Through Testing

The first *Prophetic Practice* subject builds on the previous course session, *The Principles of Testing Prophecy* [L1:7], giving advanced practical guidance on applying testing to personal and corporate prophecy.

Chapter 8: The Language of God

The second *Prophetic Practice* subject builds on the previous course session, *The Principles of Interpreting Prophecy* [L1:8], by examining the terminology and themes used by God to help us understand, deliver and receive prophecy more completely.

Chapter 9: Turning Revelation into Reality

The final *Prophetic Practice* subject builds on the previous course session, *The Principles of Responding to Prophecy* [L1:9], describing the main features of walking, working and warring with a long-term prophecy through to fulfilment.

Topic 4: Prophetic Warfare [extended course only]

Prophetic Warfare seeks to explain, equip and empower us in preparation for the primary sources of spiritual opposition we may encounter when moving in prophetic ministry.

Chapter 10: Understanding and Discerning Religious Spirits

The first *Prophetic Warfare* subject explains the definition, discernment and deceptions of the more common religious spirits and contains practical and experienced advice on how they operate.

Chapter 11: Understanding and Discerning Controlling Spirits

The second *Prophetic Warfare* subject identifies the characteristics, strategies and weapons of the more common controlling spirits and contains practical and experienced advice on how they operate.

Chapter 12: Understanding and Discerning False Prophets

The final *Prophetic Warfare* subject explains how to recognise the signs, symptoms and strategies of the more common false prophets and contains practical and experienced advice on how they operate.

14

THE LEVEL THREE COURSE

School for **Prophecy**

Level Three Course Profile

The *School for Prophecy* level three training course, *Engaging Your Prophetic Calling*, will help you enter fully into the lifestyle of a prophet or prophetess, equip you to build the Church and help you develop a strategic approach to your prophetic environment and its challenges. The level three training course will push the boundaries of your personal growth, train you how to release prophetic culture, and lay the foundations for long-term success and survival in challenging environments.

The *Engaging Your Prophetic Calling* level three training course is designed for those who are experienced and recognised as moving in prophetic ministry, or who have completed the level two training course, *Growing in Prophetic Ministry* [or equivalent training], and who want to embrace the call of God on their life.

It provides targeted, frank, and knowledgeable teaching on all aspects of the biblical prophetic office, a comfortable and safe environment for you to practise, and experienced advice on hand to help you grow in your calling. The small group workshops are an essential part of the course and provide the necessary learning environment and relevant practice to turn the teaching into an ongoing experience.

The standard course comprises nine sessions covering the following topics, teaching subjects, and supporting small group ministry workshops. The extended course adds a fourth topic with three more advanced subjects and ministry workshops.

Topic 1: *Prophetic Identity*

Employing Emotional Intelligence	Identity Ministry 1
Embracing God's Discipline	Identity Ministry 2
Engaging Godly Assertiveness	Identity Ministry 3

Topic 2: *Prophetic Culture*

Managing the Prophetic Environment	Culture Ministry 1
Mentoring the Prophetic Person	Culture Ministry 2
Maturing the Prophetic Contribution	Culture Ministry 3

Topic 3: *Prophetic Leadership*

Biblical Role of a Prophet	Leaders Ministry 1
Building a Prophetic Team	Leaders Ministry 2
Balancing Leadership, Authority & Accountability	Leaders Ministry 3

Topic 4: *Prophetic Strategy* [Extended course only]

Understanding God's Ways	Strategic Ministry 1
Unleashing the Kingdom of Heaven	Strategic Ministry 2
Unlocking Prophetic Warfare	Strategic Ministry 3

Every meeting will include a teaching session with an on-screen presentation, student-style teaching notes, a small group ministry workshop, coaching discussions, and the all-important questions and answers times.

Unfortunately, the training course manual is not yet available, although currently being written, but audio and video recordings of all the teaching sessions are available to purchase. If you would like us to consider running a course near you, please use the school website's contact form.

Level Three Course Curriculum

Topic 1: Prophetic Identity

Prophetic Identity looks at those main aspects of our sonship in Christ, which are critical to the long-term survival, success, and sustainability of any significant prophetic ministry.

Chapter 1: Employing Emotional Intelligence

The first *Prophetic Identity* subject introduces Emotional Intelligence, its biblical foundations, and how its approach to the vital area of self-awareness, or maturity, can help us achieve our full potential.

Chapter 2: Embracing God's Discipline

The second *Prophetic Identity* subject dispels the common misinterpretations of judgement, punishment, and negative criticism surrounding God's discipline. It provides a clear, healthy, and biblical understanding of its correct purpose, application, and response.

Chapter 3: Engaging Godly Assertiveness

The final *Prophetic Identity* subject seeks to ensure we experience our true and complete identity as Sons of God by addressing the key issues surrounding being true to ourselves and how to engage in any resulting confrontation positively.

Topic 2: Prophetic Culture

Prophetic Culture unpacks the context, capabilities, and conventions that the prophetic ministry needs to operate sustainably, maturely, and fruitfully while avoiding the challenges and common mistakes often encountered.

Chapter 4: Managing the Prophetic Environment

The first *Prophetic Culture* subject explains how to create, operate, and sustain a healthy prophetic environment, which allows biblical prophecy to operate through and in every area of the Church family and strengthen people's identity, maturity, and calling.

Chapter 5: Mentoring the Prophetic Person

The second *Prophetic Culture* subject establishes the main biblical principles for successfully mentoring those with the gift of prophecy. It addresses the many classic character profiles of prophetic people and explains how to help them discover their complete identity in Christ.

Chapter 6: Maturing the Prophetic Contribution

The final *Prophetic Culture* subject examines the crucial subject of the prophetic contribution from the perspectives of those contributing, the audience, and the leadership. It lays down core biblical principles while addressing the more common difficulties.

Topic 3: Prophetic Leadership

Prophetic Leadership highlights the essential features of the New Covenant prophet's and prophetess's calling, capabilities and commitments in their body function, team ministry and spiritual authority.

Chapter 7: Biblical Role of a Prophet[ess]

The first *Prophetic Leadership* subject explains the biblical role of a New Covenant prophet or prophetess, their primary capabilities, and how they integrate and operate within the body of Christ.

Chapter 8: Building a Prophetic Team

The second *Prophetic Leadership* subject explores the rationale and benefits of developing a prophetic team and how to organise their successful operation while avoiding classic mistakes.

Chapter 9: Balancing Leadership, Authority, & Accountability

The final *Prophetic Leadership* subject builds on the subject of *Partnering with Our Leaders* [L2:6] by looking in detail at the challenges and practical application of leadership, authority, and accountability.

Topic 4: Prophetic Strategy [Extended Course Only]

Prophetic Strategy identifies the main areas of interaction, overlap and synergy between the apostolic and prophetic ministries in revealing God's purposes and how to build the kingdom of God.

Chapter 10: Understanding God's Ways

The first *Prophetic Strategy* subject examines how understanding God's character can reveal the eternal motives for what He does and as a result, give us a better insight into His methods.

Chapter 11: Unleashing the Kingdom of Heaven

The second *Prophetic Strategy* subject explains the characteristics of the kingdom of heaven, how to fully engage with it in our daily lives, and avoid some of the more common myths, mistakes, and misunderstandings.

Chapter 12: Unlocking Spiritual Warfare

The final *Prophetic Strategy* subject develops the Level Two topic *Prophetic Warfare* [L2:10,11,12] by examining the personal warfare we face, the spirits who oppose us, and the work of our enemy in our lives and ministry.